D1596812

# Why listen to Zach?

**Jennifer Holden, VP Marketing, $5B revenue American manufacturer**

I have witnessed first-hand how Zach can take an underwhelming International Sales Team and channel and in record-time turn it into a high performing powerhouse. His depth and experience in building an international channel is unparalleled in the healthcare industry. Zach's direct and pull-no-punches style cuts through the noise and gets to the vulnerabilities and remediation plan. He also exploits the existing strengths to get high quality work and high value sales so that both the vendor and the distributor grow year over year.

Brendon,

hope we can find

a way to work together

Zach

847 4406843

**Rony Abdel-Hay, Co-Founder & Chairman of ProMedic Holding, >$100M distribution company with branches in over a dozen cities in MEA and GCC**

The way Zach recruited me and my company ProMedic as a distributor is truly unbelievable... I was not at all interested in Zach's new product and he succeeded to have me as a partner-distributor and drive us so that his product becomes our primary sales revenue representing over 50% of the company's top line and bottom line. This means 2 things: Zach is a true visionary and I trust him for that, and he knows how to motivate teams. For over a decade we took sales in the MENA/GCC from nearly nothing to skyrocket and became "Top of the World". My trust in Zach's unorthodox ways brought my company from a few millions in revenues to nearly $100M. Yet the most important thing I learned is: Trust in the right person can bring exceptional outcome. Sales process is a journey with many ups and downs and walking that journey with Zach not only brought wins and success but also the most valuable and memorable moments that I can ever remember and will always talk about.

**Benjamin Levy, Ed.D., Chief Commercial Officer, Rubean AG Munich/Tel Aviv**

I have known Zach for some time now and the best recommendation that I can think of is this: if I had the chance to hire him in the future in any sales or business development role, I would. Very, very few people around the world know the world as well as he does. If international sales are what you need, then you need Zach. The Arabian Peninsula, Europe, South America? Check. Asia? Check. Pretty much any other part of the world? Check that too. To my knowledge, Zach has sold and closed deals pretty much anywhere. And that is really saying something.

**Dr. Ahmed Adel Taha, MBA, MD, General Manager, Europe Middle East and Africa, $500M multinational manufacturing corporation**

What Zach taught me 15 years ago I still use today, and it puts money in my pocket every day.

**Karen Isaacson, Global VP HR Transformation, Chief HR Officer, Fortune 100 global organizations**

Zach is always my first call. He's led sales teams on every continent, in every market, and has been an exceptional resource to me when I've faced new challenges. Zach is creative and driven, and his non-traditional and pragmatic approaches always provide an insightful and clear path forward.

**Scott Lease, 6x Sales Leader/ 3x Founder/ 2x Author/ Sales Consultant & Strategic Advisor to startups around the world**

I have built and grown sales orgs domestically and internationally for nearly two decades now. If somebody asked me to recommend an expert in international sales orgs, Zach is the guy who comes to mind.

**Konstantinos Chatzipolyzis, VP Export Sales, Samaras SA, Greece**

As somebody who has worked for years in international sales, I look to Zach as a source of information and guidance in navigating new markets.

### Ken Baldo, Veteran VP Sales, Ranked Top 50 LinkedIn Sales Stars

If you don't know who Zach Selch is, you are not traveling around the world enough selling. Zach is the most interesting and influential sales globetrotter who has an uncanny ability to take the complex world of international sales and make it easier to navigate—breaking through the cultural barriers and uncovering the golden opportunities within uncharted territories.

### Jani Asikanius, VP Sales, EMEA, Aiven Finland

I worked with Zach on multiple sales processes. Zach is a very detail oriented planner, with good understanding of the big picture and capability to move through different layers of the organization. His people skills and capabilities to work in very diverse cultural environments made us succeed and reach our common goals.

### Andy Hall, Head of Hills Health Solutions, Australia

Zach has a proven track record in building successful international partner-based sales channels. I have had the pleasure of being mentored by him as I built my sales career over the last 18 years. As the head of a large health services / distribution company, I wish my partner managers possessed Zach's sales and market knowledge. He really knows how to navigate diverse markets and help coach sales teams to successfully close business using his targeted sales messaging approach.

**Mark Allegra, VP Sales, CEO and Co-Founder, Value Squared**

I had the distinct pleasure of working with Zach; we shared a common affinity for strategic and consultative sales. Zach was leading the international team at the time and on the occasions where Zach and I collaborated I was frequently dazzled by his knowledge of the international markets and his systemic approach to strategic and consultative selling principles--he truly brings a refreshing and much needed approach to modern, international sales. At the end of the day, no matter your strategy, it is about execution and delivering on revenue attainment, an area Zach is very well accomplished in and where he truly shines.

**Gavin Tice, Partner, Sandler Training Ruby Group**

Zach is an old friend and colleague, and the go-to for sales trainers like me when we are looking for guidance in the complexities of international expansion.

**Yahya Gaznavi, Country Manager, Pakistan, $ Multibillion Global Distribution Corporation**

As the head of sales for a large distribution company, I wish my other principals had the sales and market knowledge that Zach had... he really knows how to navigate diverse markets and help coach sales people to close business.

**Tom Payne, Executive Sales Consultant and Author of "Selling with Charisma," and "The Causes of Sales Success"**

Setting up an international distributor network is incredibly complex, and many costly mistakes await even the experienced international hand. Zach's strategic approach will show you where to start the process, how to vet and recruit the best dealers, and how to keep them focused on your product. His invaluable experience is now yours.

### Paul Hletko, Founder, Distiller FEW Spirits / Founder, Sterling Beach Fund

Building a global footprint was key to the growth of our brand and our fund, and Zach was very helpful in advising us as to the early steps for expansion. Now we sell on 4 continents and we own brands from multiple countries.

### Dr. Samer Nashaat Tamer, Regional Sales Manager, Abbot Egypt

Zach was the best professional sales teacher, leader and friend, and everything one could look for in a good mentor. Not only is he perfect at his job, but he has also proven himself to be a loving and caring person, both in our business and out in the world. It would be impossible to count all the ways that he has helped me in my career. Not only has he been a fantastic mentor to me, but he taught me how to mentor other people, and was a great role model.

### Antoine Trannoy, Managing Director and Board Member, Hoist Group France

Zach perfectly understands how to build partnerships abroad.

### Pax Lindell, Director Channel Sales, Workhorse Group Inc

I met Zach when I was the Director of International Sales. For me, Zach was a tremendous resource; he possesses a deep knowledge of the global healthcare market. Zach acted as a mentor and was always willing to discuss strategies and share his market knowledge and key contacts.

### Maya Hoshino, VP International Sales, Paramount Beds, Tokyo Japan

Zach worked very well between the US and the Japan teams to connect the different cultures in business to lead to success for both of them.

**Thierno Sall, CEO and owner, Africa Life Science, Senegal**

I have been running a distribution company in Western Africa for decades and I have worked with dozens of principals. No principal understands Africa and nobody understands how to get channel partners to perform like Zach. if this is what you want to do, learn from Zach

**Charbel Rizkallah, Director Offering Management & Commercial Excellence at Honeywell, UAE**

Zach is a unique type of professional businessman that you enjoy working with and compete against. I have worked with Zach for 5 years, as his partner, in which he demonstrated extensive leadership skills and an excellent business global mindset. Later on, I competed against him for four years in which he showed great ethical traits. I am proud to have Zach as a friend, no matter which side of business we are on... and I will always be!

**David Goren, Vice President of Operation & APAC Affiliates Manager, Contguard, Israel**

Zach is a brilliant sales manager, pulling together a very diverse team, and coaching everyone to develop their strengths and minimize their weaknesses. By restructuring the sales process and coaching the team to work together, Zach was able to drive the sales growth substantially past anything that was anticipated.

### Joe Henley, CEO, Prometheus Consultancy Services Ltdr

As an experienced sales coach and salesperson who's worked across numerous western countries, I can't recommend Zach enough for his vast international sales experience and knowledge. In the time I've known him, he's consistently demonstrated the highest level of professionalism, coupled with great decorum and a love of culture and travel. He possesses knowledge you can only gain by working at a local level - many tips missed by the competition.

### Oliver Dowson, CEO, International Corporate Creations, Author, Podcaster

Selling to your home market is one thing, selling internationally is an entirely different art.

### Ernie Watts, VP International Sales, Executive Director Global Chamber Chicago

Establishing and building successful businesses globally is a challenge for even the most experienced professional. Zach's ability to use a process driven approach that identifies critical success factors translates to proven results in any industry.

### Grace Preston, Director of International Sales

Very few people have the level of in-depth knowledge of international business as Zach. This knowledge is drawn from years of experience and not just theory. This is why over the years, whenever I have a complicated international situation, I go to Zach for insight and guidance. I can attribute many of my international sales successes to learning from Zach. Zach knows everyone and is very well respected in the international business community.

**Daniel Corredor Ferrari, General Manager Latin America and the Caribbean, multi-billion-dollar manufacturing corporation**

Working with Zach was inspiring every day. His guidance, vast experience, support, and leadership taught me to strategically focus on key international sales management and business development areas, allowing me to successfully lead my sales teams and channels in every territory, achieving consistent profitable growth over the years. This, while building strong long-term commercial relationships with sales channels, consultants, commercial offices and customers. I cannot thank Zach enough for his international sales mentorship, which became such an integral part of my career. I hope to inspire others as he has inspired me.

**Marc Bodner, Veteran VP, Sales**

As a consummate sales professional, Zach's insights are something I've always valued and considered. However, when it comes to selling on an international level, he's definitely my " go to" resource.

**Raleigh Wilkins, Founder and CEO, Sales Platoon**

As a lifelong sales leader and passionate student within the profession of sales, I've had the opportunity to travel to and work with international sales teams. Navigating the subtle differences that exist between international cultures can be challenging. Zach has developed a thorough understanding of the sometimes subtle cultural norms, mores and traditions that directly influence the sales process. As such, I have come to regard Zach as my go-to resource for all matters concerning international sales.

**Mark Baxter, VP communications, $2B corporation**

I worked with Zach on a corporate team as the VP of marketing to his GM of International Sales. Over several years, I watched him expand our global footprint in the Americas, across the Pacific and Mideast. His understanding of complex sales processes in far corners of the world, combined with his vast knowledge of cultural differences, proved invaluable in driving our market presence and revenue.

**Obiely Tayoro, CEO Wit Consulting SARL, Ivory Coast**

Zach knows more about selling to Africa and building African channels than any Westerner I have ever met. Learn from him.

**Sarabjeet Singh Bhasin, Business Head Kontron India, former product leader Nokia**

Zach has a fantastic understanding of the Indian culture and the Indian business culture and was able to bring in fantastic results with the team because of that understanding as well as his hard work and great team leadership.

**Roberto Pizzotti, VP Sales, distribution company, Brazil**

As vice president of sales in Brazil, I worked with Zach for almost 20 years and no American knows how to boost sales in Brazil like Zach does. His insight and approach taught us to increase sales in Brazil in a dizzying way. Our approach changed, we made the market understand that buying with us was an investment, we started to find key people in organizations, our customers multiplied their purchases by tenfold (transfer price), we established an unknown brand as number one in record time in our country, in every province.

www.linkedin.com/in/zselch-internationalsales
www.globalsalesmentor.com

www.themostinterestingsalesmanintheworld.com

# Bonus video:

https://www.youtube.com/watch?v=RJyEanNXejM&t=8s

# Global Sales

A Practical Playbook on How to Drive Profitable Growth for International Sales and Marketing Leaders

## Zach Selch

Global Sales Mentor Press

Because the English Language lacks a generic singular pronoun that indicates both genders, we have used the masculine pronouns for the sake of style, flow, and brevity. This material applies to everyone, regardless of gender.

This publication may not be reproduced, stored in a retrieval system, or transmitted in whole or in part, in any form or by any means, electronic, mechanical, photocopying, recording, or otherwise without the prior written permission of Global Sales Mentor LLC., 916 Judson Avenue, Evanston IL, 60202.

Copyrighted Material

Global Sales

Copyright © 2020 by Zach Selch. All Rights Reserved.

No part of this publication may be reproduced, stored in a retrieval system or transmitted, in any form or by any means—electronic, mechanical, photocopying, recording or otherwise—without prior written permission from the publisher, except for the inclusion of brief quotations in a review.

For information about this title or to order other books and/or electronic media, contact the publisher:

Global Sales Mentor Publishing

916 Judson Ave. Evanston Il. 60202 USA

Editors@globalsalesmentor.com

+1.847-440-6843

www.globalsalesmentor.com

ISBN: 978-1-7359131-0-0 (print)

978-1-7359131-1-7 (eBook)

LCC HF5438.25 .S45 2020 (print) | LCC HF5438.25 (eBook) |DDC 658.85–dc23

Subjects: LCSH: Selling. | Export marketing. | Export sales contracts. |

International trade. | Success in business.

Printed in the United States of America

Publisher's Cataloging-In-Publication Data

Names: Selch, Zach, author.

Title: Global Sales: A Practical Playbook on How to Drive Profitable Growth for International Sales and Marketing Leaders / by Zach Selch.

**Zach Selch**

+1-847-440-6843

zach@globalsalesmentor.com

www.themostinterestingsalesmanintheworld.com

www.linkedin.com/in/zselch-internationalsales

The contents in or made available through this book are not intended to and do not constitute legal advice or investment advice and no attorney-client relationship is formed. The publisher and the author are providing this book and its contents on an "as is" basis. Your use of the information in this book is at your own risk.

Limit of Liability/disclaimer of warranty: while the publisher and author have used their best efforts in preparing this book, they make no representations or warranties with respect to the accuracy or the completeness of the contents of this book and specifically disclaim any implied warranties of merchantability or fitness for a particular purpose. No warranty may be created or extended by sales representatives or written sales materials. The advice and strategies contained herein may not be suitable for your situation. You should consult with a professional where appropriate. Neither the publisher nor author shall be liable for any loss of profit or expense incurred, or any other commercial damages, including but not limited to incidental, consequential, special or other damages. The publisher and the author do not make any guarantee or other promise as to any results that may be obtained from using the content of this book. You should never make any investment decision without first consulting with your own financial advisor and conducting your own research and due diligence. To the maximum extent permitted by law, the publisher and the author disclaim any and all liability in the event any information, commentary, analysis, opinions, advice and/or recommendations contained in this book prove to be inaccurate, incomplete or unreliable, or result in any investment or other losses.

This book does not impart invincibility, immunity from disease or protection from the elements or crime. Please use common sense and be careful. The publisher and author take no responsibility for your safety or your health.

As mentioned in this book, the US Federal Government has put in place powerful laws to combat corruption typically grouped under the 'Foreign Corrupt Practices Act' as well as a range of laws that protect and support the US Government's Foreign Relations. The author and the publisher do not present this book as training or guidelines to those laws and urge you to seek guidance from certified professionals or from the US Federal Government when it comes to your interaction with foreign governments and with customers outside of the US It is both extremely unwise and in no way recommended or supported by the author or the publisher to try to circumvent or bend US laws and guidelines on international trade. No one should try to export from the US without being certified by official FCPA training.

For general information, to chat with the author, to inquire into our various courses, strategic guidance, coaching or other services, or if you would like to inquire about speaking or presenting, please go to

www.globalsalesmentor.com

or www.themostinterestingsalesmaninthe world.com

I dedicate this book to my sister, Rabbi Charni Flame Selch, who passed away a few years ago leaving her nearly finished manuscript on her computer. Her death, and her unfinished business, may very well have given me the push I needed to apply the seat of my pants to the seat of a chair and write the book I had talked about for years.

Of course, with that, I need to thank my loving wife of more than 20 years, Tamar, who has put up with the crazy amount of traveling that I have to do, and my three children, who know the names of all my primary distributors and live their lives according to the trade show calendar.

# CONTENTS

# Foreword
## by Marcus Cauchi, author of
## "Making Channel Sales Work"

"The only way out of my network is in a box"

– Zach Selch

The timing for this book is perfect. Road warrior international salespeople have had their superpower taken from them. Few companies are willing to risk their salespeople hop on a plane to meet a prospect internationally with the possibility of quarantine, serious illness or death from Covid-19. And most road warriors have struggled to adapt to selling virtually.

But a local channel partner, can hop on their bike or drive up the road to meet a prospect with far less constraint. In 2016/17, when I wrote Making Channel Sales Work, over 70% of ALL products manufactured and sold globally across all 26 vertical markets were sold via partners (WTO, 2016, Forrester 2017). My guess is that number will rise significantly over the next couple of years and change the sales landscape for decades to come.

As I write this foreword in October 2020, we are still in the midst of a global pandemic. Based on current indications, we are likely to endure another couple of years of lockdowns. Globally, we're entering a second major spike and if human history around pandemics teaches us nothing, we will likely behave in such a way that we will have a third, fourth and fifth spike. That's why you really need to read and apply the advice in this book.

Zach Selch is no ordinary Channel Sales leader. With over 30 years' experience selling via partners in over 130 countries, Zach has been responsible for securing hundreds of millions of Dollars in channel sales. He has achieved Presidential recognition for his services to exports. He has opened up new markets not just in advanced economies, but also in dozens of developing countries. He has delivered staggering growth to his employers of as high as 4000% by taking them international via distributors. Yes, you read that right. 4000%.

Zach's book is fresh and unique in that he has incredibly high cultural and well as commercial awareness. He has embraced virtualization and has been using collaboration tools and virtual learning as part of his toolkit for over a decade. His advice on building international sales channel and distribution partnerships is not theoretical. It is grounded in more than 3 decades of scar tissue. His advice is practical. He's not guessing. Every word, every tip and piece of advice he has lived. He has learned how to solve problems others before him found impossible to solve.

Zach has learned patience when it is needed and when to apply concentrated force and take decisive action when that is a more appropriate course when context demanded it. He has worked with the highest and the lowest and has built a network over 30 years that still welcomes him, refers him and recommends him. Even his competitors trust him and refer him. Why? Because he lives by the credo that "If you are ready to lie, cheat or mistreat a distributor or a customer, you had better be ready to retire".

Internationally, culture, trust, etiquette and business practices are very different to what you may be used to. Zach has spent a lifetime learning how to navigate them. He has developed system and tools to help you shorten the trust building cycle, bypass bureaucratic and political delays, and work around your own company's tendency to get between you and bringing in profitable revenue. He identifies ways your own leadership and management will mess things up big time, he gives you clues to spot obstacles and red flags that could slow you down.

Zach shows you how to build loyalty and lifetime partnerships. And he shows you how to make your partners successful, so they stay loyal and profitable for decades.

This book is the antidote to bad channel management. It is a blueprint for those who see channel sales for what it really represents. The fastest, most effective way to scale fast, achieve sustained, controlled hypergrowth and take your business global.

Marcus Cauchi
Co-Author of Making Channel Sales Work
Chief Revenue Officer, Laughs Last Ltd
Sandhurst, United Kingdom
October 2020

# Foreword
## by Tom Kallman, CEO and President of Kallman Worldwide

Given the size and relative ease of navigation of the domestic U.S. market, the twentieth-century model for business growth in America was to establish "local" dominance, expand regionally, establish and build a national presence and then take the leap (pick a compass heading) into the international arena.

The blessing and curse of the U.S. market is that, on one hand, corporations have the world's largest GDP playground to grow up in; the curse is that upon taking the international leap corporations are often woefully unprepared for the "foreign" challenges ahead. "Culture shock" takes on a whole new meaning when attempting to sell your products or services in a market that is governed by completely different rules, standards, and language and other barriers spanning the gamut of business concerns.

Adding to our challenge to succeed is the fact that our international competitors most often grew up in a multi-lingual multi-cultural playground that has forced them to adapt to, and succeed in, conditions their U.S. counterparts have only read about in books like this. The relatively small size of the individual overseas markets has also taught our global friends the all-important lessons of collaboration, innovation, flexibility and even, especially in Asia, to be patient while the nature of business takes its course.

Thankfully, as the saying goes, nature abhors a vacuum, and given the (Google) ease by which overseas corporations and consumers can peer into our U.S. playground, one vacuum drawing us abroad is the markets (and marketeers) that desire to partner with, promote and sell, or merely purchase the high-quality U.S. products we make/represent. The other vacuum to be mindful of is the giant sucking noise which is the American economy which can find a place for just about any foreign product. Just as Americans are attacking business opportunities abroad through many of the methods outlined in this book, the international community as well has its sights set on our playground. One can look at that as a threat or a useful tool for leveraging your own presence abroad if circumstances allow.

Whether your motivation for corporate expansion abroad is fueled by opportunities (present, or those you plan to create!), or the preservation of domestic dominance through international collaboration, a presence in the global marketplace is essential for sustained corporate success. Forward-thinking U.S. firms know that the twenty first-century model puts "international" side-by-side with domestic concerns and often doesn't differentiate between the two. Thankfully for the U.S. economy, the next generation of corporate leaders grew up in a digital world where international connections are as easy as a pick-up game of basketball. The increased volume of international trade (pre-COVID-19) has certainly been influenced by this generation of global thinkers, and clearly the upward trend of global sales demonstrates heightened awareness of how to sell abroad.

Anything worth doing is worth doing right. In my 31-years supporting and organizing 400+ international trade shows and trade missions I have had to chance observe Zach's tireless, enthusiastic approach to international sales on almost every continent. His eyes-wide-open, lesson-learning, hands-on selling strategy is brilliantly compiled in this

Practical Playbook which will not only help to level the playing field for new-to-export firms, but also serve as a checklist for those of us with pages and pages of purple ink in our passports. Addressing everything from marketing and communications, to one-on-one client engagement, to the do's and don'ts of overseas trade show logistics, it is mandatory reading for my company's export support team.

My dad founded our company and started organizing the U.S. participation at international trade shows in 1963, a vastly different world back then. But one of his favorite stories is timeless, and it is about the two hikers who were walking down a jungle path when they came across an angry startled tiger. As the tiger snarled and crept low toward them, one of the fellas slowly took his sneakers from his backpack and was reaching to untie his hiking boots. His friend whispered, "You can't outrun a tiger." And the other replied, "No, but with these sneakers on I can outrun you!".

If you are involved in international trade, then you are in a jungle, friend.

If you are reading this book, you are reaching for your sneakers.

Get running!


Tom Kallman
President & CEO
Kallman Worldwide Inc.
October 2020

# October 15<sup>th</sup> 2020

I can't send this to print without acknowledging the events of 2020. Things have changed, and some things may never go back to how they were. That said, goods need to be made and goods need to be sold; the world economy will not be collapsing this year, and we will be back to selling face to face soon enough. I do believe that some percentage of our work will never go back to the way it was, but it's difficult to say if that is 10%, 20% or 30%. I will be doing much more of my coaching and training online. I hired two regional sales managers this year without meeting them face to face, as well as a few distributors. As of September 1<sup>st</sup> 2020, I had brought in about US$ 3 million in purchase orders on deals that started and closed (including finding and recruiting the partner) without any F2F meetings. But it is still very hard to get a purchase order of any significant size without meeting face to face.

When I started writing this book, none of us could have guessed how crazy the world was going to get, and how much things would change. My assumption was that in a few months life would get back to normal. That doesn't seem to be the case. Sales must go on; without purchase orders, society as we know it collapses.

Over recent months many of the basic tenets that I considered sacrosanct concerning the important of face to face meetings have turned on their heads. I have been teaching myself how to build and run a sales organization from the comfort of my home office, in my slippers.

With that, I do not believe that this book is now obsolete. I still believe that we will return to normal, and that the key to driving growth is still driving mind share through face to face meetings. That said, the lessons we have learned this year will help us survive periods when travel isn't possible, and will help us, even in a completely COVID-19 free future, to control the cost of making and managing sales.

A good friend of mine who read this book just days before I sent it off to the printer said, "Hmmm, are you sure this isn't obsolete right now? Everyone is going to be scrambling to figure out how to survive COVID-19." And she wasn't wrong.

This book gives you the tools that you need, if you wish to grow globally. COVID-19 might slow this growth down, but the tools will be exactly as effective and relevant 3 months after a vaccine is developed as they were in December of 2019.

I am now up to my neck in a second version of this book called _Virtual and Remote Global Sales 2021_ that will give you the tools needed to build and run an international sales organization remotely. As I have always been vehemently opposed to sales books written by people who are not in the purchase order business, I could not, in good faith, do this until I had closed my first P.O. start to finish remotely.

If you acquired this book before January 1st 2021, follow this QB code or reach out at www.globalsalementor.com and I will send you a free e-copy of the second version. I figure that is only fair, and we all have to work together to figure out a way through these difficult times.

# Electronic version and print version

Another good friend suggested that I add links to various bonus material, videos, lessons, additional essays etc. Spread throughout the book you will find these links. If you have purchased a hard copy, reach out to me at the links below and I will happily send you an email with all the links, so that you can easily access them. Who knew that publishing in the 21st century would become so complex?

https://www.globalsalesmentor.com/book-optin

# On Language
# And Terminology

Several years ago, my team had just closed the single biggest deal that my corporation had ever seen. The deal was dependent on an L/C. We couldn't ship without an L/C, and we couldn't recognize revenue without shipping, and we really needed this L/C to come in before the end of the quarter, to recognize revenue. Everyone was extremely tense about it. I sat through a meeting with my boss where he used the term "L/C" 20 times. "Zach, you know there is board visibility about the L/C?" "Zach, do I need to get somebody to help you expedite the L/C or will you be ok?" "Zach, we are all waiting to hear about the L/C".

As we were leaving the meeting, my boss leaned over to me and asked, "Zach, what is an L/C?"

I called my 10-year-old daughter and said, "Princess, can you explain to the nice man what an L/C is?" and handed my boss the phone. She said "an L/C or a letter of credit, is like a check, a letter from one bank to another that guarantees payment for goods, so that the manufacturer knows he will get paid and the buyer knows that he will get his goods." I think my daughter was a little surprised that an adult didn't know this, as in my household that is a term used at the dinner table.

A few things about this story. First, yes, I can be a bit of an a-hole; second, I have lived my life with a set of terminology that might not be familiar to you, so I will try to define a few things before we jump into the book, so that we are all on the same page.

**180 days** When we refer to "60 days" or "180 days" in terms of discussing a sale, we are talking about the terms of credit. We are shipping goods and the agreement with the person paying us (either customer or distributor) is that they will pay us in 180 days.

**Booth captain** The person who is in charge of the day to day running, as well as the strategy, of a trade show booth.

**CIP (see Incoterms®)** Carriage and Insurance Paid, a shipping term replacing the old term CIF (cost insurance freight). The seller arranges the shipping and has responsibility until the location named, and then charges the payer.

**CRM** Customer Relationship Management software. This is the software where the customer's details live and where we keep track of all the movement in the funnel. A good sales team will often use the CRM as their primary desktop and use it for the flow of all information.

**EXW (see Incoterms®)** Ex-works goods are delivered at the door of the factory. Buyer is responsible for all shipment costs, including loading the truck.

**Farming** Account management, sales activities associated with an existing customer.

**Forwarder** A service provider who ships your product, most often also handing the various services associated including the paperwork.

**HIS** Head of International Sales

**HQ** Headquarters

**Incoterms®** The Incoterms® are a set of 11 individual rules issued by the International Chamber of Commerce (ICC) which define the responsibilities of sellers and buyers for the sale of goods in international transactions.

**Legalization** Sometimes countries ask that any formal document be officially notarized by a lawyer or official that has been recognized by them. To send agreements or invoices to some countries, one needs to first send those documents to the embassy or consulate. This is almost always requested by developing countries nowadays, and often the revenue from this is used to partially or fully fund the consulate or embassy. In some cases the cost of this legalization can be in the thousands of dollars, although most commonly it's less than $100.

**Letter of credit (L/C)** A legal document that guarantees that one bank will pay another bank an agreed upon amount of money when certain actions are carried out. In present day practice, this almost always involves the exchange of documents. When the seller presents shipping documents and proof of receipt of goods from the buyer to his bank, and the sellers bank then presents those documents to the buyers bank, the buyers bank is legally obligated to pay the agreed upon sum of money. Many international transactions, especially between people who have not been doing business together for a long time, use L/Cs.

**LOI** Letter of intent. A less formal, quick agreement.

**Missionary selling** Selling into a market that isn't today buying this product or a similar product. This involves teaching the customer about the concept of the product.

**Playbook** A guidebook for the team, or the partners, to follow to achieve sales results or simply to work within company guidelines.

**P.O.** Purchase order. This is the official sale. Without a P.O., there is no sale.

**Regional Sales Managers (RM)** The company employee responsible for selling in a territory, usually by managing the local distribution partners.

**Regulatory** The legal requirements to sell in a territory. This is most common in products that could impact safety. You will see this in healthcare, communications, transportation but it can be in any field.

**Ride-along** When a sales manager spends time shadowing a sales asset for learning or coaching purposes.

**Sales assets** The various people that are in the sales process. In some sales process that could include a dozen different job titles. These could work for the manufacturer or the distribution partner or be agents or consultants. It is meant to be a wide net inclusive term.

**Specs (noun can be used as verb, specc'ed)** Specifications. When the buy writes in specifications for a product that they are looking to buy as part of their purchasing process. This is often done by a committee, resulting in specs that nobody can meet.

**Value dossier** – A marketing or sales enablement tool that includes a range of materials, in the estimated order that the end user will want to consume them, to be used by non-sales assets, possibly a customer employee who will share the materials with his or her co-workers.

# Introduction

## A few comments on language, style, and communication

As a young man I was an infantry sergeant, and then I went on to work my way up through the ranks in sales leadership. For the last 25 years I have not reported to anybody who really understood what I do. Very often I had to fight my bosses long and hard to do things the right way, while pushing my team to do things the right way, in order to achieve results. I offer this story as a bit of an explanation for my choice of language. My copy editor suggested that I tone down and possibly change some of my language, and I chose not to take her advice, but I will explain myself.

I am going to assume that if you have found your way to picking up this book, you would like to grow your career, or the value of your company, or a combination of both, by driving growth in international sales. There is no better way. On the other hand, studies by *Harvard Business Review* as well as UCLA have shown how risky it can be. Following the correct steps in international sales can be an extremely powerful way to drive success; doing a poor job of it can sink your company. You can over-extend your resources, defocus from your core business, and get pulled into competitive situations that you could have avoided.

When faced with books like this, we often think, "This is great, but maybe I will pick and choose what parts I like..." I get that. You will find that I often use what my mother would call "salty language" when I want to warn you not to do something stupid. The best example of this is that I say some variation of "don't screw your distributor" 18 times. I mean it, don't. If all you get from this book is that message, you will still be a better international sales manager than about 50% of the people in that job right now. Most religions spend an awful lot of time and energy trying to keep people away from sexual immorality. That probably indicates how attractive it is to people to do these forbidden things. Not to get into the morals of it at all, but having been born in 1967 of a generation where about half the people I know came from broken homes, I can attest to the potential trail of pain that is left behind when these rules aren't followed. I can imagine that many readers will read my first 17 warnings not to screw over their partners and think, "But I am so justified in this particular case, because I like money so much and this will make me money..." I can only hope that my choice of language and my 18 repetitions will push you back on the straight and narrow path.

Another thing I have to say about language: I use mostly male pronouns thought the book. I am a 53-year-old cis male. I have worked for, and with, many great professional women, but most of my customers, most of my salespeople, and most of the salespeople I know in the field are men, and that is the way the language flowed. I am also the father of girls, and I can hope that the future will present them with more and easier opportunities than it did for my generation. I apologize if my language is offensive to anyone; it was not meant in that way.

# The job

When I was a little boy, my heroes were not Superman or Spider-Man, but two Saturday morning cartoon characters. Johnny Quest and Commander McBragg, a little boy and an old man, who had traveled the world and seen everything and made interesting friends. That's what I wanted out of life; I wanted to see the world. As a child this seemed about as far out of my reach as leaping over tall buildings or spinning webs.

Once I was talking to one of my friends who lives in my comfortable North Shore Chicago suburb about campers and trailers, and I mentioned that when I was a boy I had lived in a trailer. She said, "Was that some kind of a family adventure?" I laughed and said, "No, that was extreme poverty."

When I was 11, I lived with my family of five in a 29-foot trailer on cinder blocks behind a gas station in rural Pennsylvania. Down the street from the gas station was a flea market where I met Dave, a retired outlaw biker with facial tattoos representing crimes and acts of violence, a gap where his front teeth used to be, and four stalls in the flea market. Dave gave me a job selling cutting boards and welcome mats of unknown provenance.

Dave was a wonderful mentor and taught me a great deal about selling. To some extent, the core of my sales skills was learned in the heat, under those corrugated fiberglass awnings. One day he called me over and I could hear a little bit of a laugh in his voice when he said, "This gentleman has complained about you." I felt a little twist in my belly, and I saw a large, red-faced tourist who had two of our top-of-the-line $30 cutting boards tucked under his arm, sweat dripping down his throbbing forehead. When the tourist saw me he colored, turned to Dave, and said, "I don't want him to talk. I don't want him to say anything. My wife bought one of these crazy expensive cutting boards, and when I came to return it, this little bastard sold me another one as a gift for my mother. If he starts talking again, I have no idea what I will buy."

This showed me how I was going to see the world. I realized that if I could sell cutting boards in rural Pennsylvania, I could probably sell anything anywhere. It gave me a goal. Over the years, starting as soon as I got out of the army at 21, I was traveling the world trying to launch a successful career in sales. I sold used hospital equipment in Africa and Eastern Europe in the '80s, I sold medical equipment across Europe and Asia in the '90s, and I was the head of South Asian sales for a multinational around the turn of the millennium. Over the years, I've sold in more than 130 countries, I've lived in 6, and I've really enjoyed most of what I've done.

What I've been doing is building and managing international sales organizations, whether they be relatively small teams or large forces. It's my vocation, something I love doing and something I have an aptitude for. I've been very successful. President Obama awarded me an export excellence award, as did the governor of Illinois. I was named exporter of the year by the US Commerce Department's magazine.

All of these things make me very proud, but that's not necessarily why you should listen to me. You can learn a lot from me and from my book because I've spent my whole life delivering numbers and meeting my forecasts and my promises for revenue. At least four times, I've grown an organization that other people had struggled with by more than 1,000%. I've helped drive up the value of a company by more than $100 million and I've helped add hundreds of manufacturing jobs in factories by growing international sales. For much of my early sales career, I didn't really pay attention to people who were doing similar work—I figured things out myself. I read books, I took courses, I came up with best practices. Over the years, I've gotten to know a lot of people who do this work, and very few of them follow these best practices. Many people fall into this line of work almost accidentally. It's very common for an international sales manager to have been a regional manager (RM) who did a pretty good job and then somebody offered him the job of international sales manager. It seems exciting, but he has no real understanding of how to do it. He does it for a few years and he doesn't completely screw it up; then he shifts into another position without ever really learning how he could've done an excellent job. Then his replacement is in the same situation.

Much of what I talk about in this book delves pretty deeply into details, tactics, and mechanics. A lot of it will seem very labor-intensive and possibly expensive to implement. You don't necessarily have to do everything that I talk about, but if you do, you can dramatically increase the sales of your company, assuming you have a reasonable product that is selling in your home territory. If your product is terrible, I probably can't help you. Everything that I go into here is doable, and much of it is the type of thing that people will argue about and say is unrealistic. Almost 100% of the time, though, my methods produce results and the naysayers are proven wrong.

In my last job, the company tried for 30 years to grow international sales, which had never been worth more than about 1% of the total company sales. The owner wanted to retire and sell the company and realized that a solid international footprint could drive up the value of the company. I was able to boost international sales by close to 2,000% within about seven years and drive up the value of the company by probably more than $100 million. The company sold for $370 million, and the new owner mentioned specifically in a press release that one of the main reasons he bought the company was because of the global footprint. Despite this, I was constantly in conflict with people in the company who didn't understand what I was trying to do.

There was a pattern: I would say I wanted to do something. We would discuss it. People who had been with the company for years would say that it wouldn't work, that it was a ridiculous idea. I would push, we would do it my way, and then two years later they would say, "I can't believe that worked so well. That's amazing!"

I'm not saying this to brag or show off. I'm saying it because you will read the book and think, "That's extreme. I don't think it's worth the effort." If you really want to drive 1,000% growth, you have to look at this holistically and not just as a list of suggestions. I'm sure you could drive 20% or 50% or 100% growth by implementing a handful of suggestions from the book, but you can achieve much higher growth if you implement the whole thing as a process. Although, from a legal perspective, I'm not guaranteeing anything, it worked for me over and over and I think it can work for you—but don't take me to court over it!

This book focuses on business-to-business sales or business-to-government sales and not so much on consumer sales. There may be a lot you can pick up and understand here that will help you for consumer sales, but the focus here is on distribution sales, because if you are a smaller to midmarket company, the way you will grow your sales and your company is with channel sales.

One thing that I like to try to do with any endeavor is ask myself, "What is the single most important thing that will dictate success in this project?" And here goes: getting buy-in from the right distributors is your goal if you want to grow internationally. Distributor mindshare is the name of the game.

The key to everything is to support the assets that your distributors are putting in place to sell your product. In order to do this, we need to make it easy for the distributor to sell profitably. We need the distributor to trust us, and we need to build the mindshare within the distributor sales organization. Everything I talk about in this book is going to relate to those aspects. And this is what will make you think that I'm crazy. What we are trying to do is be the preferred vendor for our distributor salespeople; the more we can achieve that goal, the more we will sell. The difference between a successful company in this field and an unsuccessful company will come down almost entirely to distributor mindshare.

If you are a small to midlevel manufacturing company, this should work well for you. It might not work for you if you export commodities that you extract from the ground or commodities that are grown. It might not work if the majority of what you do is sell to end user consumers. If you sell manufactured or designed goods that are sold to people who use those products to solve problems, or to make money, or to service their customers, and if your overall sales are under approximately $500 million, I will stick to my position that your success will be tied to selling through distributors.

Your primary assets are your distributors' salespeople. If you go into a territory and sell, let's say the maximum you're able to travel is 140 days a year, taking into account that some of those days are transit and maybe you can do two meetings a day. Let's say you're doing 200 meetings a year, which is extremely ambitious.

Once you have three regional managers who live in territory, they will each be making 200 meetings a year, which means between the four of you, you're handling 700 meetings a year (assuming that you have other things to do).

Once each of your RMs has five distributors, your organization is doing 2,200 meetings a year. When each of your RMs has 15 distributors, now perhaps you're at 10,000 meetings year. That's up quite a bit from the 200 meetings a year, and you can reach that in maybe three to five years. While nothing is ever completely linear, there's a very good chance that by increasing from 200 meetings to 10,000 meetings a year, you will be increasing your sales top line volume 50-fold. This is the value of distribution.

There are many types of distributors, and there are lots of ways that they can contribute. I would say that 90% of distributors recruited by American manufacturers are effectively worthless to that manufacturer. Signing up a distributor who isn't a good fit for you is worthless; signing up a distributor without a good onboarding plan or training plan is worthless; signing up a distributor that you can't coach or support is basically worthless. Signing somebody up will not necessarily get you the business. It is getting that mindshare of the right distributor, in the right market that is going to get you the business.

I'll discuss this over and over in the book: every morning, every distributor's salespeople are deciding where they will put their efforts that day. In every case the salesperson has multiple products to sell, and he doesn't really care where he puts his efforts. What he cares about is getting results—making money with as little work as possible. His overriding concern is that he won't be embarrassed in front of his customers or for somebody to damage his reputation in the market.

So, the key to your success comes down to making sure that this distributor salesperson believes that he can make a lot of money with little effort on your product and that you're not going to screw him. This is really the fundamental sentence of the whole book. If this isn't something you can get behind, this probably isn't the book for you.

Many people think that being a channel sales manager is what you do when you haven't been very good at selling but the company doesn't want to fire you. Very often they don't even want to call it sales; they want to call it marketing. The way they see it, you appoint a distributor and then you sit at your desk and every now and again you send an email to your distributor asking what's going on. A couple of times a year your distributors send you an order. There are lots of companies that survive that way for generations.

What we will look at in this book is something completely different. For me, international channel sales is three-dimensional chess while direct selling is basically checkers. We need to do everything that the domestic salesperson does—as they used to say about Ginger Rogers—backwards and in heels. We're dealing with a fog of information because we never have access to as much information as a direct sales organization does. We are dealing with complications that involve shipping and financing payments, and we're dealing with multiple cultures. Your regional manager may be from one culture, your headquarters another, your distributor a third, and your end user possibly a fourth.

The hardest part of being responsible for the international sales project is to manage expectations and to prevent meddling from headquarters. Probably the biggest cause of failure in global expansion is people at headquarters who believe that they understand international sales but have really no knowledge of it and insist on getting involved.

I could give you hundreds of examples. The best example was with a company I advised that had a fantastic, innovative product. The company spent several months putting together a global expansion plan that was agreed on and signed off on by all parties. Then, after about six months—after signing up dozens of distributors that represented our 50 most attractive markets, training distributors, equipping them with sales enablement tools and demo equipment, and getting 30 or so major projects into the funnel—a senior company shareholder met a CEO from a completely different field at a party and, over drinks, essentially decided to shift global distribution from the existing network to this new friend's network. To be fair, the new friend did have an extremely impressive wristwatch.

This meant the company had to terminate agreements with distributors around the world for no good reason, hugely damaging their reputation. They essentially had to lose the entire funnel of sales opportunities, and ended up going from the best or the second-best potential distributor in a territory for the specific product, to companies that had no idea how to sell a product like theirs. The company lost millions of dollars in sales over a handshake at a party made by somebody who knew nothing of selling or international business or how distribution worked. It was probably the single biggest mistake I've ever personally witnessed, and I compared it, when I told my wife, to Coca-Cola changing its recipe in 1985.

It is key for the person managing the international expansion project to work with the team to formulate a plan and then for everyone to sign off on the plan **and stick to** that plan for the period of time it takes to work through that plan. That is the basis for keeping peace and maintaining support between the sales organization and headquarters.

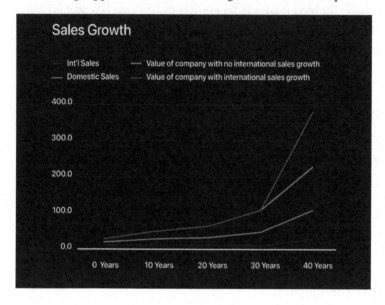

# Why Expand Internationally?

Growing your international sales footprint will grow the value of your company, probably faster and better than any other form of growth. If you are selling $50 million a year domestically, your company *might* be worth $100 million, depending on the area you operate in and the potential for overall market growth in the future. If you grow that by $10 million domestically, that might not add anything to the value of the company; it might still be worth $100 million. But if you grow that by $10 million internationally, the company might now be worth $150 million, because it is now a global player with significantly more potential to grow.

The middle market of the United States and many western industrialized countries is full of manufacturing companies that were founded between the 1930s and the 1950s. Many of these companies are now in the third generation of family ownership, and the owners have to decide how to go forward because often there is nobody to take over. The best way to double or triple the value of one of these companies is to grow the international footprint and go from being a major US player to a major global player.

That would be the number one reason for building internationally, but let's not forget the shorter-term value of ongoing revenue. Very often we have products that are excellent for the international markets— sometimes even more of a fit for international markets than for domestic markets.

We often have products that either are not a good fit for our domestic market or that the market has outgrown but that would be a good fit for foreign markets. That gives us potential additional revenue for a product that has already been aged out of our domestic market.

More than once, I've worked for a company, especially in the healthcare field, where the primary product addressed a healthcare problem that was becoming less and less relevant in the US market. I've sold medical devices whose main unique selling point was being able to work for several hours off an internal battery. By the year 2000, poor electric supply was not a problem at most US hospitals but was a huge problem in parts of the developing world. Another product I sold was developed for mass vaccination campaigns and was more suited to the developing world than to the US healthcare system.

Another good reason to build internationally: often when you have taken a significant market share in your domestic market and are the market leader, every additional point of market share comes at a high price. While international growth isn't easy or cheap, it may provide a better return on investment that fighting for additional points of market share in a hotly contested domestic market.

The cost of bringing in $10 million from a new market like Saudi Arabia may be significantly cheaper than the cost of adding $10 million to your existing $80 million in the US market.

If we have a solid domestic position and a global competitor is attacking our domestic market, reaching out into their home markets may be a good strategy to tie them up and fend them off our market. I have been hired to do that more than once, and it can be very successful. If we start affecting what they consider their bread and butter, we may even get them to pull completely out of our market to focus on protecting their own home market.

What isn't a good reason? Any reason that you can't back up with numbers. We are in this for the sales. If, deep down, the reason that you want to expand isn't tied to sales or profits or market capitalization of the company, you are probably setting yourself up for disaster.

Expanding globally is about as dangerous a thing as a company can do. It's expensive, it dilutes focus, and it can cause huge stress on the operating systems of a company. Many companies sink or cripple themselves when they attempt it and fail. You shouldn't do it if you don't have good, solid motives to do it; ego or a desire to travel isn't enough.

You also need to define success before you start. If you don't know why you want to build up your international sales you are taking on a huge amount of work that can put your career, and possibly your business, at risk. If you don't know what you are trying to achieve, you can't plan a strategy.

These are all good, solid business reasons to expand your international market. This is a common theme throughout this book. What I've seen often is people get into international sales for the wrong reason. It's not uncommon to see small business owners or sales managers get into international sales simply because they want to travel more. Or they read an article about a specific market that sounds attractive and sounds like it's going to be a good fit, and then they throw resources at the project without putting enough thought or study into it.

What I am going to do in this book is put my 30 years of experience, selling in more than 100 countries, building market share and driving revenue for more than a dozen companies, into clear and concise guideline that can help you bypass the mistakes and failures that most companies experience. The key is to do this with intent—to look at driving your international footprint the way you would look at driving your manufacturing capacity—as something that requires thought and clear-cut concepts and accountability.

This is as good a time as any to talk about expectations. Very often our companies have absolutely no idea what we're doing in terms of global expansion. While we typically will have colleagues who have been involved with companies that sell internationally, it is very rare to have multiple people who have actually been involved with the responsibility for global expansion working in a midmarket US manufacturing company.

A typical conversation starts with, "We will not be seeing a bump in revenue for 18 months because it will take that long to put in place this list of factors and activities. We all need to be in agreement." Everyone agrees, but about nine months later they're saying, "I don't see a change in revenue; maybe we should change the plan." And over the next nine months or so this chatter becomes more and more shrill and urgent and often results in companies changing or throwing away their plan midstream to try a whole new plan that will take another 18 to 24 months to succeed. I've seen this multiple times. It is critical that we put together a good plan and then hold the course. Barring new pertinent evidence, making changes due to cold feet is never a good idea.

This is one of the very definitions of chaos—when changes occur too frequently for relevant feedback to be registered. The standard management cycle is planning, execution, and measurement of success, followed by a newer plan based on lessons learned in the previous cycle. Cycle after cycle, it is the feedback gained through measurement that makes it a nonchaotic, predictable system. But if you have a system where you make new plans and take action without waiting for feedback, it is chaotic and unpredictable.

Of course, every leader who likes to operate like this will deny that this is chaos; he will talk about his gut feeling, or how with all of his experience he knows when something looks like it won't work or something like that. But it is clear that it is, by definition, unpredictable and therefore chaotic behavior.

Four-digit international sales growth cannot be built overnight. The type of change required to drive significant growth often takes 12 to 24 months to take effect. The path to this is to formulate a plan with milestones, agree to those milestones, monitor those milestones, and stick to the plan.

We live in a world that appreciates agility. I often say, "It isn't the big that eat the little but the agile that eat the slow." Pursuit predators like cheetahs are the most agile of creatures, and they carefully plan their use of energy based on the path of their prey; they do not change course randomly. Over the past 30 years I have been able to grow sales organizations by over 1,000% multiple times. Each time we followed a predictable path: strategic plan, approval, implementation, market validation, adjustments, repeat. Chaos has no place in sales growth.

## Bonus article: Why Chaos Has No Place in Sales Growth

https://www.forbes.com/sites/forbesbusinessdevelopmentcouncil/2020/06/12/why-chaos-has-no-place-in-sales-leadership/#3908d4eb21d5

## Bonus lessons:

MIT bootcamp – *How to Systematically Grow Your International Market*
https://old.bootcamps.mit.edu/how-to-systematically-grow-your-international-market/
https://www.youtube.com/watch?v=pElqxNOaCD4&t=21s

# WHY GROW?

## Good reasons

Drive value of company

Drive revenue

Attack foreign competition to keep them off our home markets

## Bad reasons

To see Paris in the spring

Anything that you can't quantify into a revenue number

# Chapter 1
## BASIC CONCEPTS

Remember that selling internationally is essentially selling. There are lots of different models for talking about selling. For me, the most important element in terms of growing international sales is continuous improvement of the sales process through controlling that process.

What do I mean by the sales process? Again, there are a dozen different models to look at this, and I don't really want to change the way you model your sales process as long as you have a way of modeling. If you don't, then I am going to suggest you use mine. For the purposes of this book I will use the model I am most comfortable with. You can insert into this any other sales model that helps your understanding and your ability to get your arms around the concept.

For me, the sales process comprises two core activity components: building rapport and trust between the seller and the buyer, and helping the buyer internalize that my product solves his problem.

These components are preceded by finding and identifying the customers, which happens before you can start the other groups of activities, and followed by the mechanics of delivering product, after-sale service, end user training, getting paid and making sure your product meets government approvals, and so on.

Let's call these components Finding, Rapport, Solution, and Delivery. Everything that we do should be tied to one of those components.

Let's look at the very basic difference between international and domestic sales. We may already know all of our domestic customers or, more likely, they might know us. When we are entering international markets, chances are that everything we've built in terms of representation domestically and all of our domestic marketing, all of our domestic name recognition, may be totally worthless. I've worked for more than one company with great name recognition and reputation in the domestic market. Basically, everybody knew us in our domestic market and our marketing materials depended on having a very high level of name recognition. The company felt that we didn't need to tell anybody who we were, the company history, company achievements, etc., because everybody was familiar with the company and our product. Starting out in the international market was a huge shock and required major changes in sales enablement tools and marketing tools.

Likewise, in our domestic market we might have a huge network of satisfied customers who have used our product in one organization and then moved on to another, spreading goodwill about our company and our product. We may have a huge base of existing relationships that we can leverage for future sales and possibly future growth in the domestic market and we do not have this internationally. Just as important, it might be much harder for us to establish relationships of trust with people in other countries.

I've worked for companies that had such a strong Midwestern culture in their company it was very difficult for employees who had grown up within this culture to establish rapport with people in Asia or Africa or the Middle East or Latin America.

This really isn't uncommon. Aside from specific cultural mismatch, for instance, between somebody who's grown up all his life in Omaha, Nebraska, and somebody who lives in Riyadh, Saudi Arabia, if you grow to be a 40-year-old salesman with 18 years sales experience achieving your sales goals and being a well-regarded regional sales manager, would you ever have had to deal with anybody who isn't a white, Christian, English-speaking American engineer? Suddenly being thrown into an international arena and having to develop rapport with people from dozens of countries and multiple religions and a wide range of backgrounds can be daunting.

Helping the customer internalize that we have a solution for his problems... This sounds like it might be universal, and it really is close. But we have to break it into pieces.

We don't know that we're **solving** the customer's needs if we don't **understand** the customer's needs. The way customers might manage their workflow and their lives may be very different in different countries. One of the product lines that I sold successfully over the years was a hospital communication system developed for the US market that dealt with improving workflow, safety, and time management for clinicians and patients throughout the hospital. It was a very well regarded, market-leading product and very well developed for its core market in the United States.

None of the people involved in product development had ever seen a hospital outside the United States, and they found they had no understanding of the workflow needs or even the physical infrastructure of hospitals in the target markets. So we were offering benefits to the customer that simply were not perceived as benefits by most of our customers—until we started to understand their workflow and positioned our messaging around the needs of these new customers.

Another element of this is the differences in how different cultures process internal information. In some societies hierarchy is more flexible than others. In some societies people are more likely to want to get information at the beginning of the discussion as opposed to the end. In some societies people are more open to receiving information before they have established rapport, while in others it is strictly sequential; no information can be acknowledged, accepted, or certainly internalized until rapport and trust have been built solidly.

What may actually be the biggest and toughest obstacle to global expansion for many US companies is the last part of those four components in the sales process—the logistics/administration/mechanics—moving the product, making sure the product gets through customs, training the end user, getting paid, and regulatory. I would also say that 95% of the training books and workshop seminars aimed at new exporters only deal with this last part, possibly because people realize very quickly that they have a problem.

Let me explain. If I'm selling you something in the domestic market, you and I are meeting face to face. You see the product. You give me money, I hand you the product. We are dealing with a very specific time and place that don't necessarily even have to be discussed. If you don't pay me cash, there are multiple forms of payment where I know that I will be paid. If you don't pay me, I simply call a collection agency and I'll get my money. You know that you're getting the product because maybe you can see it or you know where my warehouse is. You know where my shop is and delivering that product to you is simple because it's something I do on a daily basis. We're working with the same tax structure, so any taxes or any government interference or regulatory approvals are things we have both dealt with on a regular basis and we're comfortable with. We know all of that, it's all simple, and we trust and know the system."

Now let's say I am selling you something internationally. I might have to discuss when and where ownership transfers to you. Maybe you are in Singapore and I'm in Chicago. Ownership may transfer in Chicago, Singapore, or San Francisco. Ownership may transfer at the door of your warehouse, the door of my factory, or the dock next to a ship. Payment may be cash in advance, it may be 180 days, or it may be a letter of credit issued by one bank to another and a second letter of credit issued from the other bank to me. It may be impossible to get the goods out of the airport without documentation that is specific to your country, as with, say, Saudi Arabia. The legalization costs on that paperwork might be 5% of the whole value of the purchase order.

All these issues are unknown, and variables may change with different markets. This is typically the component that most scares people, but it shouldn't; it's all technical and you can hire people who know these issues and can deal with them for you. But if you don't have the right people on the ground forming relationships of trust and helping the customers internalize the value of your product, you aren't going to be able to sell.

## Force multiplication

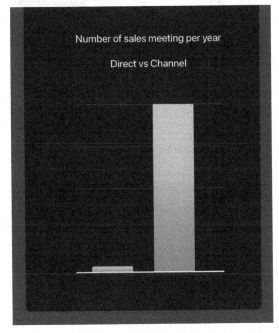

Number of sales meeting per year

Direct vs Channel

The United States Army Special Forces, colloquially known as the "green berets", are very famous, probably due to the John Wayne movie. What, exactly, do they do? Well, they're excellent soldiers, but their primary advantage in warfare has been in force multiplication. One green beret can recruit, train, and lead a larger force, which means that instead of having one rifleman who can hit his target 25 times a minute accurately, we can have 200 riflemen who can each hit his target 6 times a minute accurately.

In terms of scaling up international growth, it is key to get more boots on the ground and more sales assets selling our products. For any company that is in the small to midmarket range, what that means is a distribution network.

In the purest sense of the word, most people would define a distributor as a sales organization that buys your product, takes possession of it, stores it, and sells it. In this book I will be referring to your nonemployee sales assets as "partners". Let's talk about some of the types of partners we may work with. The key to everything in our plan is putting together the right force that consists of these assets and our own employees. If you are a $20 million company, you might have a vice president of international sales and three regional sales managers, along with a force of distributors or a mixture of some combination of the following assets.

***Global distribution agreements:*** One possibility, especially used by smaller companies, is to form a global distribution partnership with a larger corporation. This corporation may not even be a distributor; it could be a manufacturer of a similar product and related noncompeting products.

***Distributors:*** This is the most common relationship, and whether they actually take physical possession of your product in today's world may be a moot point. These are people or organizations with whom you form a legal, binding relationship. You may have one or more in the territory covering different customers or sometimes overlapping on customers, and they will promote your brand, your company, and your sales goals within their designated territory during the designated time frame of your partnership.

***Agents:*** Very often we blur the lines between agents and distributors in a pure semantic sense. An agent is somebody who deals with your customers but never takes possession or ownership of your product in return for a finder's fee or commission on sales. Depending on the nature of your product, your solution, your customers, and your market, using agents may be the best way to go—but it does have a reputation as a less committed relationship. In some cases, though, this really makes the most sense for everybody.

***Manufacturer's representatives:*** Manufacturer's reps are not dissimilar to agents, and again the line gets a little blurred here. I would say a manufacturer's rep is a single sales asset possibly supported by an office staff but really not a company or a team of people. It's common to use them as interim or fractional regional sales managers because they often cover multiple territories.

*Consultants:* In many cases we may use consultants who don't have a long-term relationship with us but are involved in a specific project or deal or are involved in creating a relationship, gathering information, or helping us with the logistics, documentation, payments, etc. I will lump them all together as "consultants," but these are people who are either getting paid for a specific project, amount of time, or deal but do not have a long-term relationship with us. I try to avoid working with consultants like this, aside from one very specific area where I think they bring the best value—gathering and organizing market intelligence. We often struggle to gather market intelligence, and one of the biggest mistakes we make is to use nonprofessionals or to trust our distributors or RMs with our market intelligence. There is huge value in employing people who are specifically paid to gather professional market intelligence, whose value to everybody is accuracy of information.

What are the motivations and fears of our partners? Obviously, distributors are in this to make money. But a distributor isn't just selling our product; depending on the stage of growth and stability of the company, the distributor is trying to grow its own brand name, company, and business.

We could have a distributor with a small number of products that is looking to add names to its portfolio in order to grow the reputation of its company. We could have a distributor with hundreds or even thousands of products in its portfolio that has grown too fast or too much and doesn't have the capacity to correctly represent all of these products, but still thinks that its place in the market is to represent the most interesting products coming in.

What do distributors fear? In general, they fear putting effort into selling your product and then not getting return on investment. This could be because the product is not as good as anticipated or the product has stronger competition than anticipated. It could be because of you—of the manufacturer's inability to supply against orders. It could be due to the manufacturer changing its plans for that market and either pulling out, going direct, or changing distributors in an unpredictable manner. The fears in the market are often tied to the unpredictability of the manufacturer, so one of the things new exporters need to learn and understand is that part of their job is helping the market come to trust that they will not act in an unpredictable manner.

# Trade

So what what's the basic structure when we're dealing with international sales and trade?

There are multiple models for this. Traditionally and historically, I have a commodity—let's say allspice or volcanic rock or tin—that is found where I am and is needed someplace else. I take that commodity and I transport it to the market where it's needed or to some type of market in the middle where traders from that market come to meet me with some other type of commodity that I might find attractive. An excellent example of this was the trade in gold that took place in West Africa. Lumps of gold and lumps of salt were laid out, a conversion rate was established, and each side took the traded goods home. Similar trading went on throughout the world.

Very often the involved parties might not have two commodities that they each wanted or whose price they could agree on. In that case, often, people would take one commodity traded for a more universally accepted commodity like silver or gold or salt and then use that as a trade good. For instance, the value of silver was pushed up dramatically because silver was the only currency or commodity that the Chinese would take from Europeans for centuries.

Then came a situation where some areas developed better manufacturing or had preferable agricultural goods. For example, for many years Chinese silks and porcelains, Indian printed fabric, European firearms, and Italian and French wines were all goods that could be made in multiple places but there was a preference for goods manufactured in a specific source. In this case, an Italian farmer from the right village in Tuscany may be able to trade one liter of his wine for 10 liters of acceptable wine of lesser quality.

Following the Industrial Revolution in the 19th century and the boom of industrialization after World War II in the 20th century, some countries, including the United States, Germany, Japan, and the UK became manufacturing powerhouses and their products were in great demand—not because of something inherently American or German, or Japanese or British but because they had much higher quality and much more cost-effective manufacturing capacity as time went on. Over the years these advantages have shifted and typically follow the cheapest manufacturing ability. For years Japan had a fantastic ability to manufacture quality products very cheaply, and now that reputation has shifted to China.

For a period of time there was a new model that really didn't last very long, possibly less than three decades. Typically an American corporation would establish best-of-breed manufacturing capacity for a commonly used manufactured commodity like bathroom fixtures, for example, and then it would set up factories in multiple locations around the world, sourcing local raw materials and locally training its workforce—essentially manufacturing American products in dozens of places around the world for the local market at a reasonable price using local raw goods and local workforce.

In the 1990s a different paradigm became a little more common. Centers of excellence like New York, Silicon Valley, Munich, Milan, and Tokyo became world centers of a specific type of professional. In this model a multinational corporation may use aesthetic designers from

Milan to design a toilet, then use engineers to make a prototype of that toilet in Munich, then shift manufacturing to a plant in China where the facilities were dramatically cheaper. This was the model that I have always believed was the most effective and the one that struck me as the best for spreading affluence and success for everyone. But this type of globalization may be ending.

What we're seeing today are companies that could conceivably exist anywhere in the world. They've come up with an idea for a product or a design for a product; they buy manufacturing equipment that is available anywhere in the world and is similar or identical to the manufacturing equipment used anywhere else in the world. They employ laborers with a similar education to laborers in other parts of the world, so in a lot of ways there isn't an inherent advantage or benefit to the location of many manufacturers in the 21st century over manufacturers in other parts of the world. They do not necessarily have an advantage of better transit, better or cheaper transportation routes, better or cheaper energy sources, better or cheaper labor sources, better or cheaper supply of raw materials. And this is important to remember in terms of quantifying the advantage that the manufacturer has over a possible competing manufacturer; it pretty much comes down to the design of the product.

There are a few more things that we need to remember when we look at being an American exporter and understanding the basics of international business.

What are some hurdles that new exporters face and typically are not expecting or didn't think of before they got into the exporting business?

Let's say you are a manufacturer, and you are number one in the US market for a specific type of widget, used by other manufacturers to create a premium product in the automotive industry. You sell $50 million domestically year after year, with approximately 8% growth annually. Your goal is to get 20% of your sales internationally within five years. What hurdles will you face?

First, is this even a market that exists internationally? Do European, Asian, African, or Latin American customers have a need or want for the solution that you provide? Is this a need or problem that they're facing today? Very often we like to assume that all consumers would like to buy something like what's being sold in the US market, but we don't know that. So the first hurdle is determining if there are customers with this need and if there are, where they are and where we can get to the most customers with this need with the lowest cost of sale.

Next we have to figure out how to sell to them. Today, who can reach these end users? Let's say that your widget is reaching end users in the United States 90% of the time when they buy a new car, and the remaining 10% is aftermarket sales through authorized dealers. Is that the same path to the end user that you can use internationally? In my experience is it very rare that the international path is identical to the domestic path, so you need to understand how you will get to the end user customer in the market structure you choose.

Your end user customers as well as your sales organization and the channels involved in your sales process are not going to be familiar with your company, your reputation, and possibly even your product. You may be selling a type of widget that nobody else is selling internationally and you may be faced with missionary selling activities, which would involve showing the market why they want this widget, what problems it solves. The problem may very well exist but isn't at top of any mind right now.

This ties up with the questions that we ask ourselves at the very beginning of the process. You may face hurdles involving government regulation. In most industries—food, healthcare, transportation, communication, IT, and others—there are government regulations, and often the government limits or controls what is imported, requiring that new products go through the regulatory process. That may be quite rigorous and can be different for every market. Many manufacturers in the healthcare or communication business have in-house regulatory affairs people to deal with the government or they have an existing, ongoing relationship with a regulatory affairs consultant.

A new exporter may very well face hurdles related to logistics and payments as well. I have worked a dozen times or so with companies that are either new to exporting or trying to significantly ramp up their exporting. In every single case, they have underestimated what they needed to learn in order to ramp up their exporting capacity. To go from not exporting at all or exporting 1% of the manufactured output of the company to exporting 20% to 25% of the manufactured output of the company will require significant changes in workflow and will require either hiring new people to help you understand exporting or retraining existing personnel in depth.

The final, biggest, and most important hurdle to international growth success that I talked about in this introduction is completely internal. Again, every manufacturer that I know of underestimates the turmoil and change involved in growing export sales. In every company the biggest battles, the most rigorous selling, and the biggest waste of time occur in internal arguments with people resisting change.

Increasing the overall sales of an existing ongoing manufacturing company by 20% through growing the international sales has huge return on investment for the company and has huge impact on the value of that company in the event of future resale. The revenue and the profit streams also bring with them large benefits to the company. The cost of that internally often can be difficult to swallow. There may be requirements to change quality processes throughout manufacturing. There may be requirements to tweak the manufacturing process. There will be requirements in the shipping and payment areas; often the existing management and the sales management are faced with changes to the paradigms they understand and are familiar with, and this can cause a great deal of tension internally.

In summary, growing internationally is possible for most American manufacturers, whether small, midmarket, or large. This international growth can bring in additional ongoing revenue streams that may not be available in the domestic market, may be significantly larger than is possible in the domestic market, or simply may have a lower cost-per-dollar growth in the domestic market. Most important, there is no better way to grow the value of a mature existing company, and often a newer startup, than growing a strong international footprint. That said, growing international sales involves changes that may create tension and stress throughout the company, and an unsuccessful attempt to grow internationally can be dangerous and hugely detrimental to a manufacturing company. When a company decides to grow internationally, it needs to be ready to throw its resources and culture into the plan.

If we want to grow international sales, certain things will have to change. That's a given. We can't say, "We will grow sales, but we're not changing how people do things." It doesn't work like that. You will find, as the head of the international sales project, a certain amount of pushback. People don't like change. People aren't going to be enthusiastic about the change. People aren't going to understand why this change is taking place. And in a perfect world, everybody reading this would be building up a new sales organization from scratch, which is much easier than rebuilding something that needs to be fixed.

In most cases, you are inheriting a poorly performing sales organization, and the poorly performing people within the organization are most likely not going to agree with you and say, "Yes, we are poorly performing and you should fire us and start over." They're going to say, "We're doing a great job. The reason sales aren't happening is outside of our control and you don't understand how rough it is and there's really nothing that can be done to improve things."

I've heard this time and time again over the course of my career. Quite often, you might have people who are very good at something and it's not international sales, but they are in that job for a variety of reasons. They thought that it would be exciting, that it would be easier. Somebody from another department might have wanted to get rid of them. Or they thought this would be a great way to advance their career and it didn't work out very well for them.

Or, they may have been transferred to international sales by their kind hearted boss after failing at regional sales, instead of being let go.

You might have a department like that, but I will assume that the reason you're trying to build this up is because the department or team or unit of international sales simply isn't functioning as well as it should be. On the other side are the distributors, and if you're trying to build this up and you're struggling to grow, then obviously the distributors aren't functioning the way they should be and they will be even more resistant because often, these are people who have their own business; they could be very successful in other things. They are putting the amount of work and effort into your product that they feel is appropriate, and they're probably richer than you are.

Often when I came into a company there were distributors who weren't selling my product very well, but boy, they were pretty rich. They might have private yachts and private airplanes and cars, much nicer than my cars. But they're not selling my product and they always have good reasons why they're not selling my product. So here we are coming in, and everybody's going to resist change.

Then there's a third group, the non-salespeople within your company, and you will come in and say, "We really need to improve the way we do our shipping. We really need to improve the way we handle our finance, our international sales payment finance."

Everybody's going to resist it. Everybody's going to say, "This is the way we've been doing it for years. I don't see any reason to change." I've come into companies probably 10 or 12 times over the course of my career. Nobody was doing shipping well. There's always room to improve shipping but nobody believes that they're not doing it well. When you say, "I'm really hoping that we can increase our shipping internationally by 500%, by 1000%, by 3000%, and if that happens, shipping is going to be very important." I can tell you horror story after horror story from a salesman's perspective. Every shipping department I have ever worked with has resisted improving their preparedness for growing international shipping.

It's very important to let people know why we're looking for change. What does that mean to a company? For a midmarket manufacturer or a smaller company, increasing the international footprint, leading in a 20%-30% increase in overall sales, has the potential to more than double the value of the company. So if we're the type of company where I have a piece of the company or we all have stock options, or we just take pride in the company and we want it to grow and we want to make sure that our future is secure, all of these things are tied up with international growth. The reason we're making changes is to drive top line sales of the company, in order to drive profitability of the company, the market cap of the company. Everybody should understand this within the company.

You can find creative ways to incentivize people in your company to help them understand the value of change. Sometimes I create little cards that read, "The recipient of this card did a favor for the international sales organization to help drive sales. This card can be exchanged for one drink at our annual thank you party." I hand the cards out to people who make indirect contributions—not salespeople, manufacturing people, engineering people and administrative people. I would just say, "Thanks a lot. What you are doing is helpful. It's helping move forward our international sales, and I appreciate it." And then, once a year, when I have my regional sales managers in headquarters, I have a pizza party in the afternoon.

That evening I invite people out to a bar. In my last company we had about 700 people at the factory. I'd invite everybody, and about 40 of them would come. They would be very excited that I did in fact invite them, and the people with the cards got a free drink. Some of these people had five cards, and they had been saving them on their cubicle walls or in their wallet. It was a token of appreciation that they really did like. It was something that was effective in getting a little more help from people who didn't gain direct financial benefit from doing what they had done to support my team.

Ideally, the head of international sales should be part of the management board discussing change at meetings, and be able to raise discussions like "This may involve a million dollars' worth of investment on final product, but we're looking at getting a return of $20 million in additional annual sales over the next six years, so we're easily going to recoup our investment." Or you might say, "We need to spend $10 to $12 million to make this change. It might be five years before we get that money back. Maybe this isn't the investment we need to make. Maybe we should be looking for markets that don't require this change." You might discover that your product, without that change, can't be sold in certain markets. On the other hand, that change isn't cost effective. You won't see good return on investment, so you have to focus on other things.

Those are options also, but you want to make sure people understand why you're working on these changes—see the value of the changes. You don't want anybody putting effort or time or money into changing a product without good commercial justification.

# A few words on corruption and illegal activities

At one point in the early 90s, I bought a very fancy Armani tie, which I stopped wearing after a few years. About a decade later, I was in charge of the South Asian Market for a Fortune 1000 corporation. My biggest deal during that period, and until now the biggest purchase order of my life, was a $30 million deal with one of the three biggest corporations in India. I was pretty conspicuous in the Mumbai business scene at the time, due to the size and impact of this deal. Over the course of about two years, about 200 people approached me to tell me that they could influence the deal in my favor. A very famous actor and several famous cricket players, people who said that they were friends of the CEO, and people who said they were his children's teachers and bodyguards; a wide range of people. They all said that they could get me a private audience with the CEO and that they had the influence to get me the deal. I carried around my old tie, confident that it was the only one of its kind on the subcontinent, and I would say to people, "I will be in the office on Thursday and I will be able to see the CEO. Take this tie, if you can get the CEO to wear it, I will believe that you have enough influence to do this deal…" Nobody took me up on the offer, and I closed the deal with not a stitch of strange voodoo help. Normal, sales process selling, just like I would have if the deal had been in Cleveland and not Mumbai. I learned that you don't have to believe things are done funny in different countries. Business can be done in a straightforward way pretty much everywhere you operate, if you know what you are doing.

I've closed purchase orders from 135 or so countries around the world over 30 years, much of those dealing with governments. A handful of those, like Cuba and Iran, are countries that the US government does not like people selling to. I have been shaken down on every continent by some government official, with the exception of Australia.

In Russia, I waved at the security camera that the agent was clearly trying to avoid while trying to get me to pay him a bribe, so he quickly waved me out without having to pay. In one African country the passport agent said, "Mr. Selch, it seems that you forgot to put money in your passport for me", and I laughed him off and waited until he sent me through. In another African country I waited by the side of the road for a policeman to let me go after he threatened to detain me until I bought him lunch. The theme is you can get business done, perhaps slightly more slowly, without paying bribes.

With that, I was extremely careful not to break any laws. I have not paid bribes; I have filled out all the correct paperwork needed for shipping to restricted countries. I have not even tried to bend the rules. Annoying the federal government is not something that I want to do.

I am not going to give you legal advice, but I am going to say that you should check the legal issues of every aspect of international trade carefully. There are differences in how you can ship goods to Syria or Cuba or Iran, and you shouldn't bend the rules. I once sold a million dollars' worth of goods to Iran, and I can still feel the deep pain in my gut as I carefully went over the dozens of pages of forms that each had very clearly on the top and bottom the warning that any dishonesty or mistake could be treated as a federal felony, and I signed my name, taking personal responsibility for the accuracy of hundreds of details on the forms.

Everyone who works for an American company that sells internationally should probably take anticorruption training, but you should follow the instructions of your human resources and legal departments, not me. What I can tell you is this: do not treat this as a joke or something to try to get around.

# Product Change

This may be the most controversial statement I make when I'm having these discussions, but I like to say I've spent 30 years selling in more than 130 countries and earned hundreds of millions of dollars in sales without ever making a major product modification for a specific international market. It is my belief that getting into the business of making modifications for every market can sink anybody who isn't an enormous company. I'm certainly open to the fact that there may be exceptions to that, especially for fast-moving companies whose products are mostly software or whose business model is making specific projects one off for customers or if you have the flexibility to change products quickly at a reasonable price. You might be completely outside of this rule. But for the most part, changes will be much larger in scope and much more expensive and much slower than you foresee.

One thing that I remember from Marketing 101 at Wharton many years ago is that selling is essentially taking the product you have and getting people to buy it, and that marketing includes the process of trying to figure out which product is going to be a good fit for the market. In a perfect world, I would love to be in a company that was big enough and rich enough and fast-moving enough so that I was constantly improving and developing new products for new markets as well as my existing markets' developing needs. I would also really like a flying unicorn. I don't think I will get either of those things.

In the real world what we are trying to do is take a product that somebody developed, figure out where we can sell it, and sell as much of it as we can as profitably as we can. I always tell the people who work for me and with me and my distributors that this is our primary mission.

I've even said that if I'm talking to a distributor and he mentions three times during the recruitment process the potential products that he would like to sell in the future, I will decide not to work with him because it's obvious he's not comfortable with the existing product line.

I do not want to work with a distributor whose focus is on products we may or may not develop in the future. Again, this is a little controversial because obviously I understand that the distributors are concerned about their future and concerned that we as a manufacturer are thinking about future products. On the other hand, if they don't believe they can sell the product I have today, I don't want to work with them.

Likewise, I want to make that crystal clear to both my company's salespeople and my distributors' salespeople. I have a reputation for being quite brutal about this. I once had a fantastic salesman start with me. He went through several training sessions in the first week, and every evening when I would ask the trainers for feedback, everybody said he kept suggesting changes that could be made to the product to make it better. That Friday I took him out for breakfast before any other meetings and I said, "It looks to me like you're not happy here. I think we can still try to get you your old job back, no harm done," and he completely freaked out. "Zach," he said, "what do you mean? I'm very happy here." I said, "Well, if you're so happy, why do you keep suggesting that we change the product? This is the product we have, and I can only assume that you don't believe that you can sell it if you're asking for so many changes." Then he spent the next hour telling me all the reasons he loved the product. I then said, "I see you love the product. I agree with you that we have a good, solid product. It might not be perfect, there may be room for improvement, but our job is to sell the product we have. There will be opportunities to talk about what we can do to change the product, but product training is not the right time to be talking about changing the product."

With all that said, sometimes we do change products. What I do strongly believe in is products that are designed for multiple international markets. The best example is having software that works in different alphabets. American companies often will create products that have screens or interface with screens that are designed to only work with Latin alphabets. With minor adjustments and a minor investment early in the process, the same products can work with virtually any alphabet. While easily half the world is happy working with the Latin alphabet, that leaves us with about half the world that would require changes to the screen or software. Why leave that other half off the table?

Aside from that, while many East Africans or Arabs from the Gulf region are probably going to be pretty happy working in English, they will be thrilled if the product is offered with software in Swahili and Arabic. Even if nobody will ever use it (and you really don't want to tell this to your vice president of research and development), this can dramatically drive sales. Anything that gets sold to the government has the potential of putting in a tender line or specification line that says, "must work in the local language." If you sell something that is used by governments in the Middle East, having software in Arabic gives you the ability to crush your competition.

That said, there are a lot of countries, like Japan and Russia, where the local language is really critical to selling your product. You are probably not going to be able to sell anything software-based to Japan without Japanese language.

When presenting this internally to make changes, you always want to talk about the potential for grouping multiple countries together. Again, it would be a disaster to make your product work in Japanese without also giving it the ability to work in multiple other alphabets. What you don't want is for somebody to invest $250,000 for a single language when $300,000 would get you languages that cover most of the world.

Language is probably the most relevant change in a product. The second most relevant is addressing a fundamental difference in electricity or plumbing or installation in different markets. This really is difficult to get past and, in the end, avoiding the changes might involve such a large sales effort that your profitability drops dramatically. I've done it a lot, but I do feel it's expensive.

I sold a product that was installed inside and on the walls of hospitals. In some countries, back boxes—boxes positioned on the walls for devices like ours and others to be placed into—were too small for our devices. These boxes were different shapes around the world. Because many of our customers wanted features that we had, they were willing to pull out the market-standard back boxes and replace them with back boxes we supplied.

By changing this element, we were able to make it easier for customers to buy our product and incrementally increase sales. Putting in electrical current adapters in today's world is pretty much a no-brainer. They are relatively cheap and small and can be put in just about anything, but ideally your products should be ready to be installed anywhere in the world and work. That will take away one more objection that your customers may have.

On the other hand, with the same company, one of our fundamental benefits was that by doing a great deal of very expensive research and development, we were able to cut down on the cost of wiring by 80% or so. The overall cost of our systems was about one-third product cost, one-third installation cost, and one-third margin for the distributor and us. There was one very large market that had several indigenous competitors. Our product was a great deal more feature rich and so more expensive, but when you took into account the lower cost of wiring, our product then became about the same price as the others, but with a great deal more features. The local manufacturers banded together and pushed the local government to put in place a regulation that outlawed our type of wiring in government buildings, effectively meaning that we had to throw redundant wires into our system and increase our cost for no good reason. Our local distributor sort of slept through this, as did the previous head of international sales. When I understood what was going on, I told the local distributor and the regional manager that they needed to get this regulation changed. I said there was no good reason for this regulation to be in place, and it was eating into our profitability. At first there was a lot of pushback and even some anger, because both the RM and the distributor thought that this was a constraint that was outside of our control. My position was that this was a problem that could be and needed to be solved with sales tools, not engineering tools. Within two years the distributor was able to fix it. It wasn't a problem once he accepted that it was a sales issue and not an engineering issue.

On a regular basis, people may say to you, "To sell in our market you have to change the color" or "We have a customer that's asking for a specific product change." Over the years I have seen a lot of companies chase those changes, and it really can eat into your profitability, sometimes to the point of making the whole international expansion unprofitable. Customers are always going to ask for changes, and they are always going to be looking for things that resemble what's available today in the local market. Your distributors and the distributor reps will be looking for the easiest way to make money, and the easiest way for them to make a little money is for you to change the product to meet exactly what the customer is asking for. That doesn't mean it will be profitable for you.

Yes, we want products that the customers want. What we really want to offer them is something that meets a need. If customers are hung up on a cosmetic issue or a minor operational issue, that means they have not internalized the value of our product as a solution that meets their needs. And that is a fundamental problem in the sales process.

Let us say that you offer a product that can dramatically reduce deaths from cardiac arrest in a hospital by cutting the response time to a code blue by 90%. And you know that there are thousands of deaths like this every year in the target market, and you know that the hospital is penalized for these deaths. Then the hospital comes back and says they require your product to be painted blue because it will fit in better with its color scheme, and the competition offers a blue product even though the product doesn't solve this problem. If this is the situation you are in, then the customer hasn't internalized the value that you are offering them. And if you change the color of your product, that may solve the short-term problem, but it still doesn't solve the problem that your distributor or your sales organization is not doing their job, which is helping customers internalize the value of your product and understand that it solves their problem.

In many fields, especially healthcare, communications, transportation, and security, there are market requirements that are not specified by law; they are simply the requirements that one or another organization has created. (Usually there are legal requirements as well.) From the first group, these requirements have often been designed to protect a local manufacturer. When people tell you about the needs of the market, you need to clarify whether this is a legal requirement or just what the market is used to.

For instance, to be sold in the European Union, most products require a CE mark. Without a CE mark, I cannot get the product out of the airport. On the other hand, many medical products that have a German competitor have requirements that the product act in a similar way to the German product. And people will tell you, "To sell in this market you need to meet these requirements," but that is convention or tradition, not law. Obviously, it's not easy to change convention or tradition, but it's very different from changing the law. There are ways to change this, and even though I'm not going to discuss it in depth here, my best strategy is to find one or two very unhappy key opinion leaders within the market who don't like the local manufacturer or the local manufacturer rep that they have to work with, and I leverage them to get one reference site in the market. Once I have one reference site that has broken with convention, the wall is cracked and then I can get into other places. But if there are legal requirements, that's a different story. No matter how good your product is and how much somebody wants it, if it doesn't have CE certification, for instance, you won't get anybody in Europe try to change the law for you.

When you do decide to make changes to products, you need to have somebody from the international sales team interfacing on a regular basis with the engineering team. And it's best to quantify the value of the changes. For instance, if you claim that if a product is made with 12 languages you can sell $1 million, and then you find out that they've changed the spec and it will only have one extra language, you have to make it clear that this means you anticipate selling only $100,000. You need to document these things.

It is very important not to let your distributors or your end users know the timetable or product feature package for these changes or new product. If your distributors believe that you will release a substantially superior product within a short time frame, there's a very good chance that they are simply going to stop selling your present product and wait. If your distributors mention to your end users that you're coming out with a new product with a new feature set, it is really possible that the end users will decide to wait.

I've seen many instances where this has actually resulted in end users deciding to go with the competition because they perceived that the competition was offering a latest-generation product and we were offering a product that was about to become obsolete. It didn't matter what the feature set was of the existing product or the price point; they simply didn't want to buy a product that they thought would be obsolete in a year or so.

When you know for sure when you're releasing the product and what the feature set is going to be, you plan a product launch, first with your regional managers and then with your distributors. Typically, you then do one in-market with your distributors and end users. This will usually run about 90 days from the RM training to the end user workshops.

If your company is flexible enough to carry out fast product changes, that's a great thing for international expansion—to create multiple products that fit the different markets very well. I have never seen a company like this. You really have to be clear if you can do this or not; in my experience, changing a product takes much longer than anybody anticipates, is extremely painful, and never goes as smoothly as expected.

Somebody once asked me a very specific question about this: "What if, for instance, I make cosmetics and I want to launch into the African market? I will need to make very different products for this market."

That's definitely true, but is this the best way for me to use my expertise and resources? Will I require knowledge or raw materials for cosmetics for African markets used by Black People, that I don't have when I'm dealing with Caucasian-targeted cosmetics? That's something that has to be thought through. In addition, we're not doing this specifically for, say, Ghana; we are talking about the whole continent of Africa or a large part of it. To me that makes perfect sense.

Ideally, I would offer a product that is a good fit for the US market, one for the European market, one for the Asian market, and one for the African market. Those products should, between them, work for Latin America, for the Middle East, and for other markets around the world, making the whole world accessible. If we're a big enough company or an agile enough company, maybe that range becomes 12 or 14 or 20 products, but I find that questionable in terms of profitability. It truly depends on what the company is able to do.

Even though this is something that I am very hesitant about, I always carry a notebook of product change requests that come from the market. People are making product change requests all the time, and I want to document them in case I can utilize them in the development of the future product. What I don't do is run around and try to make changes based on what one or two customers said.

I am going to end this chapter with a warning on that issue. I love to take engineers from headquarters out to visit the market. Typically, they have no cross-cultural communication skills and sometimes their personal communication skills in general are not that strong. But they are very excited to get out and meet customers, and it's very helpful both in terms of strengthening their connection to the market and actually teaching them things that the market may need. But it is particularly important to control and curate their experience.

I worked for a company where the son of the owner was an engineer responsible for developing a new product for the international market. I believe he saw this as his opportunity to prove himself to his father, and he really wanted to be able to show that he could handle it. He knew nothing about any international markets, and he had extraordinarily little actual professional experience. We took him out to visit some customers, and he decided to take off for a couple of days to tour some hospitals without close supervision. Later, he decided to make some changes to the specifications that we had requested based on some of the things that he had seen. Now this may sound like great initiative on his part, but we were trying to develop a product that would be good in 50 or 60 markets, utilizing feedback we had gotten from people in 50 or 60 markets, and he was changing those specifications based on visits by one person in one market over a period of two days. So you must be extremely careful about how your headquarters engineers learn about market needs and make sure that it's done in an organized and methodical manner.

You need to brief these people on how they respond to customer requests, either from end users or distributors. What is very common is that a distributor or an end user will say something like, "I really need this product to be green" and then your vice president of engineering, who has absolutely no intention of making this product green, will say, "That's a wonderful idea. Thank you for that feedback; let me evaluate this back at headquarters and I'll get back to you." At this point the distributor or end user has understood that your VP of engineering is going to make this change and this change might happen any day now. So why should he bother selling an inferior product when you will improve your product very quickly and it will make it easier to sell it?

When you tell him that this might not be happening for a while, or at all, he may blame you. After all, the VP of engineering told him it was happening and you're telling him it's not happening, so he has to assume that you're trying to sabotage it. I've seen this happen many times. At one company where I worked, there was a very senior engineer who was very polite and friendly but not much of a salesperson or businessperson. When I came on board, a lot of my distributors said that certain product changes had been promised to them by our engineering department, but there was no documentation anywhere about how these promises had been made. There was actually a fundamental flaw in one of the products, and I asked repeatedly why we had put this change into the product. I kept hearing from different people that it seemed like a good solution to the problems that had been raised in the market, but there was no documentation of how it had been decided to make this change or if there'd been any type of return-on-investment study done. Be careful of this.

In international territory, all contact with end users, customers, and potential end users, especially when it has to do with potential changes to the product, should be discussed clearly with the head of international sales to make sure that the messaging and communications are aligned.

# Basic Concepts

The more skilled, motivated and trained people that are selling your product, the more you will sell.

Your success is directly tied to distributor mind share.

If you screw your distributor, you need to find another profession.

Do not try to cheat, bribe or ship product to places that your government doesn't want you to.

Don't confuse a sales problem with an engineering problem – it is very seldom profitable to change products to fit each market.

If you aren't going to change a product, be clear about it.

If you are going to change a product, don't tell anybody until you are clear that it won't impact your short term sales.

# Chapter 2
# THE VERY FIRST STEPS

The first thing we will do is choose the markets that will have the best business impact. In order to do that, we have to start asking ourselves questions. We have to clearly understand why people buy our product. I find that when I have these discussions, this becomes a part of the process that people get frustrated with and want to skip. It really is the very foundation for everything that is going to come after. We think we understand the problem that the customer has and buys from us to solve, but often we're not thinking it through in the right way to help us choose the correct markets to expand into globally.

Who is your customer? Who buys your product? It's critical to answer this early on. We will use the answer to this to build our plans—where we expand, what types of partners we work with, etc.

I've seen this done poorly more than once. One company I worked for made products that were installed into the walls of hospitals; the traditional idea had been that the maintenance person bought the product, did so in order to meet a regulatory need, and was willing to pay $50 per bed or about $100,000 per hospital for it. The IT manager of the hospital had needs that we met and had a budget of $1,000 to $2,000 per bed for a solution like ours. By simply answering correctly "who" buys the product, we could drive up the price the market was willing to pay. Now, of course with that, addressing the IT market required completely different distributors, sales training, sales enablement tools, etc., so we needed to reach that understanding early on in order to prevent wasting money time and effort.

By changing the direction, by changing the benefits that we highlighted to our end users in the international market, we were able to drive the price per bed by hundreds of percent and added a very important differentiator between ourselves and our competition. These things, taken with other changes in strategy execution, drove almost 2,000% sales growth within a handful of years.

# Who is the customer?

The answer doesn't have to be a job title—it could be newly middle-class people, the aging population, or people with two cars. The more you understand the target customer, the better you will build your plan. Of course, plans change, and understanding changes. Don't throw away the project because you don't have a good understanding of the customer at this point; you can make adjustments if you have to later on.

# When does the customer buy?

A boss of mine taught me a concept about 20 years ago that has been very helpful to me over the years: the compelling event. We were using it in a macro sense to help us plan our sales process with individual enterprise customers. I have since adopted and modified this concept for my own planning purposes. I talk about macro and micro compelling events.

A macro compelling event is an economic, political, legal, or demographic event that can influence the market to buy my product, for instance, an aging population, a law that mandates seatbelts, a trade war that makes Chinese product more expensive to the consumer.

A micro compelling event is something that will cause people to buy on an individual basis but that can be looked at across a market. For instance, buying a home might trigger buying a lawn mower, or building a hospital might trigger buying hospital beds.

So if I know that people who are first-generation middle class, or people between 12 and 19 years old, or countries that have recently passed laws mandating security applications on the internet are good markets for me, I can plan. If I know that customers often buy my product within a year of buying a new car, I can plan.

Let me give you an example of a macro compelling event influencing my choice of market. I sold a product that provided better patient experience in hospitals and was correlated with newly middle-class markets. So by focusing on markets where a large portion of the population had entered the middle class in the past 20 years, we did extremely well.

Another time I sold a product that was an extremely accurate medical monitor but was slightly more difficult to use than the gold standard monitor. Our founder and our original VP of sales had built a strategy of pushing the gold standard out of the market due to our perceived benefit—higher accuracy. But the market liked the ease of use of the alternative solution. What I found was that customers wanted to buy our solution about a year after they had introduced the alternative solution, to supplement but not replace. The main manufacturers of the alternative solution were publicly traded companies, so it was relatively easy to see exactly where they sold, and we could follow behind them and sell our solution.

## How does the customer buy?

The customer is going to have a preferred purchasing pathway or system in place. I'll discuss later on how we want to react to or deal with their existing system. In general, I'm a strong believer from the sales process perspective that we do want to control the purchaser's pathway as much as possible. That said, to establish our activities, we need to understand how the customers typically want to buy. What is the evaluation system? Tendering? How will the distributors find and interact with the customers typically? Understanding this is going to be key to deciding what markets and what partners are good for us.

Why should that be? Well, if some markets will be very strongly locked into a tendering process and if at this point our product will not navigate that tendering process, it may be an indication that this isn't a market for us.

If the customer wants to buy our product at retail chains and we don't feel that is our strength, that may influence our choice of market, as another example.

## Why does the customer buy?

Why do people buy our solution? The answer is often not what you think, and it is always worthwhile trying to figure this out carefully. I once sold a very robust ventilator with a six-hour battery that had been designed with the idea that it would be used in patient transport in first-world countries. Our designers hadn't taken into account the market specs for a solution for transport and hadn't caught that ambulances have extremely reliable power supplies, so the product wasn't as attractive to the intended market as planned. It was extremely attractive to markets that had poor power supply; as a critical care ventilator, it met the market specifications almost exactly. By adjusting that target slightly, we were able to thrive and eventually be acquired by a large multinational.

# Building a customer profile

Once I've answered these questions, I've taken the first step in choosing which markets will be the right ones to target. And being very truthful and a little imaginative in this process is key.

If you can't come up with a good reason people should be buying your product, you may want to seriously reconsider the whole activity. I have seen a product developed that founders of the company then struggled, after developing the technology, to find an application to take the technology to market. The best that they could come up with was that this product could help save about 14% off the cost of a medical procedure. This became the primary, unique selling point the strategy was based on. The customers who could buy this product had no real interest in saving money on this procedure, and the people who were tasked with saving money had no real influence over the clinical decisions.

The reason we're going through this process is that the next step is going to be to develop a customer profile. Who is buying our product? Understanding this will help you understand where you want to sell, because effectively what you're looking for are the people who will buy your product in the greatest concentration with the lowest cost of sale to reach those target customers.

Let's go back to some examples. The most recent product I sold had the most focused customer profile I have ever seen. I was selling products that were used for mass vaccination campaigns for poor, large countries. My customer was essentially the decision maker in the ministry of health who dealt with vaccination. I knew the title of that position—the "Extended Program of Immunization Manager." I had a rather good profile of what that person would look like career-wise, education-wise, etc.

In a previous job, I knew that the target customer was the IT manager of hospitals of a certain size that were either going to be built or going to undergo a major renovation. That meant that our sweet spot was for countries undergoing a large growth spurt of the middle class. Why? Because one thing that I've noticed is that as countries or economies enter the middle class, the level of demand in medical care increases dramatically, so products that provide a better patient experience are in demand in countries with a growing middle class. A growing middle class equals new hospital builds and hospital renovations.

## Choosing the right markets

Let's say I'm looking for markets with a growing GDP with a growing middle-class. I can quantify that by saying there is a growth curve of the per capita GDP of at least 10% a year for the last five years, with an anticipated continued 10% yearly growth. I can quantify level of population, say markets of more than 15 million people. That gives me clear target markets in those parameters.

Demographics of course aren't the only indicator of whether the market will be good for me. Often changes in regulatory or legal issues can trigger a demand for my product; this is common in healthcare, food, communication, and transportation industries.

Once we have identified who our target customer is and what their profile is, we can think of compelling events that would lead somebody to buy my product. In my field, which is healthcare, a boost in hospital building is a fantastic compelling event that can drive my sales. So, for instance, when I hear that Ethiopia has plans to build 2,000 beds in hospitals and clinics, or that Saudi Arabia is building a new medical school complex that includes a large, high-end hospital, those are the types of things that may make the market attractive to me in the short term. They are compelling events that are directly linked to purchasing my product.

While I don't necessarily consider things like trade agreements and treaties to be the most important element of choosing markets, they can also be very helpful. If I realize that my prices are higher than most of my competition's and I realize that there may be higher tariffs in certain markets, that might indicate to me that I will be priced out of those markets and it might be better to avoid them depending on how confident I am in the advantages that my product has over the cheaper competition.

Over the years I have sold to places like Cuba, Iran, Syria, and Venezuela, but I try to avoid them unless I know that the market is an excellent fit for my product because of the administrative and legal difficulties of selling to and getting payment out of those countries.

Likewise, even with all good intentions, there are countries that getting cash out of is difficult either on a semi-permanent basis or on a temporary basis. I have had a great deal of trouble over the years getting money out of Argentina and Russia, depending on the regime and the fiscal policy at the time. And so you have to decide if that is a market that you want to put your effort into.

Another factor in choosing markets is what I call geographic proximity. I find that working with three to five countries that are close to each other is a good way to spread cost of sales. If I find, for instance, that Colombia and Peru are good markets for me, I might go into Ecuador as well even knowing that might not be my primary target market. If I'm already going to be in Peru and Colombia, taking another day to visit Ecuador is not that expensive, and I can train the distributors at the same time.

You'll notice that I haven't mentioned that I choose territories because a distributor or a customer has reached out to me. People say all the time that if a customer reaches out to them from a territory, at least they know there is some demand for their product in that territory. I try very hard to avoid that concept. I believe that having control of the sales process, having control of all the activities, is extremely important. When you get pulled into a market because somebody reaches out to you, you are losing control and you are getting involved in something that you did not plan and you did not thoroughly research. The fact that one person is interested in your product from the market does not mean that you have a market in the country. You don't know anything about that person or how well they comprehend the market or what their motivations are or what they really know about that market.

That said, if I know that there is a good distributor who is enthusiastic about my product in the market, that might be a good enough argument for me to decide in favor of a market that I was on the fence about. I'm not sure it's enough to push me from a market that I don't think is a good fit to deciding to go into that market, but if I'm undecided or I feel that the market has potential, or I feel that there is a good distributor who is interested and enthusiastic, I might decide in favor of that market.

Note how deeply and carefully I am qualifying this. I would never do this if I was contacted by a distributor and didn't have an opportunity to meet with them, evaluate their knowledge of the market, and size up their capacities. So, for instance, let's say that I'm not sure Ecuador is a big enough market for my efforts, but I will be in Colombia and a distributor there has reached out to me. They've sent me a profile telling me about their company and they seem to be a serious company. Then I may meet with them and if I judge that they are serious and that they do understand the market and they do have the right connections, their enthusiasm might be enough to convince that I want to enter into that market.

Of all the stages of preparation for expanding globally, this one can be the riskiest in terms of the source of your data and how you make your decision. In the same way that we have a tendency to try to sell to people we like, we have a very strong tendency to try to expand globally in countries that we think will be interesting.

I can't tell you how often I talk to a company that had a failure in their global expansion. When asked where their first markets were, they went into France, Italy, and Japan, and you know that they chose those markets because somebody on the team thought it would be fun to travel there.

The other mistake people make in this part of the planning is using the wrong advisors or consultants. A while back I was at a conference and there were experts on the stage talking about global expansion. Somebody asked a very specific question: "If I'm a small healthcare manufacturer and I'm looking to expand in the Middle East, and I can only afford to go into one market, where would you recommend?" One of the consultants said, "I would recommend going into Morocco. The United States and Morocco recently signed an agreement that will make it easier for you to repatriate revenue earned in Morocco than it would've been previously." This expert was an American diplomat based in Morocco who had been involved in this agreement. I raised my hand and said, "I hope you don't mind my asking this. The Saudi Arabian medical device market is $2 billion. The Moroccan market is $200 million. Are you suggesting that this agreement and its ramifications outweigh the attractiveness of the Saudi Arabian market over the Moroccan?" Of course, the diplomat had no answer for that. That is why my wife says we don't get invited to more parties.

I've also dealt with consultants over the years who call themselves global expansion consultants or global marketing consultants or that kind of thing, and they all have a geographic focus. It's very difficult to find somebody who's sold in more than 10 or 12 countries, especially among these consultants. Actually, most of them have never brought in a purchase order before. They've been diplomats someplace or they've been service engineers someplace or maybe they are academics who have been involved in anthropological studies of that county. They are very comfortable with the former Yugoslavia or with Japan or with Saudi Arabia. Very seldom are they comfortable with multiple markets, and they get typically paid on an hourly or per diem rate, so from their perspective that means that if *they* contract with you to help you expand globally then they're going to recommend that the former Yugoslavia is the best possible market for you to get into. So I have seen many companies going into the wrong country because either somebody within the company or their first consultant made recommendations that were completely inappropriate in terms of what they were trying to achieve from sales and revenue goals.

Once we've answered some of these questions and we have an idea of what our customer looks like and what a good market for us looks like and why people buy from us, now we will start really evaluating different markets.

Let's start by trying to get some information about different geographic markets so that we can compare.

What are some good sources? I really like the CIA World Factbook, and the World Bank Open Data website. They basically give you good, solid demographic and economic information about approximately 280 countries and territories around the world.

While I sometimes hesitate to suggest working with government agencies, it's not because I don't trust their abilities; it's because it's easy to become too dependent on them. As with all groups of people, you have stronger and weaker individuals. In this case, if you're an American or your company is American, you want to reach out to the US Commercial Service. Get to know your local office desk manager and talk to them. See if there are any relevant on-the-shelf studies that you can read. These are typically free. While my book is focused on exporting from the US, I can tell you that the Israeli, German, Dutch, Danish, British, and Canadian governments (and possibly many other countries) offer similar programs.

Very often the Commercial Service has meetings where as many as 30 commercial officers from around the world will be available to talk to American manufacturers during a two- to three-day period. These meetings can give you an excellent idea of what different markets might offer you.

In general, the Commercial Office is a great place to start, although, like with every other source of information, you need to be careful and you have to realize that in the end you are responsible and you need to treat all information as suspect. Understand why people give it to you and what their motivation is.

I have never been very musical. When I was about nine years old, I came home one day from struggling through a saxophone lesson and told my mom that my teacher had said that if we bought a new $1,000 saxophone from her, my playing would get much better. My mother asked, "How does your teacher make her money?" I said, "She gives music lessons." My mother replied, "Yep, we pay her $7 a lesson. How else does she make money? She sells $1,000 saxophones." I learned a solid lesson that day that is very applicable in the world of international sales advisors. Always keep an eye on everyone who advises you and how they make their money. Many people in the advice business are specialists in specific markets, or they are specialists in making product changes. You don't want to make strategic plans based on the fact that your advisor knows that he can bill you for changing your product or because he figures he can get more work from you if you choose a market that he is a specialist in.

Let's say you have $500,000 as your budget from the company for global expansion. You've decided to expand into ten test markets. You choose seven of them poorly (perhaps all of them are chosen with poor or weak methodology, but three of them are reasonable markets and seven of them are big mistakes). So most of your investment is wasted, and after two or three years, everybody deems the global expansion experiment to be a large failure. At the point of this evaluation, many companies will decide the global expansion is a mistake and not something that their company can do. The whole attempt at global growth and global expansion and growing the value of the company could be aborted simply because you use poor methodology in this element of the project.

I believe that methodology and process are key to all of our success here. In some households you have a baker and you have a cook, and you can cook without necessarily following process, but you can't successfully bake without following process. You have to think of this international growth as baking, as something very complex. Poor methodology and poor processes at any given point can cause failure in the project of international growth and can be a complete disaster if this is important to your company and to your career.

One of the elements that I see as problematic in the process is people seeking advice from the wrong people. There are two key elements that I look for when I'm taking advice. I want to understand how people get compensated for helping me or giving me advice. What do I mean by that? The world is full of people who call themselves "global business advisors," "global advisors," and "global expansion advisors," and most of them do not have a background in what I would call the purchase order business. What do I mean by this?

Picture an international sales team for a successful company with 30 or 40 people on the ground. This can be a territory manager with several regional sales managers or account managers and a half-dozen administrative people, technical support people, and marketing people. From those 30-plus people, possibly only three or four are actually responsible for working with the customer to get a purchase order. Everybody's contribution is valuable, but their understanding of strategy, of interaction with the customer, and of the sales process will not be on par with those people who are actually in sales. Now in the same way that if you want to develop a device or build marketing content or set up an office you go to a specialist, when you're talking to somebody about selling, somebody who has been watching the sales process from the sidelines isn't necessarily going to be that helpful.

Another group that is heavily represented among these global advisors is ex-diplomats. After a few decades in that job, many ambassadors and consular officers will try to get consulting roles in the private sector. Having worked with a many very talented and personable members of the diplomatic corps from many countries, it's my understanding that none of them have a commercial background.

The ability of somebody who spent 10 years stamping passports in Uganda or 10 years assisting American citizens in trouble in Korea to help you set a commercial strategy for your midmarket widget manufacturer for global expansion is about as high as that of a drum major from your local high school marching band. Even though these people have global experience and they seem and may very well be very cosmopolitan, their understanding of business is no better than your typical citizen's.

The other group that's heavily overrepresented in this group of consultants and advisors is academics—sociologists, anthropologists, and the like. While understanding social norms in Argentina may be very important to doing business in Latin America, it is still one small piece of a very large and complex puzzle. So if the key benefit for the key skillset that your paid advisor brings to the table is a PhD in Latin American studies or a postdoc in the anthropology of central Europe then they might not be in a position to give you solid business advice.

Where *can* you go for this business advice? There are essentially three to four levels of taxpayer-supported government help for exporters at the federal level, the state level, and often at the municipal level, plus the Small Business Administration, depending on your size.

For instance, in a big city like Chicago or New York or Minneapolis, you will have a federal US Commerce Department representative, a state commerce representative, and then the city commerce representative. If you are a manufacturer that employs less than a specific number of people, possibly 500, you may also be eligible for SBA export assistance. These organizations typically have people based in the United States as well as in local markets. In terms of choosing the correct market to enter, the people based in the United States are the strongest choice for advice, because they work with multiple markets and they are compensated and rewarded if you are successful, no matter where you are successful. If you talk to the commercial officer based in Japan, he will be rewarded if you succeed in Japan, he will not be rewarded if you succeed in Spain, and nobody except you is going to lose anything if you are not successful anywhere. So each commercial officer who represents the territory has a pretty solid incentive to tell you that that market is attractive to you, whereas the commercial officer based in your home city has an incentive to help you figure out the actual best market to go into.

There are also advisors who make their money by making changes to products. They are typically engineers with work experience in multinational manufacturing companies changing, adjusting, or designing products for export. Those people can be helpful later on in the process, but they are extremely dangerous in the early stages. Why? They typically get compensated by the hour or by the project when you hire them to make major changes to your product to enter markets. So if you talk to them about what market would be attractive, the best way for them to make money is to advise you to go into markets that will require major technological changes to your products—markets like Japan or Russia or some of the Arabic speaking countries, where there are specific software changes required to enter those markets, for example. Now those markets may or may not be attractive to you for a variety of reasons, but what you know is that there will be a cost to making changes to enter those markets and that should be carefully taken into consideration when you're evaluating these markets.

If you are new to global expansion or exports, I would also try to establish the best possible network with other export managers to exchange information and advice. Don't let pride get in your way; it is not uncommon for people with 20 years of solid sales experience to lack understanding about how to sell internationally and to get caught up by basic mistakes. If you can find a group or mastermind or even a few friends through LinkedIn to share ideas, that could be very helpful.

Over the years I've almost always had such a network. It can be relatively easy on LinkedIn to find 10 such people who sell products that are somewhat similar to yours but in no way compete. In some cases, you can even be friendly with people who have some type of competition and overlap. I would highly recommend reaching out to people like this, establishing a relationship, maybe taking them out for coffee or lunch and talking to them about the appeal of different markets. You might find that some can't really help you very much, but you might also find that some are excellent sources of information. I belong to several such groups on LinkedIn and while some of them are essentially a complete waste of time, others can be very helpful. Over the past 30 years I've made literally dozens of friends who are global VPs of sales or directors of international sales or regional sales managers, and having that network is very helpful. I can pick up the phone and ask questions and discuss things. The sooner you start building this network, the sooner you will have trustworthy people to advise you.

As with many things, when you're gathering information the key is asking the right questions. We've tried to identify who buys our product and why, so we will put together a short list of questions that will help us identify the correct markets. These questions will relate to the demographics of who buys a product, macro compelling events, and things that might put us at risk in specific markets.

Let's say that I'm selling a product that I know is highly appealing to markets with a rapidly growing middle class. Could I define what is a rapidly growing middle class by quantifying a growth curve on per capita GDP? I also know that this is an attractive product for markets that are building new hospitals. My next question is whether I can identify where they are growing the number of hospital new builds. What is the number that is attractive to me? I can tell you that probably two-thirds of the hospitals in Ethiopia and two-thirds of the hospitals in Mexico, while on paper they call them hospitals, they might not be a target customer for the products I sell. In that case I might have to quantify what exactly I mean, and I could say I'm looking for a market that has plans to build more than 50 new hospitals, each one of which will have at least 50 outpatient beds and at least 50 inpatient beds.

What could be a red flag to me in that market? Well, if that market has legally codified a restriction that is designed to protect a local manufacturer, that may be something that will keep me out.

So where can I find the answers to those questions? Well, it's relatively easy to identify the population, the GDP, the per capita GDP, and a five- to ten-year growth curve of GDP from the CIA Factbook. If I send an email to all the US commercial officers around the world with one or two simple questions, they will typically answer me. If my question is "At present how many hospitals are there in your market, and what are the published plans for building new hospitals over the next seven years?" I will usually get a solid answer.

The red flag issue becomes a little bit more complicated in terms of how to get information. Let's say you decide on going into Brazil. You invest in recruiting the best possible distributor, you hire a regional sales manager for Latin America, and because you think Brazil is a good target market you base that regional manager in São Paulo. He translates your manuals. You invest in a trade show. You have all these different expenses, not to mention your VP of global sales is spending 10% to 20% of his time focused in this market.

Then you find out that Brazil has put in place a rule protecting the local manufacturer that makes it impossible for you to sell in Brazil. In a situation like this, who loses aside from you? Possibly the local distributor has put some efforts into your product that they're not going to recoup. Aside from that, the big loser and really the only loser is you and your company. So anybody that you asked for advice about this situation really had no good incentive to bend over backwards to find you an accurate and true source of information on this.

Here is where I would invest in good local advice that I would pay for. The best way I've found to do this is to reach out to either colleagues doing business in the market or the local commercial office or possibly the country's American chamber of commerce. What you're looking for is a regulatory consultant or a lawyer who can identify and clarify rules that can keep you out. Again, I recommend this for your most attractive markets that you've decided to invest effort, time and money in, maybe not all markets. Typically a research project like this, if you know what type of regulations or laws you're looking for, will cost between $1,000 and $10,000 per market, depending on the cost of labor and that market potential. The savings from not getting surprised in the future can be huge. These types of regulations and laws are most common in healthcare, food, communication, transportation, construction, and IT and less common in other fields, so perhaps it's not something you have to worry about.

Having identified the demographic elements and compelling events that might make a market attractive to us, and potential red flags that might make a market difficult or impossible to get into, I now have a list of potential markets. Now I can put together a list of questions that will help me identify which markets are the best for me. I try to keep this to a short list of less than 10 markets. Once I have identified a short list and I have put them in order of priority, I should have a list that corresponds with the number of countries that I believe I have the bandwidth to cover the initial two years of expansion. Then I can look for potential red flags and decide if I want to avoid one or more.

Another excellent step in choosing the right market is to look at what other companies are doing. I like to keep track of two groups of companies. One would be those that I consider my direct competitors. In all cases you have a direct competitor, somebody who solves the same problems you do and sells to the same people you sell to—possibly at a similar price point and with a similar group of benefits.

At this point, you can try to identify where their best markets are. If they are a publicly traded company, there's no reason not to buy a share of their stock to get a copy of their report, which will tell you exactly where they're selling and where they anticipate growth. You may be able to get this from their website or from their press releases and from finding out what trade shows they participate in. On LinkedIn you can see them doing things like congratulating their local distributor for a fantastic year or even celebrating who their best distributor is in a given year. If a competitor who offers a similar product at a similar price point has been selling very well in Saudi Arabia, there is every reason to believe that Saudi Arabia or similar Gulf countries may be good, attractive markets for you.

Likewise, I like to keep track of a group of companies that sell to the same customers that I sell to. For instance, I sold a product years ago that in the beginning my company believed would compete with a specific piece of technology. It was a monitor that measured carbon dioxide exhalation in emergency room and operating room markets. There is a product that is the standard of care called a pulse oximeter that measures oxygen saturation in the patient. When we started looking at global expansion, our initial idea was to try to convince people to buy our technology—capnography—instead of pulse oximetry, which had established itself in the market a decade or more earlier. What we found was it was impossible to convince people to buy capnography instead of pulse oximetry, but there was a very high incidence of people buying capnography a year or two after buying pulse oximetry to use together. We found that if we could identify markets that did very well with pulse oximetry, we could anticipate that the following years would be very good years for our product. The biggest manufacturers of pulse oximetry in the world at that time were publicly traded companies. Thus it was very easy to keep track of their sales by country and then use that to map out our own international expansion.

Some of our products and some of our markets target private sector, some target public sector, and some target both. In the early stages of global expansion speed is very important, and the private sector is always going to be faster for decisions but will often involve smaller purchase orders. To clarify: a focus on the private sector will probably bring in initial orders faster, but the size of each order will be smaller. A government focus will move more slowly but will usually represent bigger individual purchase orders. As I expand, I want a good mix of public and private sector if I can get it (depending on the product), but in the early stages sometimes I depend on speed and need more focus on the private sector.

Now I will talk about something that might seem a little less scientific, but I believe that it is very valid. Domestically, salespeople often talk about using things like the Enneagram or Disc™ assessment in the sales process to identify personality gaps between seller and buyer in order to bridge those gaps in communication. I embraced this decades ago, but I remember a lot of my colleagues and friends thought it sounded a little crazy.

There is a solid body of academic work that deals with cultural differences between countries. As a matter of fact, I have a companion book to this and many online classes that deal specifically with this. Every culture addresses problem solving in a different way, and there are typically between five and eight parameters that will define the business characteristics of a culture. Several of those characteristics will impact the decision-making timeline.

For instance, Israel is well regarded as a low-risk-adverse early technology adopter business culture. Vietnam is not. So if you are looking at missionary sales and you have a product that you believe would be an excellent fit for Vietnam but at present there are no solid reference sites to use, you can guarantee that Vietnam will not be your early adopter. They may very well be willing to be the second market to adopt your technology, however.

On the other hand, Israel may be willing to jump into using your product even though nobody else has moved forward, but as a much smaller country it may represent less overall revenue.

Another example: the ministries of health in the Central American countries have a reputation for moving substantially faster than the ministries of health in the larger Andean countries of Latin America.

When you are planning global expansion, you have to realize that some early success is key to the survival of the entire project. So, you might want to make sure that you have a few fast-moving countries in the mix, even if they might not be large targets. Low-hanging fruit is critical in the mix of the global expansion plan.

Once we know what we are looking for in a market, we can travel to what are the most attractive markets for us, looking at them again for signs of potential appeal and danger.

If, for example, we are selling to hospitals and we come up with 30 countries that could be a good fit for us in terms of potential customers, we then figure out which are the most attractive in terms of market potential as well as which have the potential for moving fastest and we try to make a matrix of this.

# Bonus videos:

Methodology in choosing the right market
https://www.youtube.com/watch?v=30Xb4KcWols

Israeli business culture
https://www.youtube.com/watch?v=PsyWmV5aZfw

https://www.youtube.com/watch?v=PsyWmV5aZfw&t=46s

German business culture
https://www.youtube.com/watch?v=93PyrMA6pwQ

https://www.youtube.com/watch?v=93PyrMA6pwQ&t=21s

Scandinavian business culture https://www.youtube.com/watch?v=tt-e8qEOJG4

https://www.youtube.com/watch?v=QLbfMMXCv_c&t=67s

Guatemalan business culture
https://www.youtube.com/watch?v=Z2gL5Qc0Sew&t=27s

French business culture
https://www.youtube.com/watch?v=BMO2Fu_Wy9g&t=6s

Jordanian business culture
https://www.youtube.com/watch?v=QE5rwdIFHmc

Latin American business culture
https://www.youtube.com/watch?v=_3IlkuTyUb4

Indian business culture
https://www.youtube.com/watch?v=5czuUVX3RFg

Long Term business culture
https://www.youtube.com/watch?v=HpntvKEro4U

Chinese business culture
https://www.youtube.com/watch?v=8JoOl9rHwfI&list=PLFhf-CkmK3TGDiQnl1tj1NuZmp_pNmZay

Pakistani business culture
https://www.youtube.com/watch?v=MQHhJWolq0A

Case study: why did Starbucks fail in Israel
https://www.youtube.com/watch?v=JwXdIBDj93U

https://www.youtube.com/watch?v=NdNiIwfJkPA

https://www.youtube.com/watch?v=ssLYnzDi2ms

# How many markets are we going into at once?

This is an age-old, difficult question. I am a firm believer in not putting all of your eggs in one basket. In 2012 the biggest source of my revenue was oil-producing economies. I was selling a product to hospitals. Most hospital projects were tied up with government spending, and in oil-producing countries, the higher the oil revenue, the higher the government revenue and the more money they had to spend, the more projects. Thus, for every dollar of marketing and sales effort we put into Saudi Arabia, we got back a great return, better than any other markets.

My CEO argued vehemently that we should reduce our efforts in non-oil-producing markets because our margin was lower. His idea was that we focus on five countries that were oil-producing. They would generate the most return on investment and that would be the best strategy. I pushed back with great vehemence. In 2014 oil prices dropped dramatically and our sales to oil countries dropped by about 80%. Luckily, that happened early enough in the fiscal year that I was able to shift effort and resources to a lot of our non-oil-producing-country customers so we were able to pick up the lost revenue in a lot of these other countries by working harder. But if we had followed the strategy of our CEO, we would have tanked.

In another company I worked for, somebody had the idea of shifting to a global distributor company, which would be covering essentially in the whole world. This was a serious, powerful company that looked great on paper. Due to entirely unforeseen circumstances that involved a legal problem that was completely unrelated to us, this company was sunk and the owners had to sell the company due to a legal order. The company let go most of their marketing and salespeople, leaving us with no coverage but an obligation that tied us to this company. The issue wasn't that I had any insight into the legal problems; I just hesitated to put all our eggs in one basket.

I've heard a lot of people say that one regional sales manager can only cover six to eight countries. I believe it comes down to how much contact is expected and how much work on the ground there is. It also depends on how you plan to structure your sales organization, which we will cover in chapter four. I prefer to have regional managers focused on managing my distributors and the e. I believe that in terms of cost effectiveness for a middle-market manufacturing company, that is the best configuration.

If we use additional sales assets within the company to recruit and train new distributors, for intelligence gathering, and for technical presales support, an RM can handle between 15 and 20 markets.

If you have a small team of regional sales managers, let's say five, and nonregional sales manager assets, let's say three, that probably means that you can target in the neighborhood of 25 to 40 countries over the first two years of expansion. That could change dramatically with the nature of the product, how new this type of product is to these markets, cost of the product, etc., and conceivably that number could grow or could drop, but I think targeting 25 to 40 countries within two years is very reasonable.

Once we have looked at where our potential markets are, we will choose where we place our regional sales managers. Maybe we don't need an RM for Europe or for Africa, depending on our product and our markets. If we have a product that can be sold on six continents, we might want to cover everything, but we also have to balance out the cost and what we believe our returns will be. Often, we know that our budget won't allow us to hire five or six RMs at the beginning, so we need to make a choice as to where the best investment lies. So you can play around with this to give coverage, but in the same way that I don't want to put too many eggs in one basket, I also don't want to spread my forces too thin. You don't want to extend yourself too far to be able to give good coverage to your territories.

Once we've decided on general territories, we form clusters. If I feel that we have two to three good markets in Latin America, I'll probably add a few to make it eight to ten; even if the additional five aren't the best, we can still manage them with the resources we have. When an RM is working well, he can cover four countries on a weeklong trip; once markets are set up, he shouldn't have to be in a market for more than a day at a time on a trip.

## Bonus video

Don't put all your eggs in one basket
https://www.youtube.com/watch?v=NdNiIwfJkPA

https://www.youtube.com/watch?v=ssLYnzDi2ms

## Bonus article

https://www.forbes.com/sites/forbesbusinessdevelopmentcouncil/2020/07/30/the-focus-fallacy-why-you-should-widen-your-sales-funnel/

# Basic Concepts

## Build a customer profile

Who is the customer?

When does the customer buy?

How does the customer buy?

Why does the customer buy?

## Choose the right markets

Good reasons: Lots of the right customers
Bad reasons: I want to see Paris in the spring

## How many markets to go into?

Enough so that an adverse economic event or natural disaster won't sink you; not too many to provide good coverage.

# Chapter 3
## BUILDING A SALES ORGANIZATION

### Sales process

One of the things that we have to be aware of when we start—and will then be an important element of our work the whole time we're operating—is our sales process.

I hear from people all the time, "How can I know my sales process before I start to sell?". Like a few other things that we will do at this point, you pretty much have to estimate it and then adjust it as you move forward.

I like to say that the sales process is like a pyramid. Think about the pyramids for a second. We have pyramids on every continent but Antarctica; humans have been making them for possibly as long as 8,000 years. They are effective, robust, scalable, and reproducible. You can make a 2" tall pyramid out of plastic. You have pyramids that were the tallest buildings in the world for 5,000 years. They are easily reproducible. You can teach somebody how to make one and they can go and make them anywhere. It's the perfect design.

Now imagine the sales process like that. What you want is something that is effective, will allow people to close deals, is robust. You are always going to have people who are less good at selling and people who don't follow instructions very well, so you want your sales process to be as foolproof is possible.

You need it to be scalable because the whole idea is to grow more, and you want the same process to work effectively for your smallest deals and your biggest deals. You need for dozens or hundreds of people to learn, follow, and manage your sales process all over the world in order to grow.

## Bonus Video

https://www.youtube.com/watch?v=zT0Gp6M5NEU&t=26s

Effective, robust, scalable, and reproducible.

People often are convinced that you need a different sales process for every market.

Ideally, maybe you *would* have a dedicated sales process designed for each market. But if you're looking to scale up and grow relatively quickly and cost-effectively, that should be something you really try to avoid. People will try to sell you on that idea, and they are typically people who get paid or who make money by designing and consulting on sales processes or by entering new markets. And they'll tell you that if you want to get into a certain market, you really need to design a specific sales process for that market and that they will happily design the process for you for an hourly fee. But this is really a trap that will end up costing you a lot of money. Obviously, you will have to adjust your sales process for different markets, but adjustment is going to be faster and cheaper and more manageable than a complete redesign.

Every sales process has different elements and there are lots of different systems that people use. My system isn't necessarily the best, but I will suggest that for purposes of this chapter we work with my system. You can essentially take one of the other systems—one that you might be more familiar or comfortable with—and treat it the same way. Play around with it the same way that I'm playing with this one. The key is trying to figure out how every element of the sales process will be executed.

For me there are two core elements of the sales process: establishing trust with the customer and helping the customer internalize that my product solves their problem. On top of that, there is a third element that runs through and overlaps with both of those, which I call discovery: understanding who the customer is, how they will operate, what their needs are, how they will process information, and how they will expect information from you.

There are two other elements to the sales process that are required for every sales process: find and identify your customers and deliver the goods and get paid for them.

All of these elements are present in every sale. The importance of each element can be very different in every sale, and who carries out what is going to be different in every sale. But if the customer doesn't trust you and doesn't believe that you can solve their problem, they're not going to give you money. If they can't find you, there is no sale. If there is no mechanism for exchanging the product for money, there is no sale.

In international sales everything becomes more complex. Let's first think about how you find customers. I will define customers as end users, not distributors. I think it's a huge mistake, one that can really keep you from growing and succeeding, when you consider your distributors to be your customers.

Your customer is effectively the person who's going to pay for and use your product and decide which solution they will spend their money on. It can become very complex and confusing when you're dealing with something like a car component that you sell to a car manufacturer and they put it in their car and then sell to an end user, as an example. In a case like that, your customer is the car manufacturer because they're using your component to improve their product to sell to their customers; on the other hand, if you were to sell a high-end stereo system that is offered as an option but the point of sale is a car dealership and the driver or the owner of the car will decide which stereo system he buys based on his criteria, I would say the car buyer is your customer.

Internationally, often we have no idea how to go about finding our customer. Do we use the same marketing techniques we use in the US? Do we try and buy customer lists?

Likewise, establishing a relationship with your international customers can be very challenging. There are a number of complications that make the whole thing different from dealing with a domestic sale. In some cases your customer might simply not like or not trust foreigners or may have been burned before.

In some cases, your product and company have a fantastic reputation in your domestic market, and your sales organization has never met anybody who wasn't familiar with your positive reputation until today. And now you're faced with customers who have no idea who you are. I worked once for a 100-year-old company with an excellent reputation for quality products, and essentially everybody in the United States was familiar with them. None of their marketing material talked about the company story, who they were, their quality manufacturing processes, or anything like that. When they expanded internationally the original sales managers all assumed that every customer they came into contact with was familiar with their product and their brand. It proved to be very difficult to establish trust, because the American RMs and head of international sales assumed that all they had to do was name their company and they would be trusted, because that was how every customer had treated them in the US.

Many people, even those who don't work or sell internationally, are familiar with the concept that different cultures build trust differently. While the notion that people in some cultures take years to build trust is a stereotype, it has some basis in fact. US business culture is the highest in the world for situational trust—we see a guy in a blue shirt at Best Buy and we trust him enough to buy a sound system because we have had a good experience in the past at Best Buy. When we introduce ourselves as a VP of a large company, we expect that we will be trusted immediately. While this varies dramatically between cultures, it is safe to say that every business culture outside of the US requires more than Americans do to build trust, so much so that it can completely overwhelm an American. It may actually require things that are simply impossible to achieve in a reasonable amount of time or at all. This is why having a distributor who owns this part of the sales process is usually key.

I love to eat when I am traveling, and I also love to cook. I really enjoy a bean dish from Brazil called feijoada. It started out as a slave or peasant dish made of all the cheap parts of pigs and beans. It's the type of dish that everyone's grandmother makes, and when she makes it it's an all-day affair. You can't really get it outside of Brazil, for a variety of reasons. Years ago, I decided to make some for my family, and since you really need to make a lot, I invited friends over. It's a pretty elaborate preparation; it includes meat and beans, rice, orange slices, and some other things to do it right. I am quite attentive to detail, so I made a pretty authentic spread with all the accompanying elements. I was proud of myself, and I sent pictures to my Brazilian distributor, and he commented that it looked good and authentic.

Months later he and I were talking to a very ornery customer in Brazil who had a giant facility and who was saying, "I don't trust Americans. They come down here, they try to sell, then they see it's a difficult market and they pull out. I get stuck with stuff I can't service." We were all crammed into his little tiny office, and he was actually a huge guy, so it was almost comical with him yelling about how he didn't trust Americans.

My distributor pulled out his phone and showed him some pictures. "What is that?" he asked. The customer looked annoyed. "Feijoada... looks pretty good. My grandmother could have made that. So what?" My distributor said, "What if I told you that Zach made that?" and flipped through the phone to some pictures of me in the kitchen with the pots, actually cooking. The customer gave us a $250,000 purchase order on the spot, saying, "Okay, if he can make feijoada like that, he is committed to the market."

## Bonus Video

https://studio.youtube.com/video/tmEx9qs-6FA/edit/basic

If the customer doesn't feel that he can trust the product to perform, that he can't trust the company to continue in business for as long as he needs service, that he can't trust us to give him the expected experience, he won't buy from us.

What non-salespeople typically think of when they think of selling is the element that I like to refer to as "helping the customers internalize that we can solve their problem." If the customer hasn't internalized that we can solve their problem, there will be no sale. For the most part, this might be the part that changes least from domestic to international, but there are a few things that do change. We have to remember that not everyone internalizes data the same way, culturally. For example, Americans and French typically like to see slides in a different order in a deck, and westerners and East Asians usually like to see very different graphics on advertising and presentation decks. Not understanding those differences can slow down or cripple sales.

On top of that, the basics of day to day selling, such as making calls, sending out emails, and elevator pitches, often vary from culture to culture. While it may be acceptable to cold-call in one culture, it may be hugely offensive in another. Or while we might never think of just popping by to see a key decision maker without an appointment in one market, doing that might be the norm in another.

Discovery may be the most interesting part of international sales. If you are a good salesperson or sales leader, you may be very invested in the concept of discovery. How do I get information that will help me plan out how I make an offer to my customer?

Domestically, in your home market you should be very familiar with the cultural clues that will help you in discovery. You should understand the customer's needs in general. You should understand the structure of the customer's organization. Internationally, all of those things may be totally different. On top of that we have to remember that there is a large element of trust involved even in the level of discovery. To overgeneralize cultural selling concepts, Americans typically are very willing to establish trust on a task-by-task basis. So you go to see a customer who is generally looking to buy something like what you have, you give him your business card, and he recognizes that you are a salesman from a reputable company that he has heard of. You are wearing a clean shirt and nice shoes, and he will talk to you and open up and possibly explain to you 80% of what you need to know, just based on your clean shoes and your business card.

Internationally, several of the main cultural indicators create difficulty or barriers to quickly establishing trust in some of the most lucrative countries for American exporters. In many of the countries where we sell or want to sell, organizational information is structured fundamentally differently than in the US. And this can be very frustrating to sales managers trying to gather and organize information. I see this all the time. Americans with little or no experience push for information in a way that can destroy their prospects of getting business in the long term, due to poor cultural sensitivity. I worked at a company where a very smart American with no international experience kept pushing his field people to ask for copies of internal emails from the customers they were meeting in Africa. This was something that he wouldn't have done in the US, but in the target markets this was seen as truly appalling in terms of breaking trust.

Once we take a look at the general structure of our sales process, we want to try and fill in as many details as possible; needless to say, this will always be a living document and we want to then break it into the smallest pieces that we can.

Let me give you a quick example. Let's say that I am selling a communication system that is used by hospitals to improve the patient experience and is installed essentially in the walls of the hospital. How do I find my customers? I will look for new-build hospitals or hospitals that are doing major renovations because I know they will be breaking the walls. I reach out to the positions within the hospital that I am familiar with as people who purchase my type of system—the maintenance manager, the finance manager, and the nursing manager— and I give them information on successful projects we have done for similar hospitals. How do I help them internalize that we can solve the problem? Maybe I take them to visit reference sites; I show them our technical specifications; I show them our factory solution center; I talk to them about similar hospitals where we have successfully solved what is essentially the same problem.

How do I deal with payment and delivery? Let's say we use a letter of credit and the delivery involves complex installation done by a local value-added reseller on the ground in the market. So there we have a basic example of a sales process. Now let's break that down a little further.

Find the customers: what we may be doing is going to the local government authorities to look for building permits that people put in for both new builds and renovations. We may form informal partnerships with other vendors who are looking for new-build hospitals and major renovations and agree to share information. We may utilize a service organization that serves existing hospitals and talks with hospital maintenance managers and use those people to gather information about future building projects.

We may establish trust by holding workshops and seminars in the target market, bringing in customers and key opinion leaders from other markets who are familiar with our products. We may participate in conferences that other people are holding and talk about how we have solved problems for other hospitals around the world. We may take local market key opinion leaders who are not customers to visit some of our existing customers in other markets and then ask them to speak in the target market at conferences or workshops.

Digging deeper into the issue of helping the customer internalize, we can talk to the customer about their problems and feed them information from seemingly neutral third-party key opinion leaders or our existing customers about how they have solved these problems. We can present to different departments of the organization, utilizing slides or videos that have been designed to appeal to how these particular people from a cultural or educational perspective process and organize data; we can work with technical people within the customer organization to help build their specifications around our product. This is just a tiny slice of the tools or activities that may fit into a sales process.

Now we come to why this element is so important in the planning stage. We need to identify, before we do anything else, who should be doing what in the process.

What do I mean by that? In many traditional distributor-principal relationships, once or twice a year the principal flies into the market and the distributor sets up 10 or 15 presentations for the principal to do, brings the principal in, introduces him, and the distributor expects the principal sales manager to do the presentation. You could say that there is a very clear division between ownership of the relationship and ownership of the task of helping the customer internalize.

Let's say that is your sales process. Aside from that really not being very impactful on the market, let's say that the principal sales manager has 100 days a year he can be in market. The distributor can set up 2 presentations each day. That gives us 200 presentations a year. Chances are that nobody is going to be very excited about the results you get from that, and the profitability of that is going to be abysmal.

## Let's try to build a more reasonable sales process

In terms of finding customers, most of the work will probably fall on my distributor. I'm not going to send somebody from headquarters to look through government records for prospects. But cooperation may be at the level of the manufacturer. Can I cooperate with noncompeting manufacturers where we are all looking for the same customers and share information to then feed to my distributor from HQ level?

Additionally, if I'm showing and participating in international conferences that may attract my end users, can I pull in potential leads through my website for my marketing material that I can feed my distributors? Now there's a danger here; again, it's not uncommon for international distributors to essentially expect that you will consistently feed them leads and they will not do their prospecting. That is exactly why we are defining this at the beginning. If we, as a manufacturer, are crystal clear on what we expect from the distributor and we use these expectations to identify and choose the right distributor and we document these expectations in the distributor agreement, we are setting ourselves up for success.

Building a relationship or building trust: Let's say that I am working with a culture that is mildly xenophobic, has a very high power inequality acceptance quotient, and has very high contextual communication. And let's say I am the sales manager of a manufacturing company and a 30-year-old American man. There may be a huge investment in effort for me to establish trust with customers, whereas if I work with the distributor who has existing relationship with the customer and possibly better fits their cultural expectations as to who they trust, I may be able to save years in that building of trust.

There are obviously activities that I can do to build trust, like playing golf with the customer. It is impossible to do business with many Asian cultures without spending several meals eating and drinking together, for instance. But there are additional ways to build trust in the market that are often tied with showing commitment to that market and showing understanding.

There are human resources issues that relate to the cultural skills of a specific sales asset. Does he know how to order food in China in a way that builds trust with the customer? Let's put those aside because they are not part of a scalable project. Yes, we can say it's critical to have the right people and to train your people in cultural aspects of selling. But let's focus on scalable things that we can plan as part of the process. For instance, investing time and money in the market through sponsorship of local conferences or workshops, being able to use a local address, having a local sales manager who at least appears to be a company employee—all of those things help build rapport in difficult markets.

Let's go back to dividing up who does what. In every market I've ever gone into and with every distributor I've ever recruited, the single most important issue was whether they had a solid existing relationship with the right customer. In some cases it hasn't been possible to find a distributor with exactly the right relationships, but they might have had a relationship with people down the hall from the person I want to have a relationship with. They were the right age and ethnicity to establish that relationship and they had experience building rapport and relationships with similar customers. Taken together, those would make the distributor attractive for this element of the sales process.

Helping the customer internalize that my product solves their problem: In many cases, principals give up on the distributor being able to do this and I believe that's a huge mistake. What do I mean? Well, you say, "Nobody really understands what I do but they can get me a meeting, so they set up a meeting and I come in and present." And we're back to the issue of force multiplication. This isn't scalable. Can they get enough people on the ground to scale up our sales if their people don't know how to discuss our product? If you want to scale up, part of your plan from the very beginning has to be to get a large group of distributor salespeople who can do this part of the sales process.

This means that for all products, you want to find partners that have both the contacts and the relationships, but also the ability, to present product. Now here's the trick: you may have to prioritize. It is very difficult for a distributor that doesn't have relationships to hire or train a relationship person; the relationships that the distributor has are often directly owned by the owner(s) of the distribution company or by their trusted long-term executives. People who know how to present, for want of a less clumsy word, can be hired. So you can say in your distribution agreement it is our expectation that you will have somebody with these sales qualifications who will attend the sales training that we hold, and if you do not presently have somebody who can do this, it is our expectation that you will hire somebody like this within 90 or 180 days.

Payment and installation: Unfortunately, often a company's process for selecting a distributor prioritizes financial stability above everything else. That's important, but it may mean that the company that has fantastic sales abilities but last year had a very bad situation with a customer not paying them might not fit your corporate profile. We often say our product has such a difficult installation and servicing that the only people who can represent us are companies with a

specific service organization. I have personally seen that this destroys the sales of the company. The easiest and cheapest thing that the company can add to its human resources is a service team. You can always find technicians that will be cheaper to hire and train than salespeople.

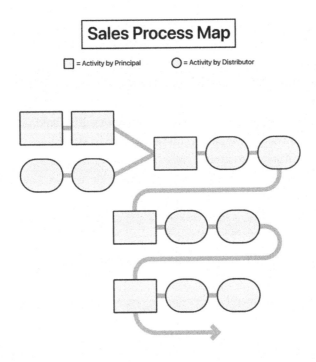

Let's take a look at two very different sales processes.

First, let's look at a process where we were selling a large installed system with average purchase order of $500,000 into a hospital.

How do we find the customers? We have a hybrid. First—some people reach out to the manufacturer based on the manufacturer's marketing conferences, website, etc. This part belongs to the manufacturer. Second—we have customers who will buy off advice from consulting companies and advisory companies around the world who advise hospitals during the planning stage or during the renovation stage, as well as large global construction companies. We can essentially leverage these organizations as though they were part of our sales channel to get more end users interested in our solutions. Third—we will work on the ground in different territories looking for signs of renovation or new build, utilizing people who are in contact today with the hospitals—typical outbound sales. Imagine all the service technicians who are going out and talking to hospital maintenance managers today for other products and leveraging their relationships to gather information about building plans for renovations and new buildings that are coming. These will be owned by the distributor. Lastly, we will be looking through records on the local level for people who have registered projects for major renovations or new buildings. That will typically be from the distributor, but it may also be a consultant employed by the manufacturer to gather information.

In just the stage of this sales process that involves finding the customer, we may have two parts owned by the manufacturer and two parts owned by the distributor.

Having identified the end user customer, now we have to build trust.

Part of that trust will stem from the marketing arm of the manufacturer. This could include reference sites, white papers, trade shows, conferences, the website, etc. All of those will help establish the trustworthiness of the manufacturer in the eyes of the local end user.

The next level could be using consultants paid by the manufacturer or by individuals with strong existing relationships with key opinion leaders, people who are influential in the market including government ministries or hospitals. Part of this could also be using an external consultant to go through the required regulatory processes for clinical studies that are needed to get the correct licenses to operate in the market.

There will be a major component of this process and rapport built on face-to-face meetings, and this will mostly fall on the local distributor.

This is why the single most important part of what I look for in a distributor will almost always be pre-existing relationships with the end user.

The manufacturer owns part of this as well. Most international buyers or buyers from countries importing 80% or 90% of their technology have experienced buying from international manufacturers that were unreliable. As a US manufacturer we may think of unreliability in a different way from how an international customer may think. We may say we are a solid 100-year-old family-owned business and make fantastic robust products and thus we are reliable. In Bangladesh, the ministry of health might be wondering whether the company will decide to sell to Bangladesh and still be selling to Bangladesh in five years. If not, that could create a problem for supply, and the last thing the Bangladeshi ministry of health wants is to buy a million-dollar system for a hospital and then find five years from now that the company that sold it is not providing support because it has decided the Bangladeshi market isn't attractive.

So this part of the sales process falls on the manufacturer within the relationship part of the process. The manufacturer needs to show commitment to the market and the local partner. Any instability in that relationship can be fatal to the project of expanding into the territory. This part of the job usually falls on the regional sales manager, although specifically in a process like this where the product is expensive and new, this is the type of thing where the head of international sales and possibly senior technical people should be brought out from headquarters to help build up trust with the end user.

In this particular case, helping the customer internalize that this is a good solution to solve their problems will require several technical discussions, presentations, and multiple exchanges of information. The hospital will depend on people from the ministry of health as well as third-party advisors that the hospital pays to help them choose a solution. So in this particular case, we are working with these key opinion leaders who aren't actual customers, plus as many as three to five departments within the end user organization. Ideally there will be at least one salesperson within the distributor who has selling skills as well as product knowledge to do all of this. In many cases this work will be divided between the regional manager and the distributor's salesperson on the ground. Very often in processes like this there will be information flow back and forth, between additional sales and technical assets within the manufacturing organization at headquarters level.

Somebody from the opinion leaders or the end user will ask a very specific technical question, the distributor will pass it to the regional manager or directly to headquarters, the question will be answered, and the answer will be sent back. This can go back and forth dozens of times during the course of the sales process.

Ideally, somebody either from the end user or the ministry of health or from an independent third-party consultant paid for by the hospital will ask the manufacturer to write the specifications. This is sort of the goal of the process, because if your specifications are written for a project like this, there is a very high probability of winning and winning profitably. To get this, one has to have established excellent relationships. The writing of these technical specifications will probably fall on somebody within the manufacturer's headquarters.

Payments and shipments: Typically in a situation like this, the distributor will be paid by the end user, often with a great deal of credit extended. The distributor will then turn around and pay the manufacturer, typically asking for even more credit than the customer asked from the distributor. If the customer says that he wants to pay you 120 days after installation, the distributor will ask for 180 days and there will be a great deal of negotiation, depending on the nature of the relationship, the manufacturer's cash flow, etc.

We may bring various credit insurance organizations into this. Let's say the government of Bangladesh is buying a $1 million system for a hospital in Dhaka. They want 120 days credit. The distributor knows they probably won't pay everything for a year. The manufacturer wants to be paid 50% upfront and 50% in 120 days. There are organizations like Exim Bank, which will guarantee that the manufacturer will receive payment and then take a piece of the deal for that guarantee.

Shipping is usually the responsibility of the manufacturer, whereas clearing the goods from customs is usually the responsibility of the distributor. I cannot stress enough how often US manufacturers mess this up. With every company I know, when they start international expansion I tell them, "You need to check all the your shipping processes and make sure that you know how to ship internationally," and they always say, "Don't worry, we know how to do this. It's under control." Then 100% of the time they lose deals in their first two years of international expansion because of mistakes with shipping.

To some extent, this is an easy fix. First, recognize that you need to fix it; second, reach out to an international forwarder and ask for help. Every major metro area in the US is serviced by shipping companies and forwarders. These companies know how to solve this exact problem. But if you think you will do it yourself with somebody who's never shipped outside the continental United States or who has shipped a couple of times, you will lose sales.

On the flip side, the distributor should have a relationship with the customs broker on the site who can get things through customs. This is key if you don't want your shipments caught up in customs. In countries that have developing economies, customs can often be very tricky. With large projects, it isn't unheard of for a manufacturer to use a local consultant on a fee-based structure to help get things through customs or deal with the paperwork locally. But the cost of that really should fall on the distributor.

In this sales process, after-sale service is very important and typically falls on the distributor. This means that the distributor, as part of their obligations in the distribution agreement, hires technical support people with qualifications specified by the manufacturer to be able to carry out technical support.

As you can see, some parts fall on the manufacturer and some on the distributor, and it might not be crystal clear from the start who should do what. That is why spending time figuring it out and carefully documenting it is necessary.

The reason you need to figure this out at the beginning is to plan what kind of people and what kind of partners you need.

Now let's look at a totally different type of product—a device doctors can use in their office or clinic to measure bone density. The device sells for $30,000 to the doctor, who bills $500 from insurance to administer the test. That is the relatively easy return on investment for doctors who run their own business.

Once again, finding customers here is split up between the manufacturer's marketing, local trade shows in market, conferences, and even advertising targeting small-practice entrepreneurial doctors and the distributor who sells a variety of new technology to a lot of local doctors. In this case you could say that about 90% of the relationship and trust element belongs to the local distributor, who has a long-term ongoing relationship with doctors' offices. The manufacturer might build on that relationship through advertising, white papers, conferences, etc., but for the most part the doctor sees a product with a relatively clear and short return on investment. He's dealing with a profile of distributor that he has a relationship with and trusts, from whom he has previously bought products that he uses in his office or clinic, so very little is needed from a distributor to build additional trust and rapport.

Now here's where it can be interesting. In this particular case, where you have partners whose primary asset is a portfolio of relationships, this profile of distributor might really focus on relationships and not really be very good at explaining how the product works or at passing information to the customer. Our primary distributor may not be able to execute this element of the sales process that involves helping the customer internalize that the product or solution solves a problem, in which case it may require an additional level. What I've done in these situations is use a two-tier distribution model, in which the distributor owns the relationship with the customer and in addition somebody else (essentially an agent that earns a commission on deals closed) is responsible for presenting. So what you have, for instance, is dozens of salespeople working for the distributor or possibly even independently. They are managed by a main distributor going around clinics and doctors' offices generating some initial interest with people who trust them based on the ROI story and then pulling in somebody for a single presentation who can help close the deal.

In the case of this product, with its relatively low price point and relatively small physical box, we used a shipping company. We would ship to a warehouse in the target country that belonged to the primary distributor, who would then ship to the customers with a manual. There was no installation required. Training courses could be handled in a central location in that country so all of the new buyers in any given month could be trained together. In today's world that training could probably be done with a video, and because of the small amount payment was done with a wire transfer between the end user and the primary distributor, who then paid the manufacturer on one hand and the two people involved in the sales process on the other hand. So that's another very different sales process.

When you look at different sales processes like this, you get a feel for how different the various distributors can be and how important it is to get the right fit for your process and product.

The reason that you need to figure this out at the beginning is to plan what kind of people and what kind of partners you need.

## Basic Concepts

## Map out your sales process

It should be effective, robust, scalable, and reproducible.

Every part of the sales process should be related to:

- Finding customers

- Establishing rapport/trust with customers

- Helping the customer internalize that you can solve their problem

- Delivering goods and collecting payment

If you don't know how something relates to those parts, don't do it until you can figure that out.

You should know who is responsible for every part of the sales process and how you can hold them accountable.

# Chapter 4
# DESIGNING AND BUILDING YOUR ORGANIZATION

## Pre-sale administration

*Shipping*

Before you start really expanding, there is a lot of preparation. Once sales start coming in, it's going to be like drinking from a firehose, so you really need to have your administration in place before you get rolling.

I guarantee that this chapter is going to get you a lot of pushback, because everybody in your company is going to tell you that they don't need to make any of these changes because they know how to do this stuff already. But if they did, you would already be selling a lot more internationally and you probably wouldn't have bought the book.

One thing that you should read up on and possibly buy a book on is Incoterms®. The Incoterms® are a set of 11 individual rules issued by the International Chamber of Commerce (ICC) which define the responsibilities of sellers and buyers for the sale of goods in international transactions. Of primary importance is that each Incoterms® rule clarifies the tasks, costs and risks to be borne by buyers and sellers in these transactions. Familiarizing yourself with Incoterms® will help improve smoother transaction by clearly defining who is responsible for what and each step of the transaction. Every 10 years they change, and over the years I've seen them change relatively dramatically in terms of how shipping is handled. Depending on what you sell and to where, a few of the terms will be most important to you.

I typically sell relatively high-value, low-weight stuff, so most of what I have been selling has been by airfreight over the years.

If you sell commodities, grain, or heavy agricultural equipment, chances are you're dealing with very different shipping, and as a result very different Inco terms will cover the majority of your shipments.

The importance of Incoterms® is that they clearly define who pays for what portion of shipment and at what exact moment ownership changes. In many cases, it's really not such an important issue until a dispute arises. In some cases, cost of transportation could be such a large part of the total, who pays for what part of shipment can be critical for profitability.

Most of my shipments over the past 20 years have either been EXW (previously known as Ex works), where the customer owns the shipment and is responsible from the moment it exits my factory, not even loading it on the truck, or CIP (previously cost insurance freight) this is actually a new one for 2020, when I am responsible for delivering it to their storage facility or offices. I have ownership until it has been delivered and I arrange freight and carry the insurance.

Occasionally a distributor or an end user will want to aggregate a large order from multiple suppliers in a specific port city like Miami or San Francisco. In that case I will be asked to ship to either a storage facility or total load onboard a ship in one of those cities.

Likewise, probably 90% of the time payment has been either wired, letter of credit, or credit payment 30 or 90 days. Years ago, when I started working, various alternative payment systems were more common. In my side of commerce, they seem to have simply died out as banking got better. You probably will never encounter cash against documents in today's world, for instance.

As you prepare to expand your international sales you will need a relationship with a forwarder. Once you are selling a lot and shipping a lot, everybody wants to be your forwarder. When you are just getting started, people will typically not find you such an attractive customer. What I have done is spoken to several forwarders and said, "Yes, at present we are only shipping $1 million worth of goods each year, but I believe that within three years we will be shipping significantly more. I need a forwarder to help me, and if you work with me now you will reap the benefit as I grow." I find that this is a pitch that forwarders are familiar with and find very reasonable.

## Why do I want a relationship with a forwarder?

Every company has made shipping mistakes, but even a simple one can cost you millions in lost revenue. I once worked with a start-up, and on one of our first deals, when we were really trying to get reference sites set up, we were supposed to ship about $50,000 worth of goods to a customer to do a small project. If that project was successful, we had a protocol, signed by the customer, that would have triggered a $500,000 order, and that order would have led to annual orders of $500,000 for a few years. The customer was a senior figure in the ministry of health in a target country, and she was going to retire the following year. She felt that launching our solution to solve a major problem they had would be a great ending achievement to her career. She was extremely excited about our product and how it could be a great way for her to make an impact on her country before she retired. We messed up the shipment and couldn't get the product to her in time, the shipment got caught up, and then we hit Ramadan, and everything got delayed a month. We missed the deadline for the pilot project. She realized that she couldn't get this done before she retired, so she lost interest. Her replacement wasn't as interested. So we lost what could have been a sale that would have really helped us in the early days of our growth, and really lost us a year, and a significant part of our growth as a company, over some shipping documents. Dealing with international shipping is not rocket science. Virtually the only thing that's required is to admit that you don't know what you're doing or admit that you need some help and to reach out and ask for some help from international forwarders. You can find somebody who can help you with all the difficult elements of international shipping, including documentation.

Unfortunately, stories like that aren't uncommon. And, while this will annoy a lot of my friends, I'd say that the biggest problem with shipping in companies as they grow internationally is hubris. The shipping manager feels that they already know all they need to know and they don't perceive that there is a difference between shipping to Calcutta or Lagos and their experience shipping to Cleveland or Los Angeles.

There are a lot of documents that are requirements for shipping internationally that will make the difference between getting product into the country and not getting product into the country. There are also huge variations in cost of shipping internationally. Think about how different the pricing can be on airline tickets. You can have 10 people in the same section of the same flight, each paying a different price for their ticket. International freight is similar. None of us is working with such a great margin that shipping costs don't matter to us.

If you have trouble finding a forwarder to work with, you can reach out to the US Commerce Department office in your city, or feel free to reach out to my website www.globalsalesmentor.com.

# What am I looking for in a forwarder?

1.  Do they cover either with their own offices or with strong correspondent relationships all the markets I think I will be shipping to in the first two years?

2.  Will they give me a dedicated contact person?

3.  Are they comfortable with small shipments and demo system shipments? These are the most sensitive and difficult shipments you will have. Customs agents often seem to think that when we ship demo units, we are trying to sneak something past them. I can't begin to tell you how many demo units over the years I have lost or had confiscated at customs mostly due to overconfident shipping people.

4.  Do they have somebody who can help me with documentation? In most good forwarding companies, there will be a department to help me write up the correct documentation to ship pretty much anywhere in the world. Again I can guarantee that the people in your office tell you that they know how to do this and it's their job, and I can tell you that half forwarders you speak to will tell you that they normally don't do this and it's usually the manufacturer's job. I can also tell you that unless you are doing a lot of international shipping, people you have on your staff in house will not have the skills and competencies to do this without screwing it up. Whatever you pay to a forwarding company, it will cost you less than one mistake in shipping.

In one of my companies, I arranged technical training for our product in Peru for about 25 new distributors. Our distributors were each sending one or two people. We rented a facility, we flew in two technical training people, and we shipped in about $20,000 worth of demo equipment for the training. The shipping person in my company was not very well organized. She had documents for several shipments her desk.

She put the correct shipping invoice in with the shipment, which listed demo units each valued at $2,000, being shipped for training and returning in one week. By mistake, she also put in an invoice for another shipment, listing this as a commercial shipment at full value (US$20,000) and a third invoice listing marketing brochures with no value. When the Peruvian customs agents saw the three invoices in the box, they believed that we were trying to smuggle in a commercial shipment without paying customs; they confiscated the shipment and almost arrested me. I spent hours being interrogated by Peruvian customs. We didn't have the training materials for our course and none of our distributor's technical people were able to be trained. This was a huge failure. You can find the very best sales managers and the very best distributors and follow the sales process perfectly and still lose business because somebody screws up a shipping invoice in your factory.

## Bonus videos

https://www.youtube.com/watch?v=QQe0TFnnrVc

https://www.youtube.com/watch?v=HhRA79kJTgQ

https://www.youtube.com/watch?v=Xk1bdTdgixo&t=4s

https://www.youtube.com/watch?v=9trQ377C9lg

## Admin and phones

The one thing that I will say about the administrative side that you will need to think about is how and when you answer your phones, your email and your faxes. You will get people trying to call or send in faxes (less so from the domestic market), and you need to think about how to deal with that. If your phones are manned from 9 a.m. to 12 p.m. and then 1 p.m. to 5 p.m., you may want to rethink that. I talk later about the concept of an Anchor, which might solve your problem or simply providing somebody in HQ a cell phone can solve this.

# Travel planning

For the most part, I'm doing a lot of this work face to face. You don't have to, but I find it hard to believe that you can really grow your sales explosively without being in the field.

More than half of American exports go to countries that have high-context, high-trust-value cultures, which means that in order to do business you really need to be in a room with somebody for them to trust you. That doesn't necessarily have to be every day or five times a year, but there will be direct, linear correlation between the amount of face-to-face time you spend with people and the amount of business you do with them in most of these countries. I imagine that one could decide that a focus on countries that are all low context and not necessarily relationship focused is a way to start to keep travel prices down, but that is sort of a novel workaround for the issue. Many people have done well selling consumer-type products or commodity-type products online, for instance.

For most of the past 30 years, I've traveled 140 to 160 days a year. I came on that number at one point in my 20s. I really don't remember where it came from, but I decided that that was the correct number of days. Anything above it wouldn't allow for normal family life. Unfortunately, I exceeded that number probably five times in the 20 years of my married life, reaching about 160–180, and I'm not terribly happy about that. I would say anything over 140 creates a huge amount of strain on the family and should be avoided at all costs. I'm not writing a book for somebody who wants to do this for a year and then burn out and go teach high school. I look at this as a book that will help people take on this type of job as a vocation for the next 20 or 30 years, and I don't think that being unable to have a family life or social life is an acceptable price to pay for an interesting and lucrative career. Obviously, I have no judgment on people who decide that they don't want to get married or they don't want children, but I think it would be sad if you did that because your company wanted you to push for a few more million dollars.

Over the years I've traveled in different ways: business class and economy class, budget airlines, road and rail (a little bit less by road because most of the markets I go to I really don't want to drive in). I've stayed in pretty good hotels—not fancy, but solid, safe, and clean. I know we all work on different budgets and with different resources, but if you can't stay in a hotel that you believe is safe, comfortable, and clean then I would not do this job for this particular company. I think that's a minimum. This is a very hard job and you need to be able to sleep at night and not be worried about safety.

I try to combine all my airline miles and hotel points and fly with one airline group and stay at one hotel group. I do that because I have a family and one of the benefits of this job is being able to enjoy the status when I'm traveling with them. In hotels, having status saves you a lot of money on things like conference rooms, laundry, eating in the hotel, etc.

There are three main groups of airlines right now. I've heard good and bad things about each of them and have held the highest status on each of them at one point or another. Right now I stick to United because it hubs in Chicago and I live in Chicago; also, I just find that I'm getting good service and good routes. I keep silver or gold status with the other two groups because occasionally I end up flying with them as well.

I fly out typically on a Sunday night; I go to a different country every day, coming back 12 days later on a Friday. As my organization and my position in the market mature, I will hit each market for a single day. In the beginning that might be harder. First, you have ramping up, which means I might be spending more days looking for partners, training the partners, etc. Then there are also emotional things; often people I am talking to will get a little offended before they know me well if I come in and leave the country without staying very long. In that stage of building rapport, I may stay longer in a country. My goal is really to be able to do nine or ten cities in a two-week trip. I'll choose a relevant spot to spend the weekend in the middle of the trip.

For most of my trips I will try and do something that looks like a geographic plan, but this really depends on the quality of my distributors and my mindshare. If I can reach out to my distributors and say, "Please set up meetings on the first" and the next one on the second, then the third, all the way across, and they do this for me, my travel is going to be very easy. If they can't, my travel becomes more chaotic.

Over the years I've inherited bad distributors or had bad distributors forced upon me. One of the things they do is come out of the blue and say something like, "The minister of health would like to meet you. I need you here next Wednesday." Then you have to stop what you're doing and make sure you're in that country on that date. But your distributors should manage that better. This poor coordination can waste literally dozens of days a year and probably upwards of $25,000 in added travel costs.

It really is important to try and get your distributors working efficiently as early as possible. If they don't coordinate or communicate with you early on in the process or they simply decide on a date without checking with you, this actually is going to cause you grief when you are trying to set these meetings up and trying to plan out your travel.

But assuming that you're planning this yourself, you know what you're doing, and your distributors are good, here's what a good trip should look like:

- Sunday evening: Chicago to Buenos Aires via Miami

- Monday: meetings in Buenos Aires
- Monday evening: Buenos Aires to Santiago
- Tuesday: meetings in Santiago
- Tuesday evening: Santiago to São Paulo
- Wednesday: meetings in São Paulo
- Wednesday evening: São Paulo to Lima
- Thursday: meetings in Lima
- Thursday evening: Lima to Quito
- Friday: meetings in Quito
- Friday evening: Quito to Bogotá
- Weekend: Bogotá
- Monday: meetings in Bogotá
- Monday evening: Bogotá to Panama City
- Tuesday: meetings in Panama City
- Tuesday evening: Panama City to San Jose, Costa Rica
- Wednesday: meetings in San Jose
- Wednesday evening: San Jose to Managua, Nicaragua
- Thursday: meetings in Managua
- Thursday evening: Managua to Mexico City
- Friday: meetings in Mexico City
- Friday evening: Mexico City to Chicago

You can plan a similar route across Europe, Africa, the Middle East, or Asia. What you're trying to do is utilize your time and money in the best way to get face time with your customers and distributors.

For most of these flights, I'll buy tickets from Orbitz using local airlines, but the original flights—Chicago to Buenos Aires and then Mexico City to Chicago—I'll book with my primary airline, United. What I usually find is the short legs in between are almost never cost-effective to book through these airlines. So I'll use Orbitz or one of the other online booking agencies. I really try to avoid it, but occasionally I'll use the local airline's website. For instance, it's basically impossible to book a ticket in

Pakistan through Orbitz, ditto for some of the African airlines. In those cases, I'll have to go on their website and book the ticket.

When you plan a trip like this, you also have to keep in mind traffic and the distance between the airport and the city. My preference is to sleep in the city not too far from my distributor or my end users. I also like to be in a place in the city where I can walk around to have dinner If I'm traveling this much; I want to at least have a nice meal.

From a purely practical perspective, staying at the airport may be the best option. As you get to know cities, you will know the traffic patterns better and so on.

There are a lot of budget carriers out there now. One thing you have to be very careful about is what airport they leave from. In some cities the budget carriers leave from an airport that is a $100 taxi ride outside of the city in the wrong direction, and then any possible savings you made by using the budget airline were lost. Most airports in Europe, in the big Asian cities, and even in South America have relatively easy, relatively cheap ways of getting from the airport to the city by train or bus. Very often from the budget airline airports you don't have that, which can detract from your savings. On top of that, the budget airlines will probably not let you take your carry-on on board, you might not be able to get the seat you want, etc. I fly a lot with budget airlines, but mostly it's because they're the only airlines that fly on the routes that I want to fly. They can be pretty uncomfortable.

I prefer to stay at one of the American or big international chains; typically you're looking at Marriott, Hilton, or Hyatt—or there are a few European chains that are pretty good like Radisson, NH, and Ibis. Status for hotels usually goes according to nights. Whereas with airlines I've had years when I was the highest status on two airline groups, if you're splitting up your nights between two hotel groups, you won't achieve the highest status. That said, it's not that bad to be gold in two groups as opposed to being platinum or diamond in one group. I know people who one year stay at Marriott and the next year at Hilton, because typically status is good for two years.

You do get a lot of good perks from that status and there really are business benefits. I use meeting rooms in my hotels often. I know a lot of people who never leave their hotel to eat. They always just eat at the lounge, which saves money. I like to get my suit pressed every day before a meeting, and I can do that for free at most Marriotts because of my status. A couple of times, mostly for trade shows and conferences, I've used Airbnb to stay in and it's perfectly comfortable. It's not a bad solution, especially for trade shows, but I still am not drawn to it enough to shift the way I work. I like hotels because I can call down if I have a problem, if I need help getting my internet working, or to get a printer.

Especially in Europe, I use trains all the time. There used to be fantastic night trains in Europe, and several times a month I would take the night train instead of spending the night in a hotel someplace. The advantage of the night train is that you can get on the train in Milan at 9 p.m. and be in Paris the following morning. You're going from the center of one city to the center of the other and you don't have to go through security. Nowadays the trains are so fast that often what that means is you actually get in at 2 a.m. so you're not getting a full night's sleep on the train and you will still need to get to a hotel. On top of that, often the people you want to meet aren't in the center of the city anymore. A lot of businesses have moved to the suburbs, just like in the US, so the whole benefit of being downtown and not having to go out to the airport can be lost. The advantage that trains do have is that you have WiFi available on the whole trip.

I very seldom rent a car outside the US. In many places you can get a car and driver for the same price as renting a car, and then you don't have to worry about driving yourself. What would happen to you as a foreigner if you got into an accident? In many places now you have Uber or driving apps like Grab, and I keep a library of those on my phone. If you see, for instance, that Uber doesn't work in a certain country, ask somebody at the hotel to tell you what app to use in that market.

You will probably find that you are changing your flights and your trips on a relatively regular basis in a way that is quite frustrating. Unfortunately, that's the nature of our job, and you'll find this very hard to avoid. In the end you're traveling at the convenience of your distributors and your end user customers, and there are so many different moving parts and so many different people involved. With time, you'll feel more comfortable estimating this. For instance, it's worthwhile buying a more expensive, flexible ticket than getting a really cheap, inflexible ticket and throwing it out if something changes.

Despite all this, I very much enjoy the element of travel in my work. I was at a trade show a while back in São Paulo, which is one of the great meat cities of the world, and an American who was there for the same trade show mentioned how happy he was that there was an Outback steakhouse next to his hotel. He said, "I guess I won't have to worry about where to eat all week; I'll just eat there every night."

I was horrified. Even if what you wanted was to have a steak every night, there are so many incredibly good steak houses in São Paulo that it would be inconceivable for me to go to an American chain steakhouse instead of having a local steak. And there are so many different options for food, why eat the same thing every night when you're in a foreign country? I know not everybody thinks that way, but I've found that you can usually grab a couple of hours to see something or eat something or enjoy something. I go out to hear live music while I'm traveling, probably 25 times a year. I have a very good meal while I'm traveling, probably a hundred times a year, and I'll try to see something unusual probably another 25 times a year. So as I'm traveling around, I might not do something every day, I might not even go out to eat every night, but I do make time for the occasional special meal or to hear music, visit a museum, that kind of thing.

That doesn't mean that I have to spend an extra day in a country. As I plan my two-week trips, sometimes I'll specifically plan to spend the weekend in the country where I want to do something specific. There are several countries in Latin America that close down the center of town to car traffic on Sunday mornings and will lend you a bicycle. If I am in Latin America on a Sunday morning, I make sure to be in one of those towns because that's a lot of fun and it's nice to get a little exercise and fresh air.

Two more notes on travel: Travel is going to be a key component of your vocation if this is what you end up doing and you keep it up. Assuming you'd like to have a normal life, you have to find a good way to balance it. You can live an unbalanced life for year or two or maybe three, and after that it will cause you grief. I don't think that any career is worth living an unbalanced life for more than three years. But that's just my opinion. You should build up habits and structure in your lifestyle that support balancing your social life, family life, and health with your work life.

I call my wife for very short conversations between three and ten times a day, usually before and after I fly, before I go to bed, and when I wake up. I don't have long conversations with her, but I want to be available if there are things she wants to tell me about. I text my wife and my kids a few times over the course of the day and they'll text me back; this keeps a feeling of connectedness going.

I try to get dates for my kids' activities as early as possible and try to put them into my calendar. *Try* really is the operative word here, so, for instance, I don't necessarily plan on being home for my kids' birthdays. I'll try, but it's a lower priority than a play or recital or something that I know is important to them. That said, if a major customer of mine needs me to come and present to his boss on that day, I'll have to do that. On the other hand, I block out no-travel days several times a year. For instance, on Thanksgiving and a couple of religious holidays I never travel, no matter what.

After that I try and put in some social nights, like date nights with my wife. I reach out to some friends literally months in advance to schedule social events; otherwise it simply doesn't work out. I schedule short trips with a family member once or twice a year and a weekend with the whole family once or twice year. I schedule a weekend with my wife once a year to get away. More or less every other year, I travel with each of my kids and my wife separately someplace. On the other years my wife will travel with the kids. When I'm home I try to do a lot of the cooking. I enjoy cooking and it takes a lot of stress off the family, which is key to longevity in this job.

The other element of this work-life balance is health. It is easy to get very unhealthy as a road warrior. It's very rough on your body, so if you don't take good care of your body, your career is going to be very limited. I do quite a range of exercises when I'm at home and on the road. I lift weights, I jog, I swim, I box, and sometimes play racquet games.

Try to find a few different things that you can do when you're traveling. Swimming, jogging, and weight lifting are three of the best because most hotels either have a gym or pool, and often they'll can recommend a place you can jog. I don't necessarily exercise as much when I'm traveling as I do when I'm home, but a little bit of exercise goes a long way toward keeping you healthy when you're traveling.

I wrote a book called *What to do with a Layover in 105 Cities around the World, from Abuja to Zurich : A travel guide for road warriors by a road warrior.* You can find it on Amazon at https://www.amazon.com/Layover-Cities-around-World-Zurich-ebook/dp/B08JY13TYG/ref=sr_1_1?dchild=1&keywords=zach+selch&qid=1601301673&sr=8-1 . It's full of ideas for what to do when you are traveling. If you have a copy of this book, email me at zach@globalsalesmentor.com and I'll send you an e-copy of the layover book.

## Bonus videos:

https://www.youtube.com/watch?v=WfXR12M0NgM

https://www.youtube.com/watch?v=4LfUkzcpxkI

https://www.youtube.com/watch?v=H25NOPI8wP8

https://www.youtube.com/watch?v=jObo1SYSvVY

https://www.youtube.com/watch?v=qR0FN3uFgOw

https://www.youtube.com/watch?v=ZB7mfEzbOjY

https://www.youtube.com/watch?v=fMVe_clGXSI

## Building your sales organization

I tend to lump all external sales partner organizations together as distributors; I like to refer to everybody as partners. The semantics here are important. We are partners in the sales process and it's critical not to think of partners as customers; think of them as part of your sales organization. Let's review briefly the various types of partners that may be involved in our sales process.

In the strictest sense, a distributor is a sales partner that is an independent company; it buys your product, owns it for a while, then sells it. The distributor takes whatever margin they can afford to on the sale of this product and they are responsible for all of their costs, usually including the legal and regulatory costs of being able to sell your product in the territory. Distributors can be one-man operations or large operations more than $1 billion in annual revenue. Distributors can focus on a single market or sell in 10 or even 100 countries. Usually, the distributor will have an office or headquarters with administrative people and other non-salespeople, including marketing people, regulatory affairs people, service people, etc. Often the distributor will have departments divided either by geographic territory or by product type. You might find a company that has construction, medical, and retail divisions or one that sells only healthcare products but has 12 divisions divided up by which end user they are selling to (private practitioner, anesthesiologist, radiologist, etc.). You might find a distributor that has 12 divisions, each one representing a different city in the marketplace. The primary motive of the distributor salespeople, the distributor sales manager, and the distributor owner is to sell for the most profit with the least amount of effort.

Keep in mind that the distributor owner always has an additional motive, which is to leverage a product to help them sell other products. This is where a relationship with a distributor can become a little tricky. A distributor may want to add a manufacturer to their portfolio even though they know that they won't sell that product or they don't believe they can sell that product, because having a new or prestigious product in the portfolio may help them sell other more profitable products or may prevent their competition from offering that product. This is not uncommon. People who have been in the distribution business for a long time refer to these people as headhunters because they "collect heads"—signs from manufacturers—to signal how large and powerful their portfolio is. In some places in the world, these people have wealth from other sources and do this for prestige, so they have no intention of selling your products at all.

We have a formal relationship with the distribution partners, and I will talk about how we manage them later, but it's important to remember that how you onboard the distributor will be key to how successful you are. Choosing the wrong distributors is one of those things that can really sink a company's international expansion project. The very best thing that can happen if you choose the wrong distributor is that you get no revenue from that market; the worst is that you get shut out of a market for years and never be able to sell there.

Agents, from a strict definition perspective, will usually refer to sales organizations that sell our product and then take a commission or a finder's fee. They don't actually take ownership of our product and often they don't carry out any additional activities in the territory such as marketing, regulatory, etc. I find sometimes that the distinction between agents and distributors melts, and I like to refer to everybody as partners.

True agents are more likely to be in those industries where we are selling larger projects to the government and so on and not necessarily where they're selling small orders on an ongoing basis. In some cases, agents may be relatively large companies but often they are smaller than traditional distributors and more likely to be a single individual or a small office. They are also more likely to not focus on one specific area of product. They are putting work more into the relationships say with the ministry of communication or ministry of health.

There is a range of people that I would refer to as consultants that can be utilized in the international sales process. For me the big difference between an employee, a consultant, and an agent is that the consultant is going to get some type of a fee that isn't 100% related to a purchase order.

Frequently, hiring a regional sales manager in Africa is not something you can afford to do, but for a quarter of the price of a regional sales manager you can hire a consultant to be your regional sales manager for 10 hours a week, for instance. Or you can use consultants who are getting a monthly retaining fee to interact with a specific large customer for a specific amount of time possibly, with the promise of a larger payout at the end of the deal.

There are a lot of good ways to use consultants in markets where we are trying to get boots on the ground, trying to get relationships on the ground. Having these people may be a cost-effective way to do it.

Consultants can be very good during the discovery process. Sometimes employees from headquarters are not going to be able to get information from customers in countries where they have no relationship or no established trust. Your partners may not be able to get you information that you can trust from the markets, because their interests do not always coincide 100% with yours. Utilizing a standalone consultant who is paid on a monthly retainer fee system to do tactical information gathering from the customers, to enable discovery and help build out the sales process and the strategy and tactics, can be an excellent way to save money.

We can use consultants to help us with clinical studies, trials, logistical issues, regulatory affairs, local marketing—all the types of things we don't want to shift to the partner because we may not trust the partner's ability to do these successfully. By paying a consultant we keep control over the system.

Within your international sales organization, who are the key players? This will help us design our organization.

First let's talk about actual company employees.

The **head of international sales** (HIS) can be a director or VP or general manager, international, or it could simply be the company's vice president of sales who is taking on the international role in addition to the domestic role. This is going to be the person who sets strategy, chooses what markets to go into, decides how to allocate resources, and sets up personnel.

Depending on how you choose your regional managers, this position may take on more responsibilities in the markets for things that do not occur on a routine basis. What do I mean? Often RMs are much better at managing distributors than recruiting and onboarding them, so it makes sense for the head of international sales possibly to also be responsible for recruiting and onboarding and setting up markets. This division of labor can be fuzzy, depending on the specific circumstances. The HIS also will deal with anything that involves distributors from multiple territories. If, for instance, you exhibit at a trade show that you know distributors who work with two or more regional managers will be attending, responsibility for the show should fall with the head of international sales. Likewise, when we have a global sales conference and we bring in all the distributors for more than one territory, this should fall under the responsibility of the head of sales. In the same way that the head of sales may compensate for the regional managers' weaknesses, often the head of sales will step in when somebody can't get to the field or there are conflicts.

The head of international sales will also set messaging, set the curriculum and the structure for sales training, and work with marketing and sales enablement to develop the tools for selling, marketing, and sales training for use internationally. On an ongoing basis the head of international sales will interface with the regional managers and keep track of all the regional managers' funnels. Depending on the size of the company, the market, and the number of distributors that the company has, I would suggest that the head of international sales meet with every active distributor at a minimum of once a year—possibly twice a year.

Depending again on the skills and abilities of the team the head of international sales will often be involved in things like postmortem meetings following losing a big deal and will probably be involved in all meetings that involve giving a warning to a distributor for poor or under performance. In this model our expectation is that the head of international sales has a great deal of distributor management and sales management skills as well is being willing to take on a lot of the bad guy activities required within the sales organization, can travel and is a good manager and salesperson by nature.

From an internal communication perspective – the head of international sales will (HIS) will communicate with the head of global sales (probably the VP Sales and Marketing) or the CEO, will provide an ongoing sales forecast that will be used by finance and manufacturing, shipping and payments, and will interface with R&D and Product Management for product issues. HIS will also interface with the administrative parts of the company concerning their team – HR, payroll, etc.

If the head of international sales has been promoted up from a position that is not international in nature or does not have these skills, there may be a serious lack of what's needed, and this could make the whole project put the whole project at risk. This is a key position. If these skills are missing, it is key to find a way to coach and/or train the HIS. These are not skills that one learns in an MBA program.

The **regional manager** (RM), the cornerstone of the sales organization, is an employee of the company who is responsible for sales in a territory. This really is one function that cannot be weak. Ideally, the regional managers would be very strong in distributor management and would also have pre-existing relationships with the local end users.

What are the responsibilities of the regional manager? Ideally, he build up his territory—that is, he recruits and onboards distributors within his territory, is responsible for their training, and coordinates to make sure that they have the proper sales enablement and marketing tools for their markets. In my experience the RMs who do this are really the very best , but I would say they are maybe 10% to 20% of the RM pool. The RMs that I know that do this well go on to be great sales leaders later.

The RM manages their distributors on an ongoing basis. Whatever part of the sales process that we want to take place locally and that we want the distributor to be responsible for (this should account for a large part of the sales process), the RM will be managing and overseeing and supporting.

For this to work well, the RM should understand the sales process very well and should be able to carry out most of these activities himself. Probably the biggest thing that we simply can't compromise on with our RMs—and this can also be difficult to find—is the discipline and the drive to push the distributors.

The distributors are often very well established businesspeople— affluent, older, well connected, and they live in the same cities and often move in the same social circles of these RMs. This means that pushing around the distributor may be very difficult for them. That's why it's such a key element that we need to be looking for during recruitment.

The things that will be happening in the territory will involve all of the local parts of the sales process—identifying and qualifying customers (this could be through online or library research or through local conferences and public appearances, workshops, and other marketing campaigns), working to establish rapport and trust. The RM is key to the image of the company.

In some countries, especially those that I would qualify as high power imbalance, high context, and high uncertainty avoidance, and where relationships are slow to build, it may be important to have an RM of a certain ethnicity. All of those cultural factors can drive in the direction of requiring somebody who is part of an in-group. Here also lies a Catch-22. Africa is the best example. If you have a regional manager handling all of sub-Saharan Africa, there is no one ethnicity that will allow him to be part of the in-group in every country where you want to sell. Very often that leads to deciding to use somebody who is a complete outsider, for instance an Indian or a Lebanese. That said, I have been able to utilize ethnic Africans for each of the many times I have hired for this position successfully, it is a matter of understanding the regions and how they interact together and experience helps.

It's important to figure out what you want from the regional manager in terms of the components of the sales process. One of the best terms or concepts that people use when dealing with sales management is time available for selling. Often we get tied up with all these different things we want our regional managers to be able to do and we get away from what they're supposed to really be doing, which is managing the distributor. If we have RMs and we expect them to oversee technical projects or shipping or those types of things, we're taking away their time available for selling, and this will impact sales negatively.

Likewise, if the regional manager is more comfortable presenting to or meeting face-to-face with customers and actually executing the sales process rather than managing, we've lost all of the scalability and the force multiplication that comes from a distribution network.

I worked for a company where we had an extremely technical product that required installation. The people before me in the position had decided that the best configuration would be to have distributors who were highly technically competent but didn't really know how to sell. That drove them to regional managers who did all the selling themselves. So if you looked at the breakdown of the sales process, the manufacturer used our website and marketing to find customers; the manufacturer used its warrantee, its installed base, and its reputation for quality manufacturing to drive trust and rapport with the end user; the regional manager presented and met with the end user and essentially owned the component of the process that helped the end user internalize that we had a solution that could solve their problem; and the distributor only owned the installation and service effectively. Now this worked pretty well in the domestic market because there were 13 regional managers covering 48 states. But because there were only two regional managers covering the rest of the world, the cost of having regional managers travel everywhere to be at every meeting meant there was no way this could be a profitable system internationally.

By changing what the regional managers were supposed to do and by changing the profile of the distributors, we were able to drive up sales well over 1,000% in a couple of years and add about $100 million to the value of the company. That is why understanding and planning this structure is really key to the success of the whole project.

Other potential team members working on the international team who are employees of the company:

**Anchor:** I find that it is critical to have somebody in the office who is designated to provide administrative support for the international sales team. This is something that you may have to fight over because many companies really don't have administrative assistance, but we're trying to keep the total available sales time as high as possible for the salespeople, the RMs, and the HIS. There will be dozens of small administrative tasks that require time of somebody in the office. And you really don't want either your RMs or your HIS spending too much time at the desk at headquarters, so getting an administrative person even for 20 hours a week whose hourly rate is 1/5 of the HIS's is really the best way to go.

What kinds of tasks am I talking about? Signing off on distributor agreements, legalizing shipping documents, planning site visits to the factory—all of those types of things require a few minutes here and a few minutes there in headquarters, which adds up to hours and days and weeks of work over the course of a year. The anchor needs to be a diligent and responsible person with good administrative skills and a strong work ethic.

**Intelligence/research:** Often it falls on RMs or the HIS to do all of their own research. I've found that even the very best are not as good as a research professional, and their time is more valuable. There are university programs today for business intelligence professionals, and there are lots of people who do this as freelancers on an hourly rate. Some companies can afford to hire full-time people to do this.

One configuration is to have a part-time person who also acts as a project manager for using external consultants. For instance, it can be very helpful to use local people at trade shows to gather competitive intelligence, and having the right person doing intelligence and research can be a very cost-effective way to manage that part of the business.

I used somebody who I paid $40 an hour to get me the names and contact details of a large list of very important targeted customers. I would imagine it would've taken me three to five hours per name if I had tried to get the same information, whereas he was taking about 20 minutes per name. This meant we were saving hundreds of dollars in labor costs for every name we acquired. Another way I've used researchers is have them prepare country files for my RMs so that they are prepared when they go to see customers. Having a professional find economic and socioeconomic information about the customer as well as recent news clippings to prepare for a meeting is a great deal more cost effective than having RMs and HISs do it themselves.

One way of looking at it is that the job of Head of International Sales is to recruit, coach, and lead sales assets, and depending on how large your team is, you might be constantly looking for new assets. Even if you don't recruit constantly, if you have a steady, low-churn team, it's always a good idea to keep an eye on potential talent that you might find for future use.

Whatever the frequency, building and onboarding sales teams is part of the fundamental job of the international sales leader.

Like a lot of things in international sales, this is one of those tasks that is substantially more difficult internationally than domestically. Think about salespeople: Good ones and really good ones (like some regional managers) have strong personalities. They may be midcareer level. They are opinionated and strong willed.

This type of person can be difficult to find, difficult to work with, and difficult to onboard. When you add to that the international aspect, the different cultures, it becomes very challenging. No matter how well traveled or multicultural you are, understanding the personalities of people from different cultures is always a challenge.

To add to the stress, a mistake in hiring a regional manager can cost your company easily a couple million dollars in lost opportunity—maybe as much as a million dollars just in direct waste of money because you won't turn around and fire him two days later. You will probably burn through a year's worth of salary and travel expenses before you realize the problem, so this is something you want to get right.

I'm talking mostly about regional managers. You might also have other individuals on your team, like the anchor I wrote about earlier. Ideally, the anchor would have 10 or 15 years of experience and would be mature and clearheaded. Unfortunately, that profile is dying out in the US, so it might be difficult to find somebody like that.

I've also used interns for the anchor job. That's less than optimal, but you might get a hard-working, intelligent person for two years. You need somebody who is always in the office and can handle emergencies, can take administrative work off the desk of the HIS, and can help walk paperwork around the office.

There's always the question of whether international gets its own marketing person. I am very much in favor of this even if it's a half-time position, because often in the US the domestic marketing team doesn't really understand what the international team is trying to achieve from a marketing perspective. Having your own person, even if all that person does is organizing and manage outsourcing your needs to external service suppliers, can be very helpful. Again, this could be a half-time position or an intern position.

Let's talk about shipping. Does the person who handles international shipping report to the international team or the shipping team? You could go either way on this. Having them as part of the international team builds a little bit of team spirit, where they feel part of the team and they really are dedicated to making sure things work well for the team. On the other hand, this is different from sales, and they might feel more comfortable with other people who deal with shipping. There is also the question of whether it can be justified to have a person on the international team just to handle shipping—if there is enough shipping happening and if that really is the best use of personnel. I find the people who don't see themselves as part of the international team are more likely to screw things up. So having somebody dedicated to international shipping who is part of the team can be very helpful.

The very first thing you want to do is identify what the profile is for each position on the team. Let's go back to the whole idea of building my sales process and figuring out who is supposed to do what. If I know who is supposed to do what, then I know what the regional managers are supposed to do, and if I know what the regional managers are supposed to do, I can build up a profile. The single biggest thing that I want the regional manager to do is manage the sales process. Partners' salespeople are often are weak at that, and they handle a range of products, so I don't want to depend on them for the management and the ownership of the sales process. I'd rather have my RM own it. That's the single most important thing that I want from the regional salesman. Probably the second thing is his ability to present, because a lot of distributor sales reps are weak in presenting. After these two things, what I will be looking for is existing relationships with good distributor partners and my specific end users. I'll typically want somebody who has experience working with more than one market and with multiple distributors. While I probably want somebody with experience in the specific industry for the connections, I don't necessarily need him to understand the product before I hire him or know the very specific sub-industry that I'm in.

I believe that hiring people from your very specific sub-industry is almost always a mistake, even though it's very common. The bottom line is you can pretty much teach any product to somebody who knows how to sell; it's just a matter of time. If somebody really knows how to sell, they could make the right contacts that just may take a lot longer to sell product.

But if you don't have demonstrated experience managing distributors and managing the sales process then I have no way to know if you can do it or not. I'm not going to be able to teach you if you don't have the native skills, so I'm never going to take a risk with that part of the job description.

Having figured out what I want, I'll write up a job description. Generally companies have a formal HR-mandated way to write up a job description, and I have a practical way. The one I am going to use has to generate interest: I want everyone to want to work for me.

I usually talk about how important this job is to the company, how welcoming the company is, what future this position will have with the company, what type of exciting technology we have, how nurturing and mentoring the bosses are, and that salary is competitive.

I don't exaggerate and I don't talk too much about the salary. I do talk about the potential for growing your career, but I don't overemphasize it because I do want to get people who are at least midcareer.

The last time I advertised, I got more than 300 resumes per ad ,and probably 60 of them were people I would hire. I believe that's a very effective return for an ad. I'm not even going to mention who you should advertise with because every time I go to advertise, the industry has changed enough so that I'm not sure where I advertised with yesterday is going to help me tomorrow. What I can say is I want this targeted area, not just a single country. When you are dealing with RMs, they might be based in one of a number of cities or countries.

Before I advertise this, I also need to think of where I will locate this position. This is almost an art form and a science in itself.

First of all, once we define our territory, what are the potential cities or countries to serve this territory? Let's say I know I want to hire a regional manager and the territory he's going to cover is Asia, not including China, Korea, and Japan but including India. Where am I going to situate him? Could be in India, could be in Singapore, could be in Thailand.

What I might look at first is cultural fit to the way I like to work and the way my company likes to work. The reason is that if there happens to be something in a culture of a specific country that worries me, I may decide not to hire somebody from that country. Obviously, these cultural tendencies are generalizations, but they're pretty good generalizations and they help me make decisions. I once hired somebody from Greece, and he was a nightmare to manage. On paper he looked great. He was a really nice guy. Culturally, Greeks tend to have a very strong aversion to uncertainty. I have a very low aversion to uncertainty, and my company didn't have very good information flow systems. There were things in my company that were unclear but I had no control over.

I needed him to prepare a report urgently for a presentation that I was making for my CEO. We had a meeting once a year to close my organization's budget as well as goals, right before the primary company board meeting. It was essential that I had that report prepared for that presentation or we were not going to get approval for something that was strategically very important for me and the whole project might get put off by a year.

This poor guy needed some information from one of the engineering departments and they weren't giving it to him. I told him that he wasn't going to get it and he had to write the report without that information. For two months I was pushing him for the report, and he kept telling me he was working on it and trying to get the information from engineering and they were ignoring him. My poor guy just about exploded from stress. So I'm yelling at him and telling him that he has to write this report without that information, and his entire cultural being is telling him that it's impossible. He ended up going off on his honeymoon with me calling and yelling at him that I needed his report. His wife hated me more than he did. If I'd known before I hired him or if I had thought it through before I hired him that this was a cultural tendency that he had that there was no way he was going to get around, I might not have hired him.

My copy editor just about had a heart attack over the above story, so let me elaborate because this is too important to cut out over political correctness. There are a couple of great books— Erin Meyer's *The Culture Map* and Geert Hofstede's *Culture's Consequences*—that summarize fantastic bodies of academic material that explains how different cultures address different issues. Again, not everyone conforms to the cultural norms, but enough do to make it a good way to plan your international business.

The other element that I look for is a good airport. For 15 years, this was probably the most important thing to me. What you want is an airport that has direct flights—cheap direct flights, ideally—to pretty much everywhere your regional manager needs to go. So, for instance, as of 2019 Kuala Lumpur has fantastic connecting flights to pretty much every place in Asia at a substantially lower price than Singapore does, so there could be an advantage to having an RM based in Kuala Lumpur rather than in Singapore. Now there are many more good airports than there were even 10 years ago, so that part of the equation is a little easier.

Passports and visas are important, too. You need to make sure that the person you hired is from a country that allows him to travel to the countries that you need him to travel to. The worst with this is the Middle East. Nobody seems to like anybody else in the Middle East, so if you have a Lebanese regional manager, there are places he might not be able to get to without some help to get a visa. The same goes for Iraqis, Syrians, and Palestinians. So you should get a feel for how easy it's going to be for somebody you hire to get travel documentation. In some cases this really isn't important, but in others, like the Middle East, it's very important. As of today, Africa is pretty good; there are multiple countries where an African with an African passport—from Kenya or Nigeria, for instance—can go almost anywhere in sub-Saharan Africa without having to get a visa in advance.

Cost of living can be an element. In a lot of ways, Singapore is the perfect place to put somebody for Asia, but it is a very expensive place to live. So you can't get by paying somebody a low salary if you want them to be based in Singapore. Looking at the Middle East, most of the sales managers that are based in Dubai are actually not from Dubai; they're Egyptian, Lebanese, Palestinian, or Jordanian. And they might enjoy living in Dubai, but for the most part they'd actually rather be living at home with their families, and you can pay them probably half as much if you base them in Cairo or Amman as opposed to Dubai.

Aside from advertising, I may do a few other things to find candidates. I may reach out to the commercial officers in various embassies and ask them if they know somebody who might be a good fit and I'll send them the job description. They usually know anywhere from 10 to 100 salespeople in their area.

Since I've been doing this for a while, I'll network a little bit. I got a lot of very good resumes the last few times I did this. I advertised through LinkedIn, and just posting on my LinkedIn profile probably got me 25 to 50 pretty good resumes.

One thing I've done over the years is collect salespeople's business cards at trade shows. I'll just go up to the booth of a company that I know hires good people and I'll ask every salesman there for his card. I'll reach out to them later through email and ask them to send me a resume.

I got trapped once with that. I was at a pretty big booth and somebody asked me why I was collecting cards. When I told him sort of quietly, "I'm looking to hire a regional manager and I'm collecting names of people who may be interested," he yelled across the booth to his manager, "Hey, this guy came to our booth trying to recruit me for another job!" Everybody turned and looked at me and started booing at me, which was sort of funny and very embarrassing. But chances are that the person you want is going to be at that show.

Once I have a bundle of resumes, I look them over. This may be my weakness; it could be that I should delegate this, but I've had trouble articulating and training exactly what people should be looking for. So while this is a lot of work, I feel I have to do it.

In my case, I'm usually looking for somebody who clearly had a regional sales job with a serious medical device company. Off the top of my head I can think of 30 or 40 names of companies. It might be that what I should do is put those on the list so that software could look for them, but I'm also a little scared that I might forget one or two, and the nature of these companies is that they merge and change names and so on. If I were talking about somebody who's 50 years old, he could've worked for Nellcor or Nellcor-Puritan Bennett or some other company that doesn't exist today because it's been swallowed up four times, and I don't want to miss that. But it could very well be that you can do a better job than I can with the technical side of this. Basically, what I'm trying to do is identify a grouping of resumes that make sense and fit my basic requirements. If I have a lot, I will look to make sure they really cover everything I'm looking for like the number of years of experience and maybe the extras that I might want. For instance, I really like people who have experience both with the distributor and with a manufacturer. Sometimes you don't find that, but if I have 300 resumes I'm sure I'll find 6 to 10 people like that. The other might be language. I might find that I'll be looking for a core language, but I'll find people with three good languages.

I will start by essentially cutting that stack of 300 as small as possible, probably to about 30.

Then I will set up calls. I will do as many as six a day, but six is pretty hard and more than that is really hard. I'll do them to fit the time zone of the people I'm interviewing, so I'll email and ask if they could take a call at a certain time. If the answer is no, I ask them to suggest a different time. Of course, you can use call setup apps and software for this now like Calendly.

Then I'll send them an email that basically says, "Thank you very much. I'm very interested in talking to you. The structure of this call is going to be that I am going to introduce myself and tell you a couple of things about the job. Then we'll switch to you so you can tell me about yourself. I'll ask you some questions and you can ask me questions." I'll let them know how much time it's going to take so they can plan.

If I can, I use something like WhatsApp or Skype to keep the costs down on these calls. I very seldom do videos the first time, but that's not a bad thing; it might give you more information to be able to see the applicants.

I have created a sheet with standard questions that try to guage the attitudes of people, as opposed to very specific things. I don't ask any real technical questions. A lot of it is trying to fish out information about how they see themselves. So, for instance, when I say, "Tell me about yourself," I imagine that within a few seconds they're going to talk about something that has to do with selling. If they go through the whole "tell me about yourself" part without talking about selling, it's going to catch my eye. I ask them to tell me about three things that they are proud of, and one or two of them better be related to selling.

I'll be sitting there with their resume and a list of questions. There's a very good chance I put together questions specifically around things that came up in the resume. 10% of the time I'll just say thank you and goodbye to somebody after the first few questions because I'll feel right away that they are not going to be a good fit.

Usually, though, we go through the whole 30-minute call. While there are all sorts of studies that tell us that interviews aren't the best way to find your right hire, they are a very good start and really the best tool. I've had some very interesting answers on these calls, but I think you really can pick up and understand who is good and who isn't and at least narrow it down very well on these calls. By the time I'm done with the calls, I should have hopefully between five and eight solid candidates for each position.

I've used a variety of online tests, and I find them very helpful. I'm not going to recommend a specific one, but the ones that I've used give me a very solid psychological profile, and I believe they've been very accurate. There are tests that cost per person you test, but I also know a good one that charges you per person you hire, so you can test every candidate who sends you a resume. Once or twice I've ignored things I've learned about people from these tests, more because I didn't understand them than because I wanted to ignore it or didn't believe in it. I found as time went by that they were really accurate, and I understood exactly what they were trying to tell me. The testing also helps you build your set of questions, and that is also very helpful.

The next step is to set up one full day of face-to-face interviews in the candidate's home market. I'll usually do it in a hotel conference room, and if I can I'll have an HR professional join me. I have found that for a reasonable fee, I can hire an HR consultant for the day to sit in on the meetings. Having an HR professional who is part of the local culture and is familiar with the local work scene can be very helpful. To put it in perspective, I can usually find somebody like that for the equivalent of less than one week's starting salary that I will pay the candidate. Obviously, it is critical to fully brief the consultant before the meeting.

At the interview, I have in front of me the candidate's resume, their test report, my notes from my telephone conversation, and a list of questions I've tailored to them. I will ask questions for about 45 minutes and then give them a little bit of time to ask questions and talk. Then I take five minutes or so to rest and clear my head and put away my notes before the next meeting. This is how I'll pass the day. Usually there will be a couple of people that I'll just let go in the middle of the interview because it's clear to me that they're not a good fit. There'll be two or three people left at the end who are really outstanding and then it becomes a situation of how I choose between them. I will leave a full second day in market with nothing scheduled and I'll try to have each of the most promising people meet me that day for a meal, or something that seems casual. I'll try to get them to relax a little bit and open up a little more, and I'll hit them with follow-up questions and conversations.

I will prepare an Excel sheet with the top candidates and all the things I felt were important in terms of what the candidate needed to perform this job well, and then I will basically make a matrix with the candidates and get a feel for who I believe is the best candidate. I'd like to be able to make that decision before I leave the market. If I can't decide on one at this point, I might even ask for a third meeting to the top candidates.

I will ask the top candidate or candidates for references and over the next few days contact each of the references to ask them basic questions to verify facts. I'll just ask them for a quick description of the candidates and what I'm looking for again is somebody to mention something about sales or persuasion or success. I believe that if a friend of a very good salesman were to describe him, a lot of what he would talk about would be the salesman's drive and success, maybe persuasiveness.

Once I've chosen the top candidate, the next step is bringing them into headquarters to be interviewed by a few other people. I would prefer more than anything else to have them interviewed by an HR professional in HQ because typically those are the people who can fill in what I'm missing in terms of interviewing skills.

What happens in a lot of companies is everybody wants to meet the candidates. Most of these people have never interviewed a salesman, let alone a salesman from another country, and they're not quite sure what they're looking for. It's important not to let people overwhelm the candidate. If I can, I will limit the number of people who sit in on the interview to those necessary. I want to use this opportunity also to get the candidate excited about the factory, our products, all the modern equipment, our service, our support, our cafeteria, etc.

After the relevant people have met the candidate, we will have a post-interview debriefing. We'll review what people have thought, including anything that might be problematic. Then we will make an official decision.

The next step is to put together an offer for the candidate. I'm not going to talk about this too much because it's really an HR/legal issue, but I'd say that there are people you can reach out to in order to get a feel for what the market value is for these positions in these countries. Often people will lowball it when they say what they believe a salesman should make in these markets. They'll say what the average salary of a salesman is, but they may be counting retail salesmen as well as B2B salesmen in their average. You want to understand the value of a top-of-the-line person with experience, because you don't want to underpay someone dramatically and have him quit after a year because he is under stress because of money.

For most midmarket corporations or companies with under $500 million in sales, what you're probably looking at is hiring regional sales managers as consultants or external employees. You are probably not going to open up legal entities in the markets you are operating in, and employing somebody directly as an employee will probably put you into some liabilities that you're not really interested in.

So what does that really mean? What I've always done is essentially hire people with a consulting agreement. My aim is to make this whole discussion as quick and painless as possible and then forget it ever happened. So we will essentially send a request and say, "Here are the instructions: Please open up a consulting company. We will reimburse you for the cost of your accountant/lawyer to set it up. Then give us the name of the company we will put that in contract. We will pay you with a check to the name of that contract company every month. You're essentially not an employee." Once we get through that legal work, we forget about it and we treat them as employees.

Again, I am not a lawyer. I can't give you legal advice, and anything I say now should not be considered legal advice. But I can tell you how to manage a sales team, and if you want these people to perform, they have to feel that you appreciate them. It is extremely important that you respect them and treat them as part of the family and not as mercenaries. How you achieve that from a legal standpoint is for you to negotiate with your legal department.

I would suggest that the offer letter be written in a way that glosses over the issue of them being a consultant as much as possible. Here is my completely layperson's, non-lawyer position: There's a limit to what your liability is and what the possible cost of this is. It's much more likely that you will be hit in the head with a meteorite than that your regional manager based in Kenya is going to sue you. So I would suggest that your overall exposure is maybe a year's salary, with the chance of that happening probably one in a thousand. On the other hand, if you don't do this correctly, you will lose millions of dollars in sales. For me it's a no-brainer.

Like everything else in this book, we're dealing with things that go from relatively shoestring budget to relatively higher, but if we are assuming that we want regional managers who could be selling $5 million or so each and maybe as much as $15 or 20 million, and we are anticipating that we can keep them for 5 to 10 years, then we really want to invest in how we choose them and how we onboard them.

Onboarding an international sales team is one of the most critical parts of our whole project. If the cornerstone of everything is distributor mindshare and the people who are most directly in contact with distributors are our regional managers, then the mindset, the skills, and the cooperation of the regional managers are key. Among the things we will have to recognize in this whole organization is that we simply don't see the regional managers enough face to face. They spend most of their time in market so this one of the only times that we get to burn into their mentality that they are part of this team.

I will reiterate here that I'm not a lawyer and you should talk to your lawyer and your HR people. Don't take my advice if it in any way goes against what your lawyers or your HR people tell you.

For many of the people we will work with, the idea of being part of a team is more important than it is for Americans. Americans are the most individualistic group of people in the world. Some cultures are at the extreme end of that curve, some cultures are somewhere in the middle, but I've never employed somebody who's even in our quarter of that curve in terms of individualism.

You could probably get a very good US regional sales manager who is excellent at his job and a completely sane, socialized person and say to him, "I will pay you a little bit over market average and I'm never going to talk to you again. Just do your job," and he'd probably be happy with that. If you were to say that to somebody for instance from China or Thailand, it would probably devastate them and either they would decide not to join you or they would gouge you for additional money to make up for it.

Our job as international sales leaders is to get the best out of our organization, out of our distributors, out of the regional managers, and out of everybody else who helps sell. What that means is we have to understand what our regional managers require, including from a cultural/emotional perspective, to perform better. You want to look into cultural markers that include things like cooperativeness, individualism, and aversion to uncertainty. These are often the things that will impact how a remote worker from a different culture feels about working for your company. The short answer is that you want to make them feel welcome and part of the family even if they don't act like your American RMs.

I recently saw a situation where a company hired somebody for a regional manager job, and the first four paragraphs of the letter essentially reiterated that this person was not an employee, should not consider themselves an employee, and never would be an employee, and then they went on to welcome him. I understand exactly why they did it from a legal perspective.

In most countries, employees have a great deal of protection against international employers, so if you hire a local employee and he can prove an employee-employer relationship, you are opening yourself to a potential legal risk. Here's what I told this company: "What's your exposure here? A year's salary, $50K to $100K? You want this guy to sell $5 million a year and you're crushing his feeling that he's connected to the company. You're making him feel like he's some kind of mercenary. So I can guarantee you that you decrease his sales ability by 50% with this letter, so this letter is costing you $2.5 million a year." I believe that just by shifting those paragraphs to the middle or the end of the letter, possibly even without softening the language, just not having them at the beginning of the letter could have solved the whole problem.

I would find a way to embrace the legal language while also presenting a warm welcome to these hires. Again, this is business advice; get advice from a lawyer for the legal side of it.

These international RMs are key to the growth of the company. Very often, the reason you're undertaking this project is because growth domestically is stalled, or you realize that you need to do this for the long-term health of company, or you want to drive the value of the company up and everybody will see a benefit in the long-term international growth.

Whatever reason you're trying to achieve international growth, you shouldn't just be doing it for the fun of it. It's key to the company and so the international team members, and their emotional connection to the company, are key to the strategy of the company.

There is a good chance that international hires need to feel an emotional connection to the company in order to perform well. These regional managers for the most part will be gregarious, very possibly extroverted, and they have no family or friends living in the area of your factory or headquarters. So the social aspect of being welcomed into the family of this company in your headquarters is important to them and thus strategic for you. You need to include an element of making them feel welcome in your onboarding and training.

I like to train regional managers in groups of two to five at a time rather than individually. Cost really isn't very much more to onboard five than it is to onboard one, and it gives them that feeling of being part of a group and having a cohort going forward.

One word of warning here: Sometimes you will have people that really don't get along, and sometimes you can even predict this from their cultural backgrounds. So if you have people who have very different senses of time, for instance, that opens up a huge potential conflict and you might find that this distracts from the training.

I had a team training once with a guy from Australia who had a very high sense of the importance of time, and a guy from Egypt, with just about the far side of the scale. Both good performers, both nice guys. They were going to meet me for a hockey game in downtown Chicago on a very cold night. The Australian was outside waiting 10 minutes early. On the way to meet, somebody asked the Egyptian for a small favor that called for short detour. To the Egyptian, it was crystal clear— it was much more important to help a friend than to let the clock dictate your life. In the end, he was late by about 30 minutes. The Australian started calling me to complain about 30 seconds after they were supposed to meet, and about every 3 minutes after that. While I was cold, I figured that I would just kill the time with a cigar as I was waiting outside the United Center. As an aside, if you stand outside a Chicago Blackhawks game in a leather jacket smoking a cigar and you have some familiarity with lifting weights, everybody will assume you are a very special kind of scalper, apparently. While I puffed away, calls raced back and forth between the Australian, the Egyptian and me, getting more and more frantic over less time than it would take to order a pizza.

The key to this is setting expectations. If we had taken time to explain to the Egyptian the importance the Australian placed on time management, and to the Australian the importance that the Egyptian placed on helping colleagues, we might have avoided the tension.

I've tried to put people up in apartments where they have access to a little bit more of the comforts of home, but I've found that it doesn't add very much and that people prefer to be in hotels. That can be again very different, depending on the individuals and depending on the cultures that they come from. There are plenty of long-stay–style hotels everywhere nowadays that give you breakfast in the morning but also give you a microwave and a two-burner stove and a refrigerator in the room so people can do a little bit of cooking.

Before the onboarding, I send a combination of videos and reading material to give people a little bit of a taste before they come in. Most salespeople will read and possibly even study all of it before they come in.

On the first day of training I cover things like HR policies and dress codes. Don't assume that because you've spoken to somebody and he has good English, that he is going to understand how to act for a few weeks in your corporate headquarters, and don't assume that he's not going to violate your HR policies, and don't assume that he knows how to dress in your headquarters.

Just a quick word about dress codes: US business casual is incredibly frustrating and confusing for most foreign businessmen. The idea that you can wear chinos but not jeans, that you can wear boat moccasins but not sneakers, that you can wear a polo shirt with a sports logo on it but not a T-shirt with a graphic on it—these don't make any sense for most non-Americans. No matter how good people's English is, often these are the things that they will get confused about.

They can also be very emotional, because when you talk to somebody about how they dress, you're touching on their personality, and it's the type of thing that they can get very defensive about. The way I usually describe business casual to foreign people is I say that their shirt has to have a collar, their shoes can't be sneakers, and they have to have a vertical pocket on their pants. As long as they have those three, I will consider it business casual. Now if your office doesn't care, then great. I personally don't care, but I don't want a situation where I'm bringing in five people to help them build up their relationship with headquarters and everybody looks at them like they are delinquents for not following the rules.

In a similar vein, let's briefly talk about HR rules. The whole concept of "political correctness" is very strange to some people. Again, if you want to take a look at cultural markers, keep an eye on cultures that are considered hypermasculine because those are probably the ones you will have the most problems with. This is also true of cultures that have a higher power inequality. The idea that a janitor or the person who serves us lunch should be treated as our equal will be foreign to some of these people, as is the idea that we can't ask the secretary to take our laundry in.

I usually put up a list of HR rules, and I call it "If you do this, I will be forced to fire you." I also want to make sure, for instance, that people don't make off-color jokes. Some people from foreign countries think that our political correctness guidelines are funny and assume that everybody else thinks they're just as much of a joke as they do. Then they'll tell the most incredibly off-color stories at social events in the United States. Part of this is that they feel comfortable, and they find it hard to believe that the people they feel comfortable with have beliefs that are so different than theirs. I've heard people talk very casually at the table with staunch Catholics who were pro-life Republicans about having an abortion, not realizing that what they were saying was offensive. I've had people talk about visits to brothels very casually at a meal in mixed company, not really thinking there was anything wrong with it. So if you can preemptively set guidelines, it's very helpful and it will protect your team. You don't want training to lead to firing.

In preparation for training, I send out a bundle of material that includes things like the HR guidelines and dress codes. It will include the same contact list that I use for my distributor playbook that includes pictures, short biographies, and the contact details of the people that interact with the international sales team and distributors. It's good for the RMs to have this before they come in for training.

There are arguments as to whether to send the playbook and the materials beforehand or not. I'm a little torn on this. I don't necessarily want to take up too much of the time of the team before they come in, but also it's nice to be able to go over it with the people in class, so I would say I am slightly in favor of holding on to the bulk of the material and sending more annexes and supporting clinical or scientific or odd documents and support documents. So, for instance, if my product is very scientific or very engineering driven, maybe I will send the various scientific or engineering guideline documents for the RM to read before he comes in, but I won't necessarily send the playbook that talks about how we will sell this product.

Anything that you can do to make it more comfortable for your team is going to be appreciated, so if you include in their welcome packet maps, what they can do in your city, that kind of thing, it's going to be helpful. When I started with one company, there was a beautiful gift basket of snacks in my hotel room, including a present for my wife and my child.

It was a very small but much appreciated gesture. If, for instance, you put in a baseball cap or T-shirt for each child of the RM from your local sports team, that's a really nice gesture to show how much you appreciate them. If you give them something they can take back home, in most cases the RM will say something like "This is a present my boss sent for you" to their children—another little trick to create a welcoming environment for people who are extremely important to the success of your project.

Usually there are HR requirements when somebody starts. In many of the companies I've worked there were HR intake classes periodically and, if possible, I would start the regional managers with one of those sessions. That way the two to five RMs are sitting with another five to ten people, and they now have some friends in the company and a feeling of community. It also shifts some of the teaching of the basic issues away from you.

I usually spend a minimum of half a day just talking about my goals and why I hired them and what I'm trying to achieve with them, and I'll do it in the structure of the presentation. I'll then spend some time allowing each of them to introduce himself to the group, although by now they probably have had a chance to talk a little bit and do maybe an icebreaking exercise.

The next thing I like to do, and depending on the timing, this could be the second to the third day, I do presentations the way I would sell to an end user customer. I'll run through it from start to finish so they get a feel for it. Then I'll go through it again, breaking it down into the components and explaining why I do everything that I do. I will do this multiple times over the course of training, but I like to do it in the beginning so they have a feel for what exactly it is we are selling. I'm not embarrassed to say that more than once I've joined a company and I didn't have a crystal-clear idea of exactly what the product was and what it did.

In some places I've worked there has been a standard course that everybody in the company has to take. In one company I worked for, everybody had to take the technician course for two primary products because, for whatever reason, our CEO thought that everybody should understand how to install and service our primary product. At the time I didn't think it was such a bad idea, and it did teach me a lot about the product and what it looked like behind the walls. That said, I went 12 years without ever installing or servicing a system, so it probably was overkill in terms of the amount of time involved.

I like to go through my philosophy of selling, how I structure the sales process, how I interact with the distributors, how I build my planning, etc., and that can take two solid days easily. My message with that is typically "I will teach you the way I do it. You can do it however you want as long as you bring in results. If you don't bring in results, you have to go back to my way. If you can't bring in results my way, then I will have to let you go." I do want, whether or not they use it, for people to understand what I think is the best way to do things. I'll try to do this somewhat in a workshop format, allowing people to discuss but without letting it get away or roll into chaos.

There's going to be a lot of information passed around here, and I don't want it to become too difficult to absorb. I will rotate people and subjects as much as I can because I believe the information will have a better chance of getting absorbed and internalized. I will bring in people from my company to talk about alternative subjects here, so I may stagger the meat of the sales material with HR or IT or technical stuff.

We will review carefully all the available marketing material and sales enablement material and discuss where we can find it all. It's going to be very important for them to be able to find this going forward.

I will introduce everybody from the contact list face to face and have them talk for a couple of minutes about themselves and what they do, etc. I want to make it very easy for my people to contact them if they need to I don't want them to feel embarrassed or hesitant.

We will go over the accounting and expense reporting software.

We will review the legal obligations for the American Anti-Corruption Act, probably with an external consultant who is authorized to teach this, and we'll make sure that everybody signs off on having received the training.

We will learn how to perform a demo and to troubleshoot the demo equipment.

I will go over what you might call my writing style guide and suggest that people follow it. It's helpful, especially with foreigners, to give them a little bit of guidance for clean internal business documents. We'll review how we write reports. This isn't one of those things where I say, "Do it your own way as long as you're successful, otherwise do it my way." I would rather everybody do it one way because it makes it that much easier and faster to read and process the reports. What I look for is uniform reports that give a reasonable depth of information but don't take too much time from the work the regional managers should be doing. We will train them on our CRM system.

We cover how to work with IT and communications, how to get tech support, what is allowed and isn't allowed, etc. If you have an external consultant or some other type of intelligence asset for your sales team, he can talk about where reports and information are stored, how you'll find it, and how you can ask for additional stuff.

Every organization has a convention for saving and naming files and folders. Don't assume that your new reports will easily guess the structure that your company is using. You want to teach them how they can save a file or folder on the server or on the cloud, how they can retrieve it, and how they should name it so that it can be found easily.

I cover how they will book travel with the company's travel policy, etc., and I talk it through narrative style as well as giving it in written format in the playbook. I want to make sure they understand that it makes sense and it's not punitive and it's not such a difficult system to use. One thing that I tell people is that the best way for them to get fired is to abuse travel policy. It is very easy for an RM to steal a little bit of money here or there. I want to make sure that they understand that it's unacceptable and could get them fired.

Those are the things that cover the company and the system; everything else covers how to sell the product, which is really the most important part. That might be two days or thirty days, depending on how difficult the product is to sell. This is really your only opportunity to establish team culture, because for the vast majority of time from here forward, your RMs will be alone in the field.

I will generally do a variety of different presentations. I will talk about all the different elements of the sales process and what we might present at each point and what the buyer might ask at each point; I'll have a library of answers and how those answers can and should be used. I'll go through case studies where I will talk about an actual deal that was closed to really walk through what happens, what the questions were, what the discussions were, etc. I will try and get the RMs to ride along with domestic RMs so the new hires can see how the RMs work and see them in three to five meetings, and they can get a feel for how the RMs presented what they talk about, any tricks, or anything like that. These ride-alongs become one of the more valuable parts the training, and you probably want to do it about two-thirds of the way through the overall training, not necessarily right at the beginning. if I can do more than one session with different domestic RMs, I'd do one at the very beginning and then three to five days before the end of the training.

To bring the whole training to a close, I will have people do presentations in front of the group. I will quiz them on things, ask questions, ask to hear their stories, etc., and make sure they are comfortable with everything that they need to know and that it flows well. The key is to really understand the product, the customers' workflow, and how to present the product to solve problems that the customer has.

In the coming two months I will spend a few days with each RM in their home market. If my workload allows, I may take them to meet each of the distributors, or at least the most important distributors in their territory. I will also spend a little bit of time watching them present to an end user and possibly to a new potential distributor. Once I feel confident that they know what they're doing, as far as I'm concerned, their onboarding process is over and now they're a full- fledged regional manager.

## Bonus videos:

https://www.youtube.com/watch?v=DxULswF_VGI

https://www.youtube.com/watch?v=H5dkX7-DCIc

https://www.youtube.com/watch?v=CF2UAYoq5mI

https://www.youtube.com/watch?v=WiRRF8xjgTc

https://www.youtube.com/watch?v=3ziBATTis9M

https://www.youtube.com/watch?v=akUJwVudz9s

https://www.youtube.com/watch?v=tJh5VVfMhhU

https://www.youtube.com/watch?v=pJk256P9XMI

https://www.youtube.com/watch?v=FrbcJ3JQylY

https://www.youtube.com/watch?v=o5jY87nYgrU&t=29s

## Bonus articles

https://www.linkedin.com/pulse/hiring-international-regional-sales-manager-part-1-4-zach-selch/

https://www.linkedin.com/pulse/hiring-international-sales-manager-part-two-phone-interview-selch/

https://www.linkedin.com/pulse/hiring-international-regional-sales-manager-part-3-face-zach-selch/

https://www.linkedin.com/pulse/hiring-international-regional-sales-manager-final-part-zach-selch/

# Channel partners: Understanding the value chain

Everybody wants a piece of the deal. Before you are selling, it seems like there is an awful lot of money to go around. You manufacture something for $5 that you believe customers will pay $100 for. You are willing to take $40, which will cover all your expenses and keeps you going profitably and happily. It seems that if you transfer this at $40, your distributor will be happy with his profit and he'll be able to cover all of his expenses. Classic value chain 101.

Then you look at it and you realize there may be additional expenses involved. You have to ship the product You may be paying for finance insurance. You may have to pay for a local warehouse. You may have more than one layer of distributor. You may have legal fees, registration, certification expenses. These things add up.

Most of these things can't be avoided. Unfortunately, many new exporters get involved in a lot of expenses that can and should be avoided and that push up the value chain costs.

Many Americans get very excited about how exotic foreign markets seem, and they get talked into the idea that they can find some well-connected person who can get business for them by bypassing the sales process. While this is sometimes the case, it's nowhere near as prevalent as most Americans believe, and if you are working for a serious American manufacturing company, you don't want to be involved in this whole game, which is often illegal. I've been very successful for 30 years selling all over the world and more than 130 markets without resorting to playing this game. But I can tell you that almost on a weekly basis, somebody will say to me, "I met this guy who is very good friends with the president of an African country, and if we just give him seven points on everything that we sell to Nigeria for the next 10 years, he'll get us lots of business." You really have to deal with those things very carefully. It is very easy to find yourself locked into agreements like this that bring nothing but push up your price 20% or 30% before anything of value actually starts.

While this sounds clearly like something that anybody should avoid, I can't tell you how often I see smart, educated people falling for this. I know a woman with a great education, who has been successful in another field, who every week would call me up and say, "I met a guy who speaks all the languages in Africa and he knows everybody in Africa and he's driving an Uber. We should give him 10 points" or "A friend of mine from college can introduce us to the president of Egypt. All he wants is five points on all future sales in Egypt." It's a waste of time, but more importantly, it's a huge waste of money on the value chain. When you are starting out, you feel like there is a huge amount of money to play with on the value chain, but that disappears quickly.

Likewise, if you hire a distributor who cannot fulfill the functions that you have specified on your partner profile, somebody will have to pay for those functions later, and you don't want to leave that to the last minute and you don't want to be paying for it out of your points. Again, this is very common. You also want to remember that if you aren't clear with what you expect from your partners and you don't put it in the distribution agreement, you will probably end up paying later to make up for their weaknesses.

Keep in mind one more thing. The most expensive part of the sales process will be the least technical—building and maintaining relationships, managing the sales process, presenting. Those elements will be very expensive to fix later if your partner isn't good at them. Installation, technical service, even regulatory affairs are things that can be bought much more cheaply than sales skills.

## Bonus video:

https://www.youtube.com/watch?v=Xhs9YkunFOc

## Finding partners

Let's say that we reached out and found a bunch of potential partners in the country that we want to go into. I'm starting this way because one of the biggest mistakes we can make is to get pulled into meeting distributors who we don't necessarily want to meet, who might not fit our profile, and even more importantly, who might be in the countries that might not be countries we want to work in. But let's say here we are in a chosen country and we've found three to five distributors that fit our profile. I bet a lot of people reading this are rolling their eyes because they are thinking, "You know, I have trouble finding one distributor in any country." While this may sound like optimism, I've never had a problem identifying three to five distributors in the countries I have wanted to work in, even when I was working with a brand-new product that never sold outside of its own market.

Typically, the way I would start finding partners is bunching countries up together geographically. For instance, over two weeks I might interview in Argentina, Chile, Peru, Columbia, Ecuador, and Brazil, and that fits pretty nicely. Or it could be five countries that sit close to each other in Africa or Europe, but the basic idea is I'd rather not, especially at the ramping up stage, fly out to Chile to interview distributors for one country. Again, I'm talking about a perfect world and from the perspective of somebody with 30 years' experience, so you might think that's totally impossible to set up, but that's what you're aiming for.

I will try to see my three distributors on the first day in any given country. I will get a car from the hotel, setting up my first meeting 9:00, my second at 11:00 or noon, and my third, say, at 3:00. I'll try find somebody local to help me with geography, even to the extent of reaching out to the concierge at the hotel to ask, "I have these three meetings to do in one day. What makes sense in terms of order?" I'll also use as a resource the commercial attaché at the embassy. They're pretty helpful with things like this, especially when it's a targeted question.

I will also often get a conference room at my hotel in case I need to do some of the meetings there, although my preference is always to see the offices. In some of the megacities of Asia or a city like Mexico City or São Paulo, that might be almost impossible, although I once visited four distributors in São Paulo in one day. This is one of those opportunities where you might want to take an interpreter with you, although probably nine out of ten distributors I've worked with around the world over the course of my career have had very good English. The advantage of an interpreter is that there may be other people in the room who are talking in the local language and it might be helpful for you to understand what they're saying. Visiting a distributor is a little bit of a detective story; you're trying to pull out all the possible information and details you can when possibly they're trying to hide some of it.

I'll make sure that I have a stack of business cards with me. I will have a tape recorder, not so much for the meetings, but to get my notes very clear as soon as I leave the meeting. I use a fresh notebook or notepad on trips like this because these are the meetings where I will take my very best and most detailed notes. When you're interviewing 20 or more distributors over the course of two weeks, this can be a little exhausting and possibly a little confusing.

When I meet with the distributors, I introduce myself and figure out who they all are and make sure that I get their cards and their information. In today's world it's not considered rude or even unusual to take pictures of people with your phone.

# The Distributor Pitch

Let's think back to what we said the distributors are looking for, what's important to them. What they want to do is make as much money as possible as easily as possible. There are some exceptions to this. What would those exceptions be? There are distributors that I like to refer to as headhunters who believe that by gathering the most representations possible they will make their distributorship seem more important and more attractive. These people will try to take on your line even if they have no intention of putting any effort into selling it. This is something that should be avoided at all costs. There are distributors that think very strategically and understand that they can perhaps leverage your product to sell more of a more profitable product. I'm not opposed to this most of the time because they still have to sell your product for this to work, and then there are distributors that are just getting started or that are on the downward slope towards falling apart and they're desperate to get just about any line they can.

But let's assume that we've identified a good, solid distributor that fits our profile and we would like him to work with us. We will pitch to them. What they're interested in is making money with the least amount of effort. What scares them is that they will put effort into our product and then we will either terminate them and go direct, will add additional distributors in the market, or will simply decide we want to pull out of this market. All of these can cause considerable loss to the distributor. They will lose any efforts they have put in; it will make them look bad to their customers and to their competition, and they might find themselves facing legal consequences if they have committed to customers and then they can't deliver. So for your distributor, your cheating them in one of these three ways is really a disaster, one way or another.

Taking that into consideration, you want to make your pitch about showing why your product is profitable, how easy it is to sell your product, and how much you can be trusted. Everything else is superfluous and a waste of time.

What shows them that the product is profitable? That there is a need that you've identified. That the need exists in their market. That a similar country with similar needs has proven to be a profitable market. That you have advantages over any competitors that sell into this market. That your price point is reasonable for this market. That you will be delivering a product to them with enough of a markdown or discount off the end user price that they can make a solid margin.

What type of margin are they looking for? Probably an initial gross margin of 30% to 60%. We'll discuss this a little later on, because you will be able to get a feel for how much profit they need from an estimate of their overhead.

What about investment of time? There are distributors that really thrive on missionary selling and want something that is totally unique in the market. They will usually tell you that or advertise that, or you will see that their entire line is made up of unusual high-tech new products. That, however, is pretty unusual. Most distributors are looking to pick up a line that is a solid competitor of lines that their competitors carry. I'm reminded of the discussions in the TV show *Mad Men*, where the agency was talking about wanting to carry a cigarette and a car and an airline and a department store, etc. That often is the way distributorship work works, where they would like to have one manufacturer of each type of product that the customer they serve buys. As an aside and a warning, some distributors would actually like to carry multiple similar products that compete with one another to offer the market. Those are the distributors you really have to avoid, because what you don't want is for your distributor to offer your product in a way that they're not going to sell, either as a loss leader or as a higher-priced alternative. Then when the customer tries to negotiate, they pull out a cheaper product and sell that. I've seen distributors do this quite a bit in all the different permutations.

The distributor is going to be looking for something that is attractive enough that they can simply go to their existing customers and say, "Now I'm carrying this product" and the customers will buy it. That would be the perfect world for the distributor.

There are also considerations about how complex the sale is, and how risky it is. By that I mean, Is the end user taking a risk buying this product? Is it mission-critical? Could the customer suffer serious consequences if they bought your product and it failed? A customer is going to buy a less mission-critical product more quickly and with less deliberation than the more mission-critical product, and your distributors will be considering this. If the end user price is very high, while this could be very nice money and profit for the distributor, it usually indicates a longer and more complex sales cycle. Then the distributor has to consider if they would rather be spending the effort on this type of product or on a product that moves faster with less profit per unit. Will there be a wide range of potential customers in the market or will it be very difficult to find the customers? Think back to the sales process that we mapped out—and the parts that we intend to outsource to the distributor. Think about how difficult each one of those will be for the distributor, and that will give you an indication of their perspective.

Along with this, remember that there are elements of the sales process that you intend to do yourself. The more elements of the sales process you intend to be responsible for as a principal, the more resources you have to support the partner as a principal in the sales process, and the better and more professional those resources are, the more attractive you'll be to the distributor.

To calm their fears, you have to be able to show them a track record—either of the company or of the head of international sales or the regional manager—or find somebody on the board or somebody related to the company who can show that they've been doing business internationally but have a record of not screwing over distributors. You also want to show why you have a business plan that indicates that you won't screw over distributors. What do I mean by that? Can you make it clear that you have absolutely no intention in the future of going direct and/or that your business plan clearly indicates that you intend to work with the dispersed single distributor per territory and not break it into pieces? You also want to show why it's clear you're never going to pull out of this market or decide to refocus on the US domestic market or your home market.

The structure of your pitch isn't "We have the best widget in the world. We make our widgets out of 20-gauge steel. Our founder went to MIT and we have a wonderful border collie in the office." Those type of pitches make absolutely no sense and are completely unhelpful to your target audience.

Your pitch should read, "There is a problem that exists in your market and it exists for X million people. This problem causes these people extreme pain to a value of Y million dollars. In a similar market, we were able to sell Z million dollars' worth of product every year to very happy customers because we were able to solve their problem. Most of our customers fall under a very clear demographic, and we have a lot of experience identifying and finding them. Most of our customers make purchasing decisions quickly and simply, as we have seen in multiple markets. As you can see from this presentation to our shareholders, the international market is extremely important for our growth. We have hired an experienced head of international sales who has 20 years' experience not screwing over distributors. Feel free to look him up on LinkedIn and reach out to some of his connections to verify that he does not have a history of screwing over distributors."

Obviously, the above is an exaggerated perfect-world pitch, but you want your pitch to include those three parts: profitability, ease of sale, and why you can trust us. Pretty much everything else, don't worry about.

Your pitch ideally should probably be 7 to 20 minutes and should be delivered in crystal-clear, simple English. If you're not used to presenting to people whose first language isn't English, you might want to practice with the specific intention of (1) taking out words that wouldn't be understandable to, say, a third grader, (2) trying to tone down any regional accent that you have, and (3) slowing your speaking down to about 60% of your normal speaking speed.

Having delivered the pitch, I usually say, "So does this still sound like something you're interested in?" And then I'll start asking them questions.

I have some standard questions for pretty much every distributor anywhere in the world. These are very similar to what I'd ask a salesman that I'm interviewing for a job. By this point, I will have already done some research on their website and I would have asked him questions remotely through email, so I might already have answers to these questions. I'm asking them again because I'd like to hear how they answer them. I'm going to get a feel for how important different lines are to them, and I'll probably also get a feel for what they're really selling and where they're really making their money. For instance, Siemens, Philips, and some of the other large multinationals from Europe, the United States, Korea, and Japan often will have different distributors for each of their many product lines. Thirty years ago, during a short period when I was a distributor, I snagged a very, very small line from a very, very large German manufacturer. I think it was a line that they really didn't care about. But then I was able to say to people, "I represent such and such company" and that made it easier for them to give me their lines. I leveraged that line to build my portfolio, but I really didn't sell very much of it. My point is that somebody might tell you that they carry a line from a very prestigious manufacturer, and it might be a very minor line.

So when somebody puts on their website that they are a Siemens distributor, I'd like to know what part of that line they sell, how much of it they sell, and maybe how much of their overall turnover that line represents. What they sell and how they talk about what they sell is probably the most important part of the interview.

I will ask them about how many salespeople they have and how they use those salespeople. Let's think back to when we talked about what we expect from a distributor and how we are dividing up labor. Your product may be more of a marketing-type product than a sales-type product, and by that I mean maybe what you really need are good copywriters, advertisers, and people who walk around and hand out brochures or people who know how to get a retail product or fast-moving consumer goods product put on the shelf someplace. So the question is, Does this distributor have people like that? Maybe what you need are account managers, people who are out visiting specific customers on a regular basis and selling face to face. If that's what you need, does this partner have it? Maybe you need sales development representatives who will be on the phone all the time. Does this distributor have those people?

With that, what's the ratio of other people to the people you need? I once inherited a very large distributor with a fantastic reputation that had literally hundreds of administrative people and hundreds of marketing people. The ratio of salespeople to other people was probably 1 to 10. They had dozens of luxury offices. I went to one of their offices in one of the best buildings in Singapore with a gorgeous view of the Singapore eye and a full-time barista and espresso bar in the lobby of their office. From my perspective, all of that is pretty much worthless overhead. And what that meant was this distributor needed the very high margin for doing very little work. For some types of products this might have worked out well, but it was a disaster for this product. They put their money on fancy Italian coffee and not salespeople.

How do they handle different parts of the sales process? How do they divide up their lines for their territories? These are very important questions. Who will actually be selling your product? Again, I'm sure some people reading this will roll their eyes and say, "First of all, this is none of your business, and second, they're probably not going to want to tell you this." But this is definitely my business. This is what's going to help me grow my sales, and I've never had a distributor not open up and talk to me about this if I get a good solid pitch. But most importantly, I can't work with a distributor who isn't going to be a good fit. They have to have the resources that I need, and on top of that I need them to flow the information to me that I need. So if the distributor is arguing about answering questions now when he should be interested in impressing me, why would I think he's going to give me information a year from now when I ask for it?

Then there will be a lot of administrative, logistical, and financial questions. And I don't want to make these seem unimportant, but to some extent they are unimportant. Obviously, I can't work with somebody who is financially unstable, who has a history of being considered dishonest, who maybe has no logistical support if that's necessary for this particular type of sale. But there's no way I can work with him if he can't sell my product, so all I'm really interested in is one question: Can you sell my product?

A very effective way of interviewing for the non-sales part is to bring a non-salesperson with me who does the second part of the audit—the administrative, logistical, and financial questions. I've never done it this way, but theoretically you could even switch the order of the meetings and have the other guy meet with them separately to save time. There's a lot of value to having a non-salesperson look at it, because we really don't want to do anything risky and I might find somebody with a fantastic fit from a sales perspective but his books make him look like a thief, and as much as I might want to work with him for his sales ability, I can't afford to take that risk. This is exactly why we need due diligence.

I've used this two-tier process through the recruitment of over 100 distributors, and I've never had somebody tell me that the person I chose didn't pass the administrative audit. Very possibly, just the fact that I know that somebody was going to be double-checking me, looking for poor judgment on due diligence, kept me on the straight and narrow.

Then I will talk about what I expect from the distributor and see if this meets their expectations. I'll talk about how I've divided up the sales process between what I want to do and what I expect them to do and talk about the fact that we will support them in certain aspects. I might show them examples of our marketing material—our distributor playbook, our training materials, that kind of thing—if I believe it's impressive and it makes us look important and serious, but if I think it makes us look amateur, I'm not going to show it to them. I'm open to a little negotiation on this, but what I prefer is it that negotiation is more about them pushing for more training or more resources rather than the other way around. If they are apprehensive about us requiring specific sales training or about us quantifying the activities that we expect, this is going to raise a red flag.

I'll talk about the marketing efforts they do today, the sales efforts, what their various personnel are involved in across the market. I'll give you an example. A lot of the distributors I've worked with have very good service departments that provide support our end users. This basically means that the distributor has a distributor employee going into the end user facility every week or every two weeks for something, and that's an excellent tool that can be utilized as part of the sales process.

This is pretty much everything that's going to happen during the interview. Then we will go on to the next one and do it over and then possibly over again. Over the course of the day I will probably have generated anywhere from three to ten pages of notes and will have gathered catalogs and other printed material about their company. I'll put all that in a folder.

At the end of this trip I will have gathered conceivably thousands of pages of material. I probably won't have access to a scanner on the road, so I'm simply going to have to carry this with me, which is never something I like to do. What I will try to do in the car between meetings if I have time, or as soon as I can in my hotel in the evening, is to review the documentation and my notes and dictate either into an audio file, which I'll then send for transcription, or into transcription software, a summary of my notes. My handwriting isn't very good, and people won't understand my notes if they're hand-written. I don't want to sit for a couple of hours and type out my notes in a narrative paragraph format, but if I read them I can essentially interpret them into a narrative format, which I can then use both to help me in the future and to send to other people and make part of the permanent record of the company. At the end of the day, that distributor will have a folder that includes all of the documents they gave me, my notes, a printed version of the transcribed narrative notes, and any additional information that comes from either my colleague who did the second part of the audit or from third parties and references. It's very similar to the folder that I'll keep when I'm interviewing RMs or salespeople.

With any luck there will be a clear frontrunner by the evening. I've saved my second day to make a second visit for follow-up questions or to ask them to take me to a few end users to get some impressions. This gives me a bit more flexibility if I find that I can't trim down the list.

It is really helpful to go with the distributor to an end user before you sign them. It will give you a good feel for how they interact with the market and what the market's expectations and reputation for that distributor are.

Eventually, whether still in the field or later on, I will matrix out these distributors. What do I mean by that? The three primary things here are competencies, focus, and bandwidth. I will make a matrix with one axis competency, one axis focus, and the size of the marker indicating the distributor will be bandwidth. So I may have a distributor with low focus and high competency or vice versa, and I may have a distributor who has high focus and high competency but their bandwidth is very small. I will be able to look at that very easily on the graph and make a decision based on those considerations. Possibly never in recruiting a thousand distributors have I ended up with a matrix where the three distributors were relatively equal.

Again, every product, every market is going to be different in terms of what you value more, but you have to consider what you decided when you wrote your distributor profile and then compare these distributors to that ideal profile.

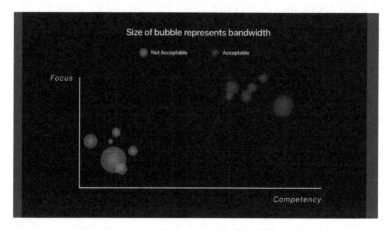

# Bonus videos:

https://www.youtube.com/watch?v=kxfdZT9_qgk

https://www.youtube.com/watch?v=VyYdGRyR1RM&t=4s

https://www.youtube.com/watch?v=br2bfv3dZXU&t=67s

https://www.youtube.com/watch?v=ajXNaQvq2-o&t=14s

https://www.youtube.com/watch?v=AsrNeLPa2w8

# Distributor agreements

You will need a distribution contract if you want to work with agents or distributors. We're going to start off structuring the distribution contract, building it from the definition of what we want our partners to be doing—what part of the sales process we want from the partners. Every company I have worked with has typically had a horrible distributor contract in the beginning.

I use a distributor agreement that I don't like very much. Over the years I've discovered that I don't really have much choice. There are things that you really do need in distributor agreements. I'm not a lawyer so I'm not going to tell you what those are, but you should find a lawyer to discuss this and get a good agreement that covers your rights. It is very important that this agreement is obviously in good faith and relatively equal. Distributors are dealing with multiple principals and the life of the distributor means that most times they're simply forced to take the manufacturers' distributor agreement, so they see a lot of them and they're very careful about protecting their rights. They can compare your distributor agreement to other distributor agreements. If you put together an agreement that is clearly in poor faith, they will understand very quickly that you're not a manufacturer that they really want to work with or can trust.

That said, here's the way I would structure an agreement. In the first paragraph you have something that identifies you as a manufacturer, and the other guy is a distributor. And then nobody's name gets mentioned until the end of the agreement where you sign it. Why? Because when you have an agreement, we have to put in each other's names 10 or 12 to 20 times over the course of the agreement; it just comes to a lot of work and you don't want to waste time on this.

Typically, I don't put anything I really care about in the body of the agreement. I know that sounds crazy, but from my perspective the agreement is to keep my lawyer happy. I'll tell you something else: Again, let me be very clear this is not legal advice, but over 30 years of selling in over 100 countries, with about 750 to 1,000 distributors I've worked with, I've never seen a manufacturer actually sue an international distributor. The only time I've ever seen a disagreement become a legal issue was at one company I worked for close to 30 years ago, when the regional manager from the company actually stole about half a million dollars' worth of materials and sold them to the distributor at a cut cost and then disappeared. But that is such an incredible outlier of an event that it's just a good story more than something to be scared of. So let me put it this way: If we spend six months negotiating a contract that could be spent selling and we want the distributor to sell $2 million a year, having a tough contract just cost you a million bucks. You have to decide if it's worth it.

I put the stuff I care about in annexes to the agreement. The first annex is territory and I'll very specifically cover what the customer's territory is, and one thing you will always want to do is to use the correct name of the country. For instance, Bangladesh is the People's Republic of Bangladesh, England is the United Kingdom. There may be legal reasons that this is important, but I do it mainly because I want to look neat and correct.

I will specify what the product is and, depending on how you operate, you might want to put the product price list in with how long your prices are usually valid and document what your rights are to change the price. When you change the price and how you change the price should be clear in the agreement.

Now here's the important stuff I will clarify right in the agreement: I will say in an annex that it is our intention to work with a single distributor in this territory. For us to continue working with a single distributor in this territory, it is our expectation that our distributor will put in place X number of salespeople with Y qualifications that are representing no more than Z product lines. The intent here is to clarify exactly what sales assets are put in place and how much of their work we will expect to get. If a salesman represents 12 lines, then I'm essentially only getting three hours of his work every week. Is this enough? For most products I don't consider that enough, but there are cases where it might be.

How do I get to this math? Let's say I need the distributor to be selling to hospitals and my target is private-sector hospitals of more than 50 beds. In this territory I know that there are 200 hospitals like that, which means that to get to every hospital once a year, my distributor has to be visiting four or five a week. I probably want them to be visiting more than once a year. That's eight times a week if they are visiting each customer twice a year. Hopefully, I have a feel for the geographical layout of the country, and I can say it's reasonable for them to visit two a day, but that's still essentially a full-time job for one salesperson. That means I want them to either give me one salesperson full-time or four salespeople at quarter time. And I want to document that in the agreement.

I will document what type of training that salesperson is going to have, and I may document what type of experience and what career level that salesperson is going to be. If they take a new person right out of school, that's going to be totally different than if they put somebody with 10 years' experience on my product. Let's say that I have a curriculum of training for salespeople. I will expect them to have the dedicated salespeople fulfill this curriculum and I will expect that they will participate in ongoing training. I might have two training sessions a year, for instance. Now to be perfectly reasonable, every hour that I'm training these people they're not out selling and there may be expenses involved with travel and so on, so I don't want this to be unreasonable and it's going to be related to how attractive my product is. If I don't have a very attractive pitch to begin with, I can ask for whatever I want and they're not going to give me anything. So everything that I want is tied up with my being able to give an attractive pitch to make sure this distributor wants to work with me.

Aside from the sales assets, I may need marketing assets. In some cases the marketing asset may be even more important to my particular sales process and product, so I will document that in the agreement as well.

I will document all the specific efforts involved. I may say it's our expectation that the distributor will carry out 400 customer visits over the course of the year. I might say it's our expectation that the distributor will participate in specific trade shows or conferences. I might say that the distributor will sponsor workshops. All of this is tied to my sales process but I can't assume it's going to be done if I don't document this in my agreement.

You may notice that something is missing here: sales numbers. This is very controversial, but I don't like to put sales numbers in the contract for the first year of the agreement if I know that my sales cycle is 18 to 24 months. I don't want to ask for specific dollar amounts during that time. What I want to ask for is activity; if I'm getting the right activity, the sales will come.

Now let's flip this around. I could say in year one the distributor is going to put in an order for $250,000. Let's say for the next 12 months the distributor does absolutely nothing. What's my remedy? I have no remedy. He could be saying that in another 12 months he will put in an order for $250,000 by the last day of our agreement and he will have met the demands and the requirements of our agreement and he is a partner in good standing. If then the last day he says to me, "We didn't sell anything. I can't put in the order," at that point what's my remedy? I can terminate him. I just wasted a year in that territory and there's nothing I can do about it.

I cannot tell you how many times I have seen this happen. Most people who write agreements like this will tell me that they're much tougher than I am and more business savvy and they're going to get the sales they want. Then at the end of the year they end up with empty pockets because they didn't think through what they were doing.

Somebody I know gave an incredibly lucrative market to a distributor with an agreement that included no activities, but a multi-million dollar order in the first year. My acquaintance was extremely proud of the agreement he had negotiated. The order never came, the distributor made no efforts, but literally for 12 months this guy kept telling me how smart he was—that he was getting millions from this territory. He told his investors that he was getting millions from this territory and in the end he got nothing. I said to him in the middle of the year, "You are not seeing your distributors making any effort and you will be sorry about this later on in the year." He said, "I have an agreement. He has to give me that money." I asked, "Does the agreement say that you can sue him and that you will get your money? No, the agreement says you can terminate him. Your distributor effectively kept you out of this lucrative market for the cost of a little ink that he signed on your agreement." He would have been much better off with no minimum order but a clear action plan in the agreement.

In this case, I don't believe that there was ill will on the part of the distributor or that he was trying to cheat anybody. I think he saw this as an option and then he decided it wasn't the product he really wanted to sell but there was no reason for him to terminate the agreement in the middle of the year. But I've also seen companies do this, where they represent a competitor and they take exclusive representation of your product with the agreement that they will put in a large order, and they've effectively kept you out of the market so that your competitor has free rein of the market for a year and you get nothing out of it. There's absolutely nothing you can do because you didn't think through your agreement from the beginning.

The way I structure this is if after 30 days or 90 days, the distributor hasn't put in place the agreed-upon sales organization and sales activities, you can basically say, "I'm giving you a warning. It's obvious to me you haven't done what you agreed to do. Do you still want to represent me, or do we part company as friends and I put in place a different distributor?" I have never seen a situation where the distributor then says, "You're right, Zach, let's part company." When we have a contract like this, typically the partner modifies their activities and meets their obligations. They see that I'm serious and they do exactly what they're supposed to do going forward.

I will put in place what the expectations are for communication, as well. The most important part of this is how I want them to report to me what their activities are and what the situation is in the market. So, for instance, I will specify that they should work with our CRM and get trained on it and that their salespeople will input data directly into our CRM. If I'm not quite that sophisticated, I will ask for an Excel sheet on a monthly basis that shows me all of their activity as well as the funnel of their prospects and their customers. But if this isn't in the agreement, my chances of getting this information without constant nagging and arguing are pretty slim.

We will put into the agreement things like how payment takes place, how shipping takes place, etc. Most of the time, what I will say is for the first number of orders or first number of months, and then things can change in the future. In the beginning they will pay cash in advance or an irrevocable letter of credit from a reputable bank. I want to clarify what is an acceptable letter of credit. Let's say I'm dealing with certain developing countries. They can easily give me a letter of credit that's worthless. I don't necessarily want a letter of credit from the Third National Bank of Sudan. So I might say it's my expectation that all letters of credit will be written by a bank that is acceptable to my bank. I'll either name my bank or I will specify letters of credit that will be acceptable to a well-regarded, large bank but I'll name it—say the Bank of America or Citibank.

The mistake that most people make is to worry about things that they should not be worried about. Here's the deal. You're not going to take your distributor to court pretty much anywhere in the world. Again, working with between 750 and 1,000 distributors over the years, I've never seen a situation where somebody says, "They didn't fulfill their side of the contract. I will send the lawyer down to Brazil to sue them." What we do is we terminate them, or they walk away from it. We want to have a very clear clause in the contract that explains how we terminate them and how they can get out of it and what the stages are for us to divorce or to separate. That's really what's important. The idea that we should spend a thousand words talking about how they use our marketing material because we may sue him in court is simply unrealistic and wasteful.

On the other hand, I want to make sure that they know what's expected of them and that if they don't do what's expected of them, I will terminate them. That to me is what's important in this agreement.

What you want to define in the agreement is what are the expected activities of the partner. Something that I find mind-boggling is that you can take a 50-page agreement written by a company for its distributors, and there won't be a single sentence about actual sales activity. You should instruct your lawyer to make sure you are covered as well as possible in terms of basic legal protection without adding anything superfluous to the agreement. What do I mean by superfluous? Well, are there insurance requirements for selling your product in a specific market in terms of liability? There may be, depending on the product. You might really need this from your distributor, but most of the time you don't. A lawyer from the target market or possibly somebody from the commercial attaché can tell you. But if you put into your agreement that your distributor needs $1 million of insurance in order to sell your product, they may very well lie to you or just suggest that you take that part out. Like any other type of negotiation, putting things in that you know will be taken out is a waste of time.

It is perfectly acceptable to say the distributor will have two people who sell our product who have undergone a specific training and who do not sell more than two additional product lines and so are devoting a minimum of 15 hours a week to our product line 50 weeks a year. That might seem very detailed but that's the type of thing that I put in all my distribution agreements. Otherwise you have no idea what type of activities they're actually going to do to sell your product.

I will also have things like specific trade shows, marketing materials, translation required, training, and even personnel that needs to be hired in a distributor agreement. I want to cover all the various sales activities so they don't surprise anybody.

Aside from the sales activities, I want to put in the communications and reporting activities that are expected as well. What do I mean by that?

Let's say my expectations are that we will have a biweekly telephone call to discuss status. Now you might find that too much—maybe you want a monthly call—but putting that type of communications in the contract means I won't be arguing about it later. I ask my distributors to use my CRM and my reporting software. I ask them for specific types of report on their sales goals.

We will put a lot of effort into onboarding the distributors. We want to make sure they understand that they have an obligation to fulfill their side of the onboarding process.

What else can I put in the agreement? I also want to clarify what their territory is and where they're not allowed to sell. I don't want my distributors selling outside their territory.

I may specify their responsibilities in terms of our relationship as a company with their local government. What do I mean by that? There may be registration processes, there may be various bureaucratic organizations operating in their country, and who is supposed to pay for those should be documented in the contract. For instance, the cost to legalize documents, which is a requirement to do business in some countries, can be in the tens of thousands of dollars. I want to make sure that the agreement specifies who is responsible to pay those costs.

I've had people argue with me about this and say that this it is unreasonable to request it from distributors. But I've never recruited a new distributor who argued with this. Typically, the only pushback I get from distributors is when they have been working with my company for a long time with poorly defined processes in place and then argue when changes are made involving more rigorous process.

We will put a time limit on the agreement, which can be one year or two years or until the end of the current fiscal year plus an additional year. The last is my preference. I like to renew all agreements at the same time of the year; it's a lot easier to keep track of. A good mechanism is to have contracts automatically renew if the parties don't cancel the contract sometime in advance—30, 60, or 90 days. So, for instance, a contract might run from September 1st 2019 until December 31st 2021 and will be automatically renewed if neither party decided to break the agreement before November 1st 2020 and triggered the mechanism, usually sending the other party a registered letter.

It is extremely important to have a mechanism in the contract to cancel the contract and a mechanism for notifying the local government that the contract is no longer valid. While I haven't done it myself, I know people who request a resignation letter in advance when they sign an agreement with the distributor. It can be very difficult to get the local government to recognize a unilateral termination of the distributor, so if the company wants to terminate the distributor later, they want to be sure they have the tool in hand to facilitate this termination.

There should also be a mechanism in place to increase the requirements in future years. So if you are asking for two salespeople in the first year, it is reasonable to ask for a third salesperson in the third year or to simply say that at a specific point in the future—say a year and a half or two years from the signing of the agreement—the requirement will be revisited and additional sales and marketing resources may be required from the distributor.

Though the distributor will most likely want pricing structure to be documented in the agreement, that does not have to be specific numbers. It could also come in the form of "distributor will be offered the best price list offered" or "distributor will be offered product according to price lists published on September 1st every year."

I have not always had freedom in preparing the distribution agreement. Recently, I was in the middle of a discussion where company CFO basically said, "I don't really care go talk to the lawyer" and the lawyer said, "I don't really care about this contract but I need to get instructions from the CFO and I can't change it without those instructions," so I went back and forth a half-dozen times. We were using a contract that had been written by somebody who had been in the company for 10 years and really knew nothing about international business or sales. It was 30-some pages long and none of it had anything to do with anything relevant.

Some distributors I work with are so well positioned that they have their own agreements, and there's nothing I can do about that. I will add my annexes to their agreements, and I will make sure that my lawyer is okay with that and I'll sign it. But I try to do that as little as possible.

## Bonus videos:

https://www.youtube.com/watch?v=nV9eVP7lk6Q

https://www.youtube.com/watch?v=k9mC3dPvr8g

# LOI

Another little trick I use is a letter of intent. I have a one-page letter of intent that basically says:

1. It is our intention to work with you as our distributor in the territory, and we are not negotiating with any other potential distributors for the next 31 days.

2. The nature of our relationship is that we will manufacture the product and you will sell the product in the assigned territory.

3. It is our intention to sign our agreement within 30 days of this letter of intent. This LOI will serve as our agreement in this territory between our companies for the next 30 days. If we cannot reach an agreement by then, I will find another partner.

4. During this time, it is our expectation that the distributor will undertake activities A, B, and C and the manufacturer will undertake activities X, Y, and Z.

Let's say I've just spent two days in Thailand. I've interviewed three distributors and on the first night I matrixed out the information I got from the distributors. The second day I had another meeting with my preferred distributor and it's clear to me that I want to work with that distributor. I will send him an LOI right away.

I have on my phone a blank LOI where I can fill in the name of the country and the name of the distributor, and I have a link to a Dropbox with the relevant early-stage marketing material and sales enablement material. Literally from the back of a moving taxi, I can send the distributor this LOI on my way out of the country. Then I fill in the details into the agreement: the name of the distributor, the territory, and what assets I expect them to put in place, and I send it to them. They'll take it to their lawyer and now we'll spend a period of time going back and forth with changes. The stronger my pitch, the less likely I am to make changes to the agreement; the weaker my pitch, the weaker my negotiating position.

By using the letter of intent, it is possible to get distributors to jump immediately into the work and not waste time. I have found it to be an exceptionally helpful tool also to help move getting the agreement signed because the distributors feel that they have a time constraint.

# Bonus video:

https://www.youtube.com/watch?v=h4dTvPnsgko

# Bonus article:

https://www.linkedin.com/pulse/how-can-we-shorten-time-between-offering-channel-partner-zach-selch/

# Distributors

Let's talk about the different types of distributors and how I'm finding them.

What were the things we said were the important parameters? Bandwidth, competency, and focus. These are like a triangle. If one of them is completely missing, the triangle is going to collapse. On the other hand, you may have a situation where you have great bandwidth or great competency or great focus and the other factors aren't very good; then you have to decide if you can live with what they have.

Let's say that I have 10,000 potential customers in my market, and this distributor visits all of them monthly to sell them something from their product list. In that case my need is to have a huge bandwidth and maybe not so much focus, as long as I know that once or twice a year the distributor will be talking about my product. Alternatively, let's say that what's really important is that the distributor have an excellent relationship with a specific individual in that country, say the minister of communication, so I will consider that a competency that is key to my sales process and I will be willing to be very forgiving about other things. I know distributors in countries the size of Nigeria and India who have only one or two sales assets in the whole company but those sales assets have excellent relationships with very specific buyers. In that case I'd rather work with a very, very small company even though the market seems to be huge because they have that very specific competency that I need. I know companies that have a thousand salespeople, but they tend to hire people right out of school and don't pay very well and don't train very well, so they have huge bandwidth but they might not be able to sell my product. So I need to find that correct balance between the three points.

The biggest trap that I see people fall into is the issue of size. People get obsessed with bandwidth. They say, "This distributor has 1,000 salespeople and that distributor has 300 salespeople and the other distributor I talked to only had 6 salespeople. Obviously, I will go with the distributor that is bigger." I would say nine out of ten times, that's the wrong way to go. When is the 10th time correct? When you have a really good relationship with the owner or CEO and you are confident that person is going to make sure that the company sells your product and puts focus into it. I had a distributor once in Dubai that was the biggest distributor of medical devices in the Emirates, and we represented about 0.1% of their revenue, but I had an excellent relationship with the CEO. I would have dinner with him four or five times a year, and I knew that I could trust him to keep the level of focus with their salespeople even though his company dealt with a thousand other lines. I've had that type of situation a couple of times in my career, but that's rare, and if you are going into a situation where you do not have a relationship with the distributor you can't bank on it. You might've had one good discussion with the owner and you might be optimistic that he likes you and that he's going to put focus into your product line, but this is one of those things that people end up crying about a year later.

Who is the very best distributor you can get? Picture a guy who is a sales manager for a manufacturer. He comes from a middle-class or maybe even a blue-collar background, he has a college degree in commerce or business or engineering, and he worked really hard to be a top sales rep for the manufacturer. At age 40 he quits, he puts a mortgage on his house, he pulls out his retirement money, and he opens up a distribution company. For the next three years he and his wife are living a very spartan lifestyle to get the company going. In the fourth year, things start going well for him, and by year 10 he gets a Porsche and a Land Rover. This is the guy you want because he's hungry, he's self-made, and he's probably going to do a good job for you if you do a good pitch.

As soon as I have an LOI in place, I will start feeding sales enablement and marketing tools to my distributor because I want them to start working and to see that I take this seriously and I know what I'm doing. I'm helping him out again, going back to the three issues: profitability, easy to sell, and trust. Typically, one of those sales enablement tools includes a deck, whatever types of white papers or scientific documents or reference material that he's going to need to sell in his market, and possibly videos. I will have a packet of that in Dropbox so I can send it to him right away. I don't want to waste a day.

When I start a project of expanding, I put together an onboarding plan for distributors before I have interviewed the first one. What does this include? Training for their salespeople, regulatory issues, and anything that may be specific to my product, for instance, technical training, service training, etc. Ideally in the taxi to the airport as I'm leaving, I can trigger this—I can send out an email that essentially says to my regulatory manager, "This is our new distributor. Please start working with him on the regulatory issues"; to my finance manager, "This is our new distributor; start working with them"; and ditto to the shipping manager and the payments manager and the training manager.

I'll cover sales enablement tools and training materials in chapter 7. What I want from my onboarding plan is essentially a schedule that says if I meet with the distributor and send him an LOI on day one, at what point is he fully in position to start presenting the product and at what point is he in position to accept delivery and install a product for a customer? Obviously, I want this to be the shortest amount of time possible. Any time that is wasted here can be detrimental to my international expansion plan.

The chairman of a company I once worked for, who had no experience selling or working internationally, dictated at one point that I work with a distributor that I did not choose, due to some personal relationship. This was a very serious organization. They were very large and had a lot of systems in place, but they just were not the right partner for us. My chairman also decided that we would let them follow their own system for onboarding instead of us driving the process.

They had a very clear process. First they did regulatory approvals, which often could take six months to a year. They had an excellent regulatory approvals department that would check every detail carefully. Once regulatory approvals were finished, they started to create marketing and sales enablement materials. They had excellent copywriters, the very best creative artistic talent—they created beautiful tools.

Then, once they had those materials, they started putting together training. They had a training department that was full of pedagogical experts and high-tech screens and projectors that would make a Bond villain jealous. After they had done training, they did a product launch. Nobody did any selling until after the product launch.

I understand and appreciate why they did this this way. If you take it backwards, how can you sell without training? Why carry out the training if you don't have all the tools ready? If you need to put the regulatory approvals on the marketing materials, you can't start making the marketing materials until you have the regulatory approvals. So, from that systemic approach, it makes perfect sense. From our perspective, this was fatal; we were in startup mode and we wanted to grow. Even more important, we had a solid competitive edge for a problem that clearly existed but possibly could be solved by a competitor in a matter of months or a year, lowering the value of our proposition. So time was essential to us, but there was no way they could work any faster due to their process.

Now here's the thing: This distributor was used to generic products that were very fast-moving and had an extremely short sales process and would have a market life of maybe decades. From their perspective, once they had the sales training, they thought that their salespeople would hand the end user a datasheet and the end user would give them an order. That was how they were used to selling. Our product had an 18- to 24-month sales process because it was a totally different type of product at a vastly higher price point than what that distributor was used to. So they wasted a year before any salespeople ever learned anything about our product. This was a complete disaster for both sides. This comes from having a mismatch in terms of profiling your distributor. If we had worked with a profile and if we had stated our expectations in the agreement, everybody would have realized from the very beginning that this was a mismatch. It wasn't a bad product and it wasn't a bad distributor. These were just products and a distributor that really should never have been working together.

The last part of the onboarding is going to involve a ride-along with the regional manager or possibly even the head of international sales. This means somebody from the manufacturer going out with the distributor salesperson to visit end users and do a presentation or discussion. Once we've done the first one and we have a good, solid feel for the competency of the sales assets, the onboarding process is now over and are shifting into routine management.

## Bonus video:

https://www.youtube.com/watch?v=3UA-xTE0yRk

https://www.youtube.com/watch?v=tU4OStKulv4

# Basic Concepts

## Designing and building a sales organization

Improve you support infrastructure before you start.

Your ability to ship goods internationally isn't as good as you think it is; find a good forwarder.

Phones: You need somebody to answer the phone when it rings, and you will need to have the ability to work with faxes, and apps like WhatsApp.

## Travel

Aim at traveling less than 140 days a year.

Try to use one hotel chain, preferably a good one; try to keep to one of the big airline groups; try to buy your long flights from the airline website and your short flights from a website like Orbitz.

Exercise and try to enjoy yourself. It will help your stamina.

Communicate with your family and friends.

## Sales Organization

Partner/distributor/agents: These are the people that are going to sell your products. There is a semantic difference, but let's call them partners. Keeping the right ones in place; having good mind share is the key to your success.

Regional Manager (RM): The person who will find the right partners and keep the right level of mind share. Probably a good idea to choose these well and treat them well.

Anchor: The person in the office who does all the stuff that needs doing but isn't important enough to pull the Head of International Sales off of travel.

Intelligence: The more you take this off your RM and on to a pro, the more you are going to succeed.

## Value Chain

It seems like a lot of money now, but you will want that money later, don't waste it.

## Distributor Pitch

7 minutes of clear English

How will they make money without too much effort selling your product?

Why can they trust that you won't screw them?

## Distributor Agreement

I'm not a lawyer, talk to a lawyer.

You aren't going to end up in court, you want to be able to get out of the agreement, not sue.

You need to clearly put into the agreement your expectations in terms of sales activities, reporting, communication, everything that you need to succeed.

Don't bother with a sales number for first 2 years.

Use an LOI, it will get them moving 90 days faster.

# What are you looking for in a Distributor?

Bandwidth, competency, focus

# Chapter 5
# REBUILDING A SALES ORGANIZATION

A lot of people reading this are not starting from scratch—just fixing a weak or poorly functioning sales organization. Rebuilding it. And this is a situation I've been in most of my career. Only a couple of times have I built something up from absolutely nothing. Usually there was organization in place that was very weak and not performing, and I was brought in to fix it.

Fixing the damaged sales organization is actually a lot harder than building a new one. The biggest problems that an international sales manager has are all related to headquarters. When you're dealing with repairing an existing organization, all of these problems become 10 times as hard. This is really a very difficult challenge for anybody. Why is it so difficult?

1.  Somebody built what's in place today and that somebody may very well still be in the company or their friends are still in the company, and now you will tear it apart and speak about it in noncomplimentary terms. There will be emotions involved. Somebody once thought that this was the best possible structure, that these were the best possible distributors, and now you're essentially tearing apart all their hard work. If you succeed, they will feel like you embarrassed or humiliated them.

2. There will be some emotional connection between people in the company and some of the distributors and salespeople that might need to be changed. I have mentioned the problems that I had had with changing some of my distributors and firing salespeople. It gets emotional.

3. The company has been doing things a certain way for a long time and now you're asking them to change and they don't understand why. It's going to be a year or more before anybody sees any results from the changes you want to implement, so in that period of time there will be a lot of pushback, with people saying, "We've always done it this way. Why do you want to change it?"

You have to put all these problems out of your mind. You have to soldier on and push through. At the end of the day, you should be able to increase what you have in place by 500% to 1,000% if you follow the guidelines in my book. I have increased existing sales organizations by over 1,000% in sales four times in the past. It's very doable. In my opinion, the vast majority of people in the US who are building international sales organizations have no idea what they're doing, so the organizations that they build are almost by definition faulty and weak. A few minor tweaks and some discipline can double sales very quickly and then possibly increase sales hundreds or thousands of percent.

The first thing you want to do is go back to the planning stages that I talked about earlier when I was talking about building a new market. Can we figure out what the right markets are for us? Let's put together a list of those markets and compare it with where we are today; I can guarantee that we will be in the wrong markets.

I would not suggest pulling out of a market where we have distributors—maybe we are selling a little bit and maybe we have some installed base—just because that isn't one of the markets that we would have chosen had we chosen correctly. That would not be fair, both from an ethical perspective and from a business perspective. We do not want to treat our partners or customers unfairly. It's not a good idea to pull out completely from these places.

We may decide that we will shift down the resources and the assets we put into these wrong markets, but that's another story. One of the people who came before me in one of my jobs really wanted to spend time in Malaysia and Australia for personal reasons. It had nothing to do with business. So he convinced my CEO that it was worth investing hundreds of thousands of dollars in him and his wife spending time in Malaysia and Australia to develop the market. Of course, no market development actually took place, and he wasted a huge amount of money for no return. When I came on board, I realized that these were just not great markets for us; they'd been chosen for the worst possible reasons. But I wasn't going to cut the market off. I was just going to downsize the amount of assets and resources we invested in those markets.

I don't think I've ever decided to completely cut off a market that my company has been in. While it might be a drain on assets and on money, I think abandoning a market sends an awfully bad message to the global market and really isn't fair to the partners or customers.

The flipside of this is we may not be in the markets we should be in. If we are, we might not have put the proper level of investment and planning into them. Very often people go into markets that they find attractive for irrational reasons. If somebody tells me that they're planning out their initial global expansion and the markets they've chosen are France, Italy, and Japan, that expansion is going to fail spectacularly. The reason is that I can't think of any product where the best possible markets will be France, Italy, and Japan (except maybe some high-end cookware). But what that means is this person has decided to go to these markets specifically because they want to take vacations to France, Italy, and Japan.

Our job is very hard, and we don't necessarily get to make decisions based on something we might want or enjoy. Our responsibility to our company is to choose the correct markets, the markets that are a good fit for our product.

Next we have to look at the team. This is never fun because if the organization isn't producing, chances are the team is weak.

We also have to consider the possibility that the team may not have had good guidance or strategy. They might have been working with the wrong messaging or selling to the wrong markets. It may not be the fault of the team. That said, it may still be impossible to turn them around.

In all of my career, I've never gone in and turned around poorly performing regional managers. I've turned around lots of bad distributors, but at the end of the day, I'm probably going to end up firing a bad regional manager. This is one of those things I don't necessarily like to say. I wish it were different, but if you have some guy who's been sitting around the job for six or seven years wasting money and not producing anything, I'm not sure I can turn him around. On top of that, he's probably going to hate me and fear me and do everything he can to undermine me. I've done this three or four times, and I basically let people work their way out until they decided to quit. I thought that was the fair way to do it—to give people an opportunity to improve and to hold off from firing them and give them the opportunity to improve. And I allowed them to quit if it didn't work out. I think I made a mistake, and today I think I would just go in and take apart the organization and fire the RMs.

As cruel as this sounds, I am talking from a practical standpoint and from experience. I am also a person who is very proud of having mentored a half-dozen people who reported to me who went on to become CEOs and maybe dozens to become VPs of sales. It's not that I don't want to help or mentor or turn someone around. I just find that this is one of those situations that is very hard to turn around.

Let's start off by talking to the team as a group, individually, or maybe both—a group discussion followed by individual interviews. What we have to make clear is that it is now our intention to turn everything around, and that this might be great for them, or it might not be what they are interested in, but it is happening one way or another. As with any team that we take over, we want to get to know each member. I have often taken people out to eat to get them to relax a bit if possible; I tried to get a feel for their experience and their skills. I would really jump into this, because it's important to figure out early on who you can trust.

This may go against just about every management book written in the 21st century, but I am not all that interested in them telling me what went wrong or how things can be improved—that is, unless I get clear buy-in that they believe things can be improved and they want to improve them.

How do I decide if these people should be let go or not? Take the job description that I built for an RM from the sales process I built. It's divided up between what our people are supposed to do and what our distributors are supposed to do. In our organization, are the RMs doing what they are supposed to do? Are they leading the distributors to do what they are supposed to do?

There has to be a reason that these RMs aren't doing their jobs correctly. I will guess that one of those reasons is that they do not have all of the skills and abilities that I would like them to have. We can ask them to go through the same testing and reviewing that we might do with a new hire. We can present this as getting to know the department; it doesn't have to be presented negatively. I will interview and get to know them, have them review their funnel with me, spend a little time with them like it was an interview.

I always like to travel with an RM to see how they interact with their markets—customers and distributors. If you're inheriting 20 regional managers, you might not be able to invest the time in that much travel in the beginning; if you're inheriting two, it's totally different; you can cover that pretty easily.

I like to travel with them and watch how they travel, because if somebody's been a regional manager internationally for five years and they are a poor traveler, that will give you a lot of information about how seriously they take their job and how well they learn how to do things.

I had a guy once who I noticed was extremely sloppy with his passport while traveling. He carried his passport and wallet in his hand, and he kept setting it down and picking it up, making me very nervous. It might sound like a silly thing, but I said to him "You will lose your passport like that," and his argument was that his suit was so tight that he couldn't put his passport in any of his pockets. He had this very fashionable very tight suit. I said, "Do you know what is going to happen if you lose that passport? You will get stuck here for a couple of days talking to the embassy to get a new passport, and the sales meetings you are supposed to execute are not going to happen and that becomes my business. So I need you to figure out a safer way to travel with your passport. Whatever you do, I don't care, as long as you put it in a safe place."

I actually ended up firing him because he was a very poor performer, and somewhere in the back of my head I thought that there was a correlation between somebody being sloppy about his important tools like his passport and somebody who is a poor performer. Maybe I could've fired him that first week and saved everybody stress.

I want to see how regional managers interact with my distributors and end users. The biggest problem you will see from poor performers is that they are essentially servicing the distributor, not managing the distributor.

The distributor calls the RM; the RM does a presentation and leaves; the distributor talks to the customer. Either the distributor sends us an order or not, or sends us a request for discount or not, or something like that, but the RM isn't managing anything.

The regional manager should be managing the sales process and should be working with the salesman and the sales manager from the distributor company to advance the sales process. If the regional manager is acting like a sales asset to the distributor, where he comes in and presents and that's it, we have a fundamental flaw.

If the distributors are treating my RM with disrespect or even contempt, that's going to show me a lot, and it's going to be about the RM, not only about the distributor. If the RM can't get respect from his distributors, he can't do his job.

On this first trip with the RM, I let the RM do everything he normally would do, and I observe. I'd like to do a ride-along, get to an end user or a few if possible. I would like to see him in action. Is he reviewing the funnel or pipeline? Is he coaching or teaching? What is he doing? I want to understand his philosophy, his strategy, and his tactics for being an RM. I have yet, over 30 years of this, to be surprised for the good.

I will chat with the distributors and the customers, but the first trip is primarily to observe the RM.

After getting to know the RMs, I decide if I can salvage them or if I have to find a way to ease them out gently. If I believe I can salvage them, I have to make sure that they are aware that we are working to help them keep their jobs. This is too serious to dance around.

Working with the team, I will try to build up all the tools that we discussed earlier—the sales process chart, the distributor profile, the target markets. Much of this may change. We might find that we are working with a team that isn't as clear on the concepts at the beginning, but we need to start someplace.

As I get to know the RMs, I will get to know the distributors. The first step is to have a discussion at headquarters with the RMs and review the various partners and their funnels. The original meeting and discussion are really to get to understand what people are thinking, how they are evaluating the distributors, what their expectations are, etc.

I then take my distributor profile and compare it to the distributors in place. When I've taken over an organization, I've tried not to terminate distributors unless I had to. In the past 15 years, I have only terminated two distributors. If a distributor has been working with us for years in good faith, even if it is the wrong distributor, I owe it to them ethically and professionally to try to help them turn it around. Fifteen years ago, I thought it was impossible to turn a weak distributor around, but I've had very good success in recent years doing exactly that.

The way I'm turning these distributors around is actually documented in the sections on building and growing a distribution network. It's not fundamentally different, except these distributors are connected to us already and they probably aren't the people I would have chosen, so there might be more work on training and coaching. I will identify the gaps in their competency, their focus, and their bandwidth, and I will work with them on a plan to improve.

You will definitely get pushback from the distributors over the rebuilding project. From the distributors' perspective, everything is going to change. Nobody likes change. You're asking them for more information, you're asking for more activities, you're pushing them in a direction that they're not happy with, and it's going to be a big, bloody fight. On the other hand, a lot of the people I work with have driven their sales up by about 300% in a few years working with me, and I try to use that as an example as to why people should cooperate with me. Still, often they want to push back and they don't want to cooperate; they want to fight me on it.

I have threatened to terminate distributors over this, basically pushing to the point where they were sure I would fire them, and then they've given in. I've never actually had to terminate a distributor that could improve but resisted improving. I threatened a lot but was able to drive compliance.

Let me point out here that you can only drive compliance if you have an offering that the distributors find attractive—that is, they believe that they can make money, that it will be easy to make money, and that they can trust you. It's just like when you recruit a new distributor, but in this case you might have to really work on the pitch if they do not value the company or trust the company or you. If the partners you have don't really value the line, then you have no leverage.

In taking over a new area or new organization, I've always gone out and met with all the distributors, talked with them, gotten a feel for how they see their business, how they see themselves, what they like. It's pretty much like interviewing a salesperson. If you say to somebody, "What's your business?" and all they talk about are other products, not your product line, they're not terribly proud or happy about selling your product line. That's going to give you an indication. If they're not necessarily a sales organization, they're more of a service organization or more of a marketing organization and what you need is a sales organization or, conversely, what you need is more marketing, that's going to give you an idea of what they can do.

If you can, talk to the customers they're comfortable with. You talk to somebody and you get a feel for how they see their business, what's important about their business, all those types of things. And you can get a good feel, just by talking to them, for what is important to them and where you rank. The bottom line is that you want to be important to them. It's difficult to establish that. But if your company's been working with them for a few years and you're not important to them, then you should know about that and deal with that. Maybe that's when you terminate them or you make a serious change.

I once went to visit a distributor when I had just taken over, and they made me wait in the lobby for about 90 minutes even though I had a scheduled appointment. I said to the regional manager at the time, who I had also inherited, "If they respected us, if they valued our business, there's no way they would keep me in the lobby for an hour and a half". For years we had to push them to sell. They were a good distributor, but they just had no focus on us, and they didn't really care about us. So, it's a matter of whether they care about you and are doing the activities that they're supposed to. And you can pick all of this up in a good trip to market.

What do I do on a trip out to market? I talk to the owner, I talk to the sales manager, I will look at their existing funnel, and I will get a feel for how they're managing their information. Are they using a CRM? Are they using a sales funnel system? Are they using other automated systems? They might not use exactly the system I would like them to use, but do they have a good system? If they don't have a good system that's going to tell me something. And if they're using a very sophisticated CRM and they're using it well, that's going to tell me something too.

I want to get a feel for the number of salespeople. I also want to understand if they are being truthful with us. Have they told us the truth about themselves? Just as if I was recruiting a new distributor, I want to evaluate these existing distributors. I want to talk to their salespeople. If we've heard about their size, I'd like to see their office with my own eyes and get a feel for that. I want to see their system for recording data. I want to see how they work with their prospects, how they carry out the various activities of selling—how they're prospecting, how they're presenting, how they're dealing with discovery, who their relationships are with, etc.

It's also very valuable to visit customers. I was once evaluating a distributor that I had inherited, and I went out with a sales manager to visit a customer. The customer mentioned something about how he had lost about a hundred pounds after having bariatric surgery since the last time he had seen the sales manager. Now, I know that you don't lose a hundred pounds overnight; it probably takes a year or more. The sales manager had just been telling me how he went to see these people every month or every six weeks. So right then and there, I knew that I had caught him in a lie, and that's the type of thing you can pick up on these trips. That's what you're essentially looking for. It also doesn't hurt to plan your trips to coincide with local shows or conferences; it makes it easier to meet multiple customers with the distributor or with distributor salespeople.

Activities: Once we have looked at the markets and the team and the distributors, now it's time to look at the various activities that were carried out before. Let's see what we need to do to improve those.

In the same way we'd do this when building a new organization, we'll put together a sales process chart that shows all the different activities that everybody is supposed to be doing within the existing organization. Now we will compare the gaps between what they are doing and what they should be doing. This is going to be a very painful activity, because the distributors will feel that they've been doing the right things because they're already selling something and they've been generating some revenue and nobody has asked them to do it differently.

The first hurdle in this is going to be getting them to report. They will probably put up a lot of resistance about giving you additional information. Without the information, it's hard for you to judge what needs to be improved. Remember the old saying: what you can't measure, you can't improve. And you can't measure anything if you're not getting information from the distributors.

Some of the things that will need improvement are how many sales calls they're doing, how they are prospecting, and how they are presenting.

Do your existing distributors have the right connections? If somebody chose the wrong distributors in your organization before you joined the organization, these distributors probably don't have the connections you need. I joined a company once where we had an extremely technical product that required very complex installation. Because of that, we built up an organization of distributors that were very technically savvy. While they were really good at providing service contracts to hospitals in their territories, our sales were horrible, which is why I was brought on board. The contacts these distributors had were typically the maintenance managers of hospitals. We used to call them the people who sit in the basements of hospitals.

Our products over the years had developed and were now very IT oriented and significantly more expensive. We wanted to be selling to the IT managers and the chief operating officers of hospitals, not the maintenance managers. Our distributors simply didn't have the right connections, which was severely limiting our sales ability.

Once we've done a good gap analysis, we can come up with an improvement plan for the distributors. Nobody's going to like it, but in the end they should be able to make a lot more money, so hopefully they will embrace it regardless.

What should this plan look like? We will strongly suggest that they hire new people with new skill sets or new connections. For instance, while they might not like it and it might be offensive, we will suggest that perhaps their salespeople don't have the ability to create connections with the right group of people but they might be able to hire somebody who can do this. We will also talk about training and how the training is something that we will drive. Again, it's going to be very similar to what we discussed about building up an organization. We will offer two types of training: training that is very specific to our product and then training in general sales skills that can be useful otherwise.

One of the reasons this organization is weak and needs to be rebuilt is that the distributors don't see value in us and are not giving us sufficient mindshare. By improving what we give to the distributors, we will also be improving our mindshare position with them as well as improving their skills and competency and, hopefully, the amount of focus they put on us.

One thing that is impossible to get distributors to do is improve bandwidth. Bandwidth requires growth in the size of the company, which probably involves the company seeking financial help or investments or loans. You have to be a very serious principal and strategically key to a distributor for that distributor to go out and look for money to add resources to keep you happy. Realistically, we should be focused on improving the distributor competency and focus, because those are attainable goals.

Within our organization, we want to look at how we spend our time and money. That is how our RMs and, to a lesser extent, the other members of the team spend their time and money. I look at boots on the ground: how many sales hours we are getting and how many meetings we are getting from our RMs. I once inherited a regional manager who traveled for about 30 days a year. When he went on a business trip he would fly one day, rest one day, meet one day. Fly one day, rest one day, meet one day. All through his trips. His cost per meeting was huge. He'd been with our company at that point for about 11 years, so he was making a significant salary plus a benefit package, and you could do the math and figure out that each meeting he was carrying out over the course of the year was costing us about $12,000. This was really not cost-effective. By shifting that position to a regional manager based in market who was a little bit more energetic and had more initiative, we were able to cut that cost down dramatically—to about $1,200 per meeting. We grew the overall sales of that territory by about 500% by improving processes and of course by replacing the RM.

When we look at replacing our employees, we basically follow the same pattern that we did in the other chapters. We talk about building, but we will carefully evaluate the work that the team is doing and see if we can improve them or we have to replace them. As I mentioned, I've usually found that I ultimately end up replacing them. If somebody has been doing an extremely poor job with no accountability for 10 years, even if he started off great at his job, it's going to be very difficult to get him to produce well after 10 years of doing bad work.

Aside from the dramatic changes such as replacing people, I want to look at all the different things we're doing within the organization. Are we presenting using the correct deck? Are we following the correct sales process? Are we writing our reports correctly? Are we using the right sales enablement tools? The core to all of this really follows what I've written about in Chapter 4 on building up a sales organization.

What we are doing is taking what we have and comparing it to what we should have, and there may possibly be some pieces worth salvaging, once we look at them carefully. However, most of the time, if an organization isn't producing very well, you'll find that every component is weak and needs to be dramatically repaired or replaced.

# Basic Concepts
# Rebuilding

Much harder

You will get more resistance internally

Try to turn around partners.

Accept that you will probably have to fire RMs.

Ride-along with as many RMs as you can; carefully note your gut feelings.

Build the team like you were building from scratch; do the assets fit what you need?

Build a gap analysis; what are you missing?

Improvements will come by changing lots of small things as much as changing a few big things.

# Chapter 6
# ONGOING OPERATIONS

## Building processes

Let's go back to what we were talking about in terms of the overall process and who does what in the organization. In some cases, you'll say "The RM should be coaching and managing the distributors' salespeople."

Sometimes you say, "He's also responsible for the training, coaching, and managing of the distributors' salespeople." In some cases, he'll also be responsible for recruitment. That really depends on the skills, strengths, and workload of the head of the international sales department.

I myself am very skilled and very experienced at recruiting distributors. I've helped out regional managers so that they weren't solely responsible for recruiting distributors, but instead responsible for the managing, the coaching, and to some extent the training. In part I would take the training on myself as the head of international sales.

You might also have a head of international sales who isn't as experienced or as strong as your RMs either with the training side or the recruitment side. You can shift that around, depending on what makes sense for your organization.

The thing is, it can be very time-consuming to recruit and onboard distributors. And often, you'll want to make sure that those regional managers are getting a feel, as much as possible, for working with the distributors—coaching them, managing them, keeping things flowing.

But these are different options. I could imagine, even, a business development manager who was responsible specifically for recruiting distributors. So you could make that a completely separate position, depending on the size of the organization, who you have, and that kind of thing. I know some companies divide up the sales process into different types of positions, but again that depends on how large the company is. You could have somebody who is dealing with new products, somebody for new customers, somebody who's dealing with the government, and somebody who's dealing with the public sector and the private sector. There are different ways you could divide this up to get more effective use of your overall sales organization and your distributors. This could be one person, or the responsibility could be divided over multiple people.

The way to do this is to lock it with your sales process and with your funnel and figure out who should be doing exactly what. There isn't any part of the sales process that isn't assigned to a specific function along the value chain between a principal, the distributors, and other people. Then, if you find that there are areas that you may need help with, you can recruit somebody to help you set that up.

I once ended up with a group of distributors that had been forced upon me and who had no real connections among the end users that I needed. The distributors weren't having any luck setting up meetings, which was really slowing us down. So I was working with an external organization that would set me up with meetings and set up my distributors with meetings. We were paying an external organization a set fee to schedule meetings with end users as a way to supplement and help out the distributor. By using this external service, we were able to significantly move the sales process forward. But having a situation where the distributor needs assistance in that particular part is unusual, and it only happened to me because I was working with a company that had major internal strategy problems. It's something that could happen, and you have to find a way to get out of situations like that that could be forced on you.

The way I like to do everything is by using a funnel system. I came across the funnel system probably close to 30 years ago, and I've been using it religiously ever since. For me, the funnel is the best tool possible for managing what's going on in the field with the customers, with the salespeople, with the distributors. You can use different models, but from my perspective they all transfer pretty well to a graphic image of a funnel. If you're using a certain type of pipeline or a another type of model, you can insert that here instead of the funnel. But what I look for is the ability to keep track of everything from the salespeople—of every element, every step of the sales process—with every one of their customers that is aggregating this information.

We've set up who's expected to do what. And we know what we expect from everybody on the team, and from my perspective that includes the people in my company—and partners. I look at the international sales leader, the regional managers, the various marketing and support people within the principal manufacturer. Then also within the distribution company, everybody who's going to take part in the various activities. And possibly anybody who's working with us. And that could include agents, consultants, maybe key opinion leaders that we may be paying, anybody like that who's involved in the whole process. We want to identify everybody who's involved, not necessarily by name, but by position and what they're supposed to do.

We will set up a system to keep track of this, divide up the labor in a systemic way, and then have some accountability.

# The Funnel

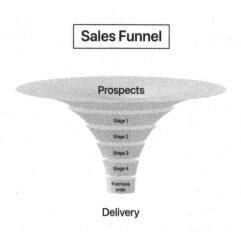

I consider the funnel the best way to manage the sales organization and the sales process. Picture a funnel with horizontal slices that divide up different elements of the sales process. In my experience, there are probably close to 30 pieces within the sales process, but for our purposes let's talk about 6. Why is this a good visual way to keep track of things? Because if you can imagine the narrow end, the bottom of the funnel is significantly smaller than the top of the funnel, so you throw in, for example, 100 prospects and 5 come out the bottom end. Thus you know approximately what your ratio is total, you're getting about 1 out of every 20 prospects resulting in a deal. But more importantly, you can then take a look at all the different slices and see that from stage one to stage two you're losing 10%, from stage two to stage three you're losing 10%%, etc.., through the funnel. That is usually referred to as the conversion rate, from stage to stage.

When you're working as an individual contributor and you're managing your own funnel only, you can take a look and get a feel for how you're doing. But let's say you have a hundred salespeople spread out over 60 countries around the world selling your product, and you're taking a look at their funnels. You have a very solid idea of how well, first of all, the whole system works. You might find that between stages four and five, everybody has a problem: everybody's losing 45% or 50% right at that point. Then you might determine that your presentations are weak or that your prices are problematic and you're not establishing value early enough. On the other hand, you might find that specific people are doing much better or much worse. Most people are following a reasonable conversion ratio and then there are a couple of salespeople who in one particular area are having a big problem. They're losing a lot of things that are falling through in one specific area.

By keeping track with a funnel system like this, you can identify who is strongest and who is weakest at every stage. You can identify specific problems. Those problems might signify that you need better sales enablement material or marketing material. They might signify that you need to be putting more prospects into your funnel in order to get more out the other end. They might signify that you need to train better in certain areas of your sales process. The funnel's going to give you the feedback and the data that you need to keep track of what's going on.

So, let's go back to the systems and the processes. I now have a structure, a skeleton sales process. I figured out who should do what. I could go through and say, "The people in the principal marketing department will deal with these elements of finding the customers. We will reach out, we will engage a researcher, an external business intelligence guy, a freelancer who's going to work on a specific part of finding information that we will use to identify potential customers." We might tell the distributor that a different part of this element of the sales process belongs to him. And when we define elements of the sales process that belong to the distributor, we will document them directly in the distribution agreement. So what we're basically saying is, "Of the 30 pieces of the sales process, these 14 belong to you, and this is how I expect you to do them, and I will put that directly into the distributor agreement. How do we hold you accountable for this?"

If they're selling something that's costs a couple thousand dollars and they have hundreds and hundreds of deals, obviously I'm not going to know the name of every customer, but if I can see a pattern in how they're aggregating this material, that'll give me a good feel for what they're doing and the shape of their business as a whole.

I don't necessarily have to understand what's going on project by project but by taking a look at the shape of their funnel, I will get a good feel for everything.

When you don't measure things, you can't improve them, and you can't keep track of things like forecasting. The funnel is a key tool for accurate forecasting, but it's also important in terms of making adjustments. Let's think about an example. We come out with some messaging and we're very excited about this messaging. We can see from the funnel if this messaging is helpful or not. If it speaks to the customers and get us purchase orders, it is effective. It could very well be that the messaging that we think is fantastic messaging is not attractive to customers at all. It doesn't speak to them and it isn't moving us forward in terms of our goals. By keeping track of the funnel, we are in a really good position to adjust any of the various tools that we're using.

Remember that we have reached a contractual agreement with our partners as to their level of activity. It's very important that we know what they're doing because that is going to help us decide whether we continue to work with them in the period before we reach satisfactory revenues from their territory. If the distributor agreed to carry out 100 sales calls a year in the first year of our agreement, then by the 90th day we should see evidence of at least 15 or hopefully more than 25 calls. If we don't, this is cause for concern and a discussion with the distributor.

What I'm looking for is information from the salespeople about what their activities are, what meetings they're carrying out, and what takes place at those meetings. I want the effort and the time needed to create this report to be an absolute minimum, and there are a few ways of doing it. Working with the CRM is a little expensive but it's probably the best way. Working with an Excel sheet is significantly cheaper and it's probably the second-best way.

The sales rep is going to come out of the meeting hopefully with a couple of pages of handwritten notes. While in a perfect world I would capture a scan of those handwritten notes, if I had a million pages of handwritten notes from all over the world on the cloud, I think that's probably bordering on hoarding. On the other hand, what often happens is the rep should come out of that meeting with his two or three pages of notes and create 300 to 500 words of actionable material to pass on to his manager (from the distributor), his regional manager (from the manufacturer), and the headquarters of the distributor and manufacturer.

What should be in the report? The information of all the relevant people we talked to within the customer organization. We use a variety of scanning software for business cards and capturing people's information. It is relatively simple. That said, there are a lot of markets where you will talk to people who don't carry business cards. In that case, if you can capture their name and their mobile number and/or their email, that's a great start and very helpful. We want to talk about who this person is and try to basically map out the relationship with people within the purchasing process.

Every market has different terminology. For instance, Personal Secretary to the Minister of Health in Egypt is a very different position than the

Permanent Secretary of the Ministry of Health in Nigeria, but neither of these positions have a counterpart in the United States or Germany. So what we'd like to do is put down the title but also a very short description of what that title means. We want to document how they're related to the sales process—for instance, is this a gatekeeper who controls access to the minister of health? Is this the person who controls the budget? Is this the person who needs to be convinced to make a decision? Everybody you talk to should fit somehow into this puzzle, even if the way they fit is they have no influence—and you can say that. You can say John Smith, assistant director of finance, doesn't appear to be relevant for the sales process.

While this might sound a little open to interpretation or very subjective, it's key for me to understand what this person is thinking or feeling. Someone I used to work with suggests a system of marking with little smiley faces in your handwritten notes what appears to be your customer's state of mind and what is yours. This might sound a little extreme, but imagine looking down at your notes and seeing a little frowny face for the customer and a little frowny face for you, a little smiley face for the customer and a smiley face for you, then a big smiley face for the customer and a big smiley face for you over the course of a discussion. It gives you a feeling of whether that customer is accepting or internalizing your discussion and whether the customer trusts you. I like to look at it as a little switch. At what point do I feel that the customer has internalized that I have a solution to their problem? And at what point has the customer internalized that they can trust me?

When you teach the sales reps to think this way and to document things this way, you can look at your sales process and at your customers and you can say, "There are three people involved in the purchasing process. Two of them trust me and have internalized that the product solves their problems; one of them doesn't seem to trust me but does seem to have internalized that I can solve his problem. Is this sufficient to close the deal?" Having this in a graphic structure is extremely powerful for the sales rep, but also for the manager and for the whole team going away from the customer back to headquarters.

It is crucial for me to structure the sales process graphically and to keep it as part of the reporting structure. This is one of the key elements of sales management. What do I mean? We've talked repeatedly about the sales process and the sales funnel, so let's imagine we have a 12-part sales process and we lay this out on an Excel sheet. The sales rep essentially is saying that he moved from stage VII to stage VIII or that he is solidly in stage X. This gives us the information we need about this deal if we do it correctly. It is also an extremely "economical" way of doing it, not wasting any of the sales rep's time or keeping the rep away from actual selling.

This also helps me understand my organization down to the smallest component. What do I mean by that? If I look at the holistic worldwide funnel of thousands of deals that are cooking right now, I can see where the deals are in the funnel and watch how they progress from one stage to the next. If what I'm seeing is that we are losing 10% on average from step to step through the process (and I'm just using that number as an easy math example that is neither a good nor bad ratio), and then I see that in one market, though those numbers are much larger we're losing 25% from stage to stage or we're only losing 3% from stage to stage or there are specific stages where either worldwide or in one market we're dropping 50% instead of 10%, each one of these examples is going to give me information that I can act on to help me improve my sales organization. I will use this information for my marketing material, my sales enablement tools, my sales training, and to evaluate my distributors. This information is key for everything I do to build a world-class sales organization.

Napoleon used to talk about reading the roll call lists of his army every morning and night—dozens of pages of numbers listing the level of readiness against specification of his forces. He said that this was the key to being a good general; it allowed him to know what was going on with

236 | ZACH SELCH

his forces. To me, the funnel serves that purpose. If you know the conversion ratio for every step of your sales process for each of your distributors and you know the situation of all the big deals in your funnel, you know almost everything that you need to know to run your organization.

## Bonus videos:

https://www.youtube.com/watch?v=mBcWa6FZyWs

https://www.youtube.com/watch?v=YUJ2HNSjkoE

https://www.youtube.com/watch?v=PedW4s3YeM8

https://www.youtube.com/watch?v=swYIFmG0SYw

https://www.youtube.com/watch?v=1s9GiOBxUX0

https://www.youtube.com/watch?v=yHVOyah9n38

https://www.youtube.com/watch?v=9pE7dBvgwN4

https://www.youtube.com/watch?v=RTRZdgipQHQ

https://www.youtube.com/watch?v=3oszD6D3wlU

## The core activities of territory management

Setting a baseline might be the hardest part to think through because there is going to be a combination of math work and guesswork involved in this. Can we estimate what our market should be in the territory? Sometimes we can get a relevant and accurate number for the territory. Let's say we sell brake pads. It could very well be somebody has made available a research document that will tell us what the overall brake pad markets are for Germany or Italy or Japan. Chances are that even if that type of research document is available for some of the larger markets, they're not going to be available for smaller markets, and if somebody tells you they have them, those documents may be very inaccurate. So what can we do?

One way people do this—which isn't necessarily accurate but does give you a bit of a direction—is to say, "What is something that correlates strongly with what I sell? Can I tell the overall number of brake pads sold in the company by knowing the number of new cars sold? From that can I get a feel for what the potential market is for my product?"

If I have annual product sales of $100 in a market with 1,000 annual new car sales, can I use that as an indicator for other markets all over the world?

Could I say that if there are 50 car manufacturing facilities in the market and they are each producing 10,000 cars, then logically the brake pad market is 500,000 new cars, plus 20% of cars in the installed base, that need to replace pads every year? Can I expect 5% of that market? Unfortunately, these are the types of questions that we play around with to try and find what makes sense for most markets outside of the large market, because there may not be better data than this available. I really don't like to say, "There are a billion people in India and if I can just get 10% of them to buy my product, I will be rich." What you really want to show is why these people should be buying your product, so you understand what really makes sense. A better way to plan is to say, "There are 100,000 ophthalmologists in India and 25% of them have a standalone surgery. I offer a solution to a problem that they all have, so if I can get a marketing channel that can reach them, it's reasonable for me to sell to 10% of the ophthalmologists in the country."

There are people who can do this research for you, including me, but probably the most cost-effective way of doing it is to reach out to the US Commercial Service.

One other way of doing this is to see if you can find estimates from some of your bigger competitors, especially public companies. A while back I put together an extremely accurate mapping out of the world market for a product because three of the players were publicly traded companies and I was able to look at what they were producing in different territories around the world. I could get relatively accurate data on their market share in the United States and then I could use that to figure out what they were selling in other parts of the world, and since I knew their market position in some of these countries, I was able to fill in the blanks and come up with a really good estimate for the worldwide market. Later on, I had an opportunity to compare numbers with an independent researcher who had put together a similar analysis, and the overlap was very high, about 95%.

So now that we have numbers, we have goals, and we are saying that if the total available market is 100%, what can we get right away? What can we get in a period of years that represents our reasonable growth curve? And it has to make sense how you will get from zero to the number that you think is reasonable. I often see people say something like "In three years we should have 25% of the market," but there's no real reason for this goal unless you have a plan to get there.

In order to put in reasonable numbers, we also have to link reasonable activities. What a disaster it is when you say you will reach 40% market share within five years and end the sentence right there. What you want to say is, "If we execute our plans and carry out the activities that I've specified, we can plan on reaching 40% market share in five years." Too many times people look at a market and say, "Sure, we didn't allow you the resources you asked for and we didn't green-light market entry into the countries you asked for, but we still want to know why you haven't hit the numbers that you promised us five years ago." The sales numbers and the speed of expansion are all going to be tied to the assets and resources made available to the project. I would put that as a footnote in any chart that you write for any record, any place where this appears, so people realize that they can't expect the growth without the resources, the activities, or the assets.

Let's say we have a series of markets where we are selling $50,000 each. We believe that the available market is $2 million each, and we think it is reasonable that within five years we will be selling $1 million in each of these markets if we follow our plan. So our assumption is probably going to be that next year there may be no increase in sales and in the following year there will be a sales funnel that brings us up to $200,000. Now we can do this in a linear way and just say over the next five years we will increase to $2 million, which means $200,000 growth per year. It's not actually going to look like that; it's going to be uneven. On the other hand, we may be able to plan it out from the opposite direction and say, "In year two it's our intention to get five governmental contracts that will represent $200,000, and in year three we intend to get an additional five government contracts but also two private-sector contractors, representing a total of $300,000. That breakdown gives you an understanding not just of the numbers, but of the activities you need to be doing and of how those numbers should break down in order for you to get the overall targets you want to achieve.

If you can do this for all the markets you want to go into, it gives you a solid benchmark from the start that you can judge and evaluate your progress against.

You can also hook this into the activities that you requested from your distributors and the target numbers you've given them. Keep in mind that if the total goals you give your distributors are $10 million a year, you really don't want to be forecasting that figure to your headquarters in the first few years before you have a solid understanding of how those numbers will work. You might forecast $8 million instead, based on the $10 million goals that you have given your distributors.

So this may be a little controversial, but I believe that if the distributor is doing the right things, and it's the right distributor with the right profile doing the right activities, we will get the best results possible. Coming out and saying, "I will estimate what those results are and if the distributor is getting those results, I will leave them alone" is sort of a lazy way of doing work. Have I ever done it? Yes, I've done it mostly because I'll take a look at the market and say, "These five markets aren't necessarily where I want to put my effort. It's not worth fighting with the distributor right now. I'd rather be working in places where I know that my return on investment is going to be much higher."

My overall long-term goal is to replace all of the poorly performing distributors and the ones that aren't a good fit. I might not do it right away. I might leave them in place and focus on working on the countries that have more potential. But ideally, I would look at all these under-performers or distributors who simply aren't a good fit and start easing them out.

Obviously, once you've identified a weakness with a distributor, you don't have to get rid of them. You can also say, "We're putting together a training plan to make the changes that we need to see from you." And this isn't uncommon. I went into a company once and inherited eight distributors, none of whom would I have chosen to begin with, but I was actually able to improve almost all of them. I only had to fire one of them, and I got the others to improve their sales by about 300% on average by teaching them and pushing them to get the right results.

I got a lot of grief about it. They didn't like the idea that I was pushing them. They didn't like me very much, but a few years down the road they loved me because they were making a lot more money and I was able to help turn them around. But it came down to the fact that I had to push them in directions they didn't really want to go.

You're starting off evaluating the distributors against the benchmarks that you've set for yourself. You're figuring out if they're the right people and if they're doing the right activities. And then, if they're not the right people, not the right distributors, you're asking them to make fundamental changes. Making those changes really isn't easy. But if they value your line enough, they will.

If they're not performing well enough and/or they're not the right partner, they aren't going to value your line enough to make the necessary changes. What type of changes would they have to make? Well, they might have to change the types of people they do business with, the types of relationships they work on. For that, they might have to hire new, serious performers.

Let's say you want them to be able to do meetings at a very high level within government ministries, but they are not able to do that. How do they fix that? They have to hire somebody, and that might be a very expensive hire. So they might decide that just isn't something that interests them. I don't often see a company making a change like that.

What else could they do? Essentially, it's a matter of having the right sales resources, having bandwidth, having competency, or possibly even having focus. Now, if you make those demands, if you say, "Here's what we want. We want you over the course of a year to make this change to your sales organization, at least for selling our product," they either will or they won't, but you never know. The fair thing is to give them the option.

Aside from who they are as a company, it comes down to the actual activities. And for this, you can come up with a plan where you would say, "This is what you have to improve." That's much more likely to get a positive response, because if they're essentially a good, solid partner, then that's a very reasonable request for us to make.

What type of activities need to change? It may come down to how well trained their salespeople are, how many meetings they go to, how they report to you. With all these things that are documented in the distributor agreements with new distributors, you can come back and say to the legacy partners, the old distributors, "Over the course of the next year, I'd like you to make these changes." It wouldn't be fair and it wouldn't be effective to say to people, "You have 90 days to make these changes," but it's perfectly reasonable to say, "I'm here to make these changes. That is what I was hired to do."

Now you might decide, as I did once, to say, "There's absolutely nothing this distributor can do." I once came into a company where somebody had assigned the entire Middle East, essentially from Morocco to Iran, to a guy who had never sold products like ours before. He wasn't a real distributor. He had retired from the car industry. He was a Lebanese American who had run a car dealership primarily serving Lebanese Americans living in Detroit. And then he decided that he would open up a distribution company working in the Middle East, but he had no real experience with it. He was a nice enough guy, but he was about as likely to succeed in this as any random person off the street.

He acted as a master distributor. He traveled to the Middle East once a year, met with distributors, and talked to them. Then some of them would sell. So we were selling about $100,000 to $120,000 a year throughout the entire Middle East. And this wasn't anywhere near good enough. To put this in perspective, within in a few years, we were selling $6 million or $7 million in the Middle East. By getting rid of him, we increased the sales in this market dramatically. There was no real way that this guy had any chance to turn this around.

I knew that our agreement was going to become invalid in six months. So I met him and said, "We're not going to renew your agreement, and I'd appreciate it if we could part company now, as opposed to waiting until the end. We'll let you make any additional orders you want, we'll deliver, and we'll sell according to the same price list. But the earlier we can get out of this, the better." Of course, he didn't take this very well. We were a large part of his revenue even though he wasn't selling very much; he was also sort of retired from his previous work. We didn't really give him any choice, and he walked away in the end.

On the other hand, I was able to turn everyone else in the company around and really nurture them and help them thrive. But sometimes there's just no way that you can turn around a distributor who's that bad of a fit.

Sometimes the fit is great. They are a great distributor; they just aren't giving you the activities that you want because nobody has ever asked them or pushed them. Now you have to say that the fit isn't the problem; they're a perfectly good distributor. They just haven't been doing the activities because nobody's pushed them. They don't to you, they don't give you information, they don't do the type of meetings they're supposed to. They're really not doing everything they should. At that point, you can come up with a plan and say, "This is where we want to go and you have to get there. You have to follow up on this plan and make sure that we will reach it and we work towards reaching it." You must hold them accountable.

Let's flip this around. If you go out and meet with your existing partners, you will also find that some of them are doing really well on specific elements of your sales process. Maybe it's a company thing or maybe it's something that can be traced to a specific salesperson, but you might be able to pick up that trick and teach it to other partners, with the partner's permission.

## Channel sales and the need for information

I mentioned before my favorite reference to Ginger Rogers - "Sure he was great, but don't forget that she did everything he did, backwards...and in high heels." The challenges faced in international channel sales are hard to grasp. People who don't understand sales or channel sales or certainly international sales often think that channel sales is simply signing up a distributor and sitting back and waiting for purchase orders to come in—and that there really isn't very much you can do in the meantime. And that's how you sell X. But if you want to sell 10 or 20 or 50 or 100 times X, you have to be actively involved in the sales process with your international channel partners. Passivity doesn't get you sales growth. This is really the core of my mission statement. I'm not going to be able to grow if I can't get this information.

Ideally, as my distributors' sales rep leaves his meeting with the customer, he's going to generate a 300- to 500-word mission report that tells me what he did and who he met. He's going to go into the CRM or the Excel tool and shift where we stand with this particular project or deal to the right spot in the sales process. In the 90s I was using Excel for this, and I still use Excel, but I've augmented it with CRMs like Salesforce and HubSpot. Today a sales rep can access a CRM from his smartphone and the whole process can take a couple of minutes. He can attach the report to Salesforce and then I'll get the report plus an update of where we've moved in the funnel.

What am I going to do with these reports? First, the regional manager collects the various reports and aggregates them. Using a CRM, there is no work involved in this aggregation. If we use Excel, there are probably a few hours of work a month pulling together everybody's Excel sheet into one report per regional manager. Then these regional managers will send that material to me as the head of international sales, and I will add it to the aggregated single global sales report.

There are a couple of graphic tools that I'm a huge fan of, even if some of them are pretty old school and low tech. I go back and forth between how comfortable I am working with the CRM and working with the "funnel on the wall," which I like very much. The advantage of the CRM is more organizational because it can be used to communicate with other departments and with a lot of other people, whereas really the funnel on the wall stops with me.

What do I mean by funnel on the wall? I have a big whiteboard and on it is drawn a big funnel, which essentially shows all the different elements of the sales process as slices in the funnel. Every project that we are quoting on around the world is represented by a different-color sticky note. The colors represent the different RMs, so I may have a cluster of red sticky notes and a spread of yellow ones and a group of blue ones spread out over the funnel when I lose a deal or we stop pursuing it. The sticky note moves outside the funnel and stays parallel to the last slice where it fell out.

What do I get from this? Here's the thing: I can look across the room and I get a feel for how the top of my funnel looks, how the bottom of my funnel looks, when potential deals may be coming. I also get a feel for how well spread everybody's funnel is because generally no territory or no individual is exactly as good at prospecting and closing and farming. Everybody has different elements of the sales process they are better at and elements they are worse at, and I will get a good feel for that as I look at the funnel.

What's fallen out of the funnel and where it's fallen out is also going to give me a huge amount of information. I've been trying for about a decade to extract from a CRM the same amount of information I get from the funnel, and I just haven't gotten there. I am sure that there are people who get much more information from a computer and much more usable information and much more comfortable information than I do, but personally I still love this. That said, it effectively means that if I'm not sitting at my desk (and I'm not 160 days of the year), I don't have my big funnel in front of me, whereas on the CRM I can see this 24/7 wherever I am, and that's a huge advantage, too.

I am a big fan of mapping out the sales process and keeping it a living document. I had an interesting discussion with a fellow sales nerd a while back about mapping out the sales process, and I realized that in his mind the process of mapping this out could take weeks or months and in my mind this was something that could be workshopped out in a matter of hours. I think we're both right. I think you can come out with a solid fast and dirty sales process in an afternoon workshop with your team, but it could conceivably be years before it is a perfect document. And the reason we were discussing this was that the question "Is this usable if it is imperfect?" came up. I believe it is, because you can start with an imperfect mapped out sales process and then shift as you gather more information and as you understand the markets better.

This may surprise you, but I will use the sticky note for the sales process map as well. Let's say we lay out all the different elements of the sales process and we start this by simply making five sections: Finding the Customer, Establishing Rapport, Helping the Customer Internalize That We Have a Solution to Their Problem, Delivery, and Discovery.

Now let's take each section and break it down into the smallest possible pieces. Discovery might include discovery of the sales process, discovery of the decision makers' names, discovery of the decision makers' personalities, discovery of the budget, discovery of the schedule, etc. Establishing rapport may consist of dozens of pieces, including establishing rapport with the financial manager, with the clinical manager, with the maintenance manager, etc.

I would like to believe that this process is standard and never changes, but the process might be different for every customer or for every market. Before I step on my own toes here, let's be clear: When I say it's different, these will be small changes and small differences. If we do this right, the structure of this should be very similar for Brazil or the US or Germany or Nigeria or Japan. What we will do is make each one of these components a new sticky note in a different color that represents who is responsible for this activity. Is it the head of international sales? The head of business intelligence? The regional manager? The distributor sales manager or the distributor rep? We want to be clear who is supposed to do what, as we can best understand it. Remember, we did this when we talked about the initial expansion internationally, but this isn't a one-time thing; we are actually going to do it on an ongoing basis. We might, as head of international sales, look at it every now and again ourselves and then maybe once a year workshop with the team to get a feel for potential changes.

Maybe we have come to know that there's another important person within the customer organization that we have to work with, or maybe we decide that the best way to do a certain piece of this is have somebody from headquarters do it, not the distributor's sales rep. Again, this is the type of thing that I love to have on my wall because it gives me a solid feeling that I can look up from my desk and see what people are supposed to be doing and compare it to what we're actually doing.

I like to matrix my distributors on a relatively regular basis. We used the matrix in the beginning to choose distributors, and once I'm working with distributor for a while, why shouldn't I compare where they are with where they were when I hired them and where I want them to be? So picture a matrix with the X axis as competency, the Y axis as focus on my product, and the size of the dot representing the distributor's bandwidth as it represents relevance to me. So that bandwidth represents how many sales assets are available to sell my product as a function of or as it relates to the size of the overall potential market. So this is going to give me a good picture of how each of my distributors looks. I can make every dot a different color representing the different regions for the different regional managers. If I want to get a little fancy, I can give each dot a tail that represents where they have moved over the past years, which gives me an indication of how the distributors have improved or deteriorated and how well they are meeting my needs.

So those are the three graphical tools that will give me a lot of information about what's going on in my organization. It is entirely possible that I am hopelessly out of date and there are much better ways of doing this, but for me this is a very powerful system that allows me to keep track of what's going on.

Now, in terms of accountability, we've set out a plan. We say the distributor's supposed to do a certain amount of calls. It's enshrined in the agreement. Then the regional manager will be saying to the salespeople, "Did you go on meetings last week? Were you on meetings for our product? Tell me what's going on. Who did you see?"

If you think about it, you have perhaps 15 or 18 distributors being managed by that regional manager. Maybe it's less. Maybe it's only 7 or 8. But it should be somewhere between 7 and 20. He's reaching out once a week and just touching base with the salespeople and saying, "Tell me about what happened. Did you do what you were supposed to do? Did you go out and talk to the customer? What came out of it? Were there problems?" Again, we will talk a little bit about how the sales manager supports the distributor salespeople separately. Thus each call is a combination of accountability but also support and coaching. The distributor salesperson is going to say things like "I did a presentation. It didn't go as well as I wanted it to." The regional manager then can say, "Okay. Let's talk through this. How could we improve this? Do you want me to send you more material? Do you want me to help you with training?" It's very important to make sure that you're in relatively constant contact with the salespeople from the distributor and are keeping track of what they're doing. If the distributor salespeople either aren't doing what they're supposed to be doing or aren't communicating, which again is part of what we specified in the distribution agreement, there should be minimum levels of communication, set types of communication.

So if they're avoiding this, they are not meeting their obligations. This gives you room to end the relationship. Again, that might seem a little harsh, but you want to set up discipline from the very beginning.

When you have distributors that don't follow processes from the very beginning, it is nearly impossible to fix it going forward. I've repeatedly come into situations where we had a distributor who simply wasn't doing what they were supposed to. They had never been asked to do what they should do, so they had gotten very lazy and very complacent. And then we really needed to push them to do their job. If you have a distributor who's been working for you for 10 years and not giving you reports, not being accountable, it's almost impossible to turn them around without a huge fight.

On the other hand, when you start from the beginning, they appreciate the fact that you're requiring accountability. You're taking them seriously, and typically will consider you a much more serious, more valuable principal. So this is all part of the discipline of the regional manager and of the head of international sales. You will follow up with the distributor salespeople. You will see what's going on to the right level of resolution.

We will set goals. And we will hit those goals. We all like to say that our goal is a certain number. But what we want is not a yearly goal that's a number. Effectively, that would mean your distributor has until the end of the year to tell you that he hasn't done anything. I've seen this over and over and over again. The remedy is that after 12 months, I can issue him a 90-day warning saying, "You didn't do what you said you were going to do." After the 90 days, I can terminate the agreement. So now 15 months later, he hasn't sold a penny. I've given him exclusivity, and I'm screwed.

This is extremely common. You take some guy who's been very, very sophisticated in other elements of business, and he is responsible for a distribution network or for a company that sells for a distribution network. And he says, "Let's just give them a number, a very high number. They have to sell a certain amount or we will terminate them." Great. And then if they don't sell it, we terminate them. That's all we can do. You can't say to your Filipino distributor, "You promised to sell a million dollars. I'm taking you to court in the Philippines and I will get my million dollars." It's just never going to work.

On the other hand, if you say, "Let's talk about this. What's expected of you in the first 90 days of onboarding? What's my role in that first 90 days? What's your role? This is what we will do. We will make available to you training in our home office and training in the field. We will make available to you certain training videos and other materials. We will give you a playbook. What we expect from you is that X number of people will learn this material to a level of proficiency. We expect you to have named individuals dedicated to this. Our expectation is that 60 days after we sign this contract, you will already be giving us reports telling us about the sales meetings that you're carrying out so that we can keep track of that. It's our expectation that your salespeople will be carrying out three sales meetings presenting our product a week, every week that we're in partnership."

And those are the types of things that you can then hold the partner accountable for, track, and keep on top of going forward. And then you will assign part of that accountability, part of that keeping track, to your regional manager and part of it to the head of international sales. This is usually the way it's going to work.

## Communication

When we have this organization up and running correctly, we can have dozens or maybe hundreds of salespeople spread out all over the world, far away from headquarters, and possibly not really seeing the people from headquarters more than once a year. We may also have a half-dozen or a dozen people in headquarters whose jobs are focused on the international market and we have to communicate information among everybody.

People like to talk about Sun Tzu, the ancient Chinese military philosopher, and I think one of his chapters that people get most wrong is the one on communication. People often don't understand the value and importance of internal communication in business and especially to sales. In warfare they say there are three elements of the effectiveness of a military unit: communication, mobility, and firepower. If you don't have communication and mobility, all firepower is simply whatever is in one spot at one time, and you can't generate additional firepower or scale up.

Why am I babbling about firepower when I'm talking about sales? If we are dealing with selling internationally and essentially a long line of people between where the product is manufactured and where the customer is, the communication must be stellar and crystal clear, and this is one of those areas with a great deal of failure.

Like everything in the issue of international sales growth, the biggest mistake people make is not looking at this holistically. Weak companies and poor managers look at this and say, "We need to improve the reports," but in order to improve the reports we need to put in place better systems and more trust. People will not feed information back to headquarters if they don't trust what will happen with that information. Additionally, every minute the sales asset is spending on communicating with headquarters is a minute that they are not selling and effectively not making any money for anybody. If we put in place systems that everybody feels wastes their time, they're not going to use them and maybe they're going to lose their level of trust and rapport with the company and the products in general.

## What is the information needed?

Every sales asset in the organization from start to finish needs to be replaceable. There is a pretty high attrition rate for salespeople within distribution organizations, and if you're dealing with good salespeople, some of them will be very rapidly approaching retirement age and you could find that they will be retiring. You must assume that your salespeople could leave you at any minute, and you want to get all the information that they have available into the system.

On top of all that, as I have said before, "You can't improve what you can't measure." And you can't measure what's going on in your sales organization if you don't have information flowing in to headquarters from your salespeople. The key to explosive growth, to driving growth up 1,000% or more, is constantly making incremental improvements. In order to make those improvements, you have to know exactly what's going on everywhere throughout the sales process.

# Distributor Information

Distributors are usually are extremely hesitant to feed us information, and they have good reason to be. Every distributor has been burned by somebody. Typically, they feed you information and then you take that information and pass it to another distributor, or you try and sell direct or something, and the distributors remember this. So you really can't cheat or burn a distributor or you will destroy your reputation. And when you destroy your reputation, you're really burying yourself; you're just not going to be able to sell.

But, aside from the fact that we will try to avoid at all costs burning or hurting our distributors, we will push them to give us more information, and we'll probably do this slowly and incrementally. When distributors say, "I don't want to give you information about my customers," I understand that. That's usually about trust and I'll work towards building up trust. But what I've also done is say, "Give them code names. You're dealing with 50 hospitals, so give each one a code name so I know that you're visiting 50 different hospitals. If you don't want me to know the name of that hospital, I can live with that, but I do need to know that you visited 50 separate hospitals. I need to know where they are in the funnel. I need to know how they've progressed. I need to know when they fall out of the funnel. I need to know what the next steps are. If you want to call them Hospital 1 through Hospital 50, I can live with that. I just need to have that information."

What's sometimes happened is that within a relatively short amount of time, the distributor says, "I'm just going to give you the name. You've proven that I can trust you. It's too much work to change the names on everything. I'll just go along and give you the names."

The other part of that is that they'll say, "My salespeople are very busy and we don't want to send them to training. And again, if you're dealing with a legacy partner—a distributor that you inherited, not one you onboarded—you don't have a lot of leverage until it comes time to say, "Okay, but we're not going to renew your old contract. We will add a new contract, and it is going to require training, so why don't you just go ahead and send your people to our sales training without putting up a fight?" And then you add, "Let's start with one. I'd prefer that you send three salespeople, but send one and see if this works for you."

Obviously, now the spotlight's on you. You have to make sure that your sales training is effective and adds value and helps them sell. But my assumption is that that's what we're aiming for. So what you want is to slowly push these existing distributors, these legacy partners, into the training habit. You can use rewards; you can punish people.

You can also say, "I need information in my funnel. You are today getting a 40% discount off of list. We are changing our default discount from 40% to 30%, but everything that you give me information on will still get the 40% discount." So you're effectively giving them an incentive to feed you information. Likewise, you can say, "Any distributor that sends three people or more to training will continue to get 40% discount off of list. If you don't send any of your people to training, your discount is going to drop by 25%."

I get to know most of the salespeople within the sales organization. Literally, that could be a hundred salespeople. I like to get a feel for their strengths and weaknesses. Over the years I've coached dozens to go on to become distributors, to become VPs of sales. When they know you are interested in their success, you get their loyalty and hard work.

Support like that can be very helpful to get the distributor salespeople on your side. They're going to make money and if you have a distributor salesperson who's been selling for 20 years, they could be making a fair amount of money. They know what they're doing. They're choosing what is easiest for them to sell, what is the most profitable for them to sell, and most distributors strongly frown on your saying to people, "I will give you an extra five points personally if you sell my products." That's the type of thing that's going to get distributors to walk away from their relationship with you or to find it simply unacceptable. On the other hand, you can give people things like a steak dinner, a dinner with their wife someplace, tickets to a Broadway show, tickets to a nice sporting event, a bottle of wine, pieces of jewelry, ties, little things like that. They'll remember you and appreciate it.

With a distributor, we're looking at competency and coverage. We want to know that they have skills and that they're getting out and doing the work they're supposed to be doing. We can compare that with our strategic goals. Let's say that we want to get into customers with a different profile. We've done very well with hospitals between 250 and 500 beds. We haven't done as well with hospitals with over 500 beds.

Do the salespeople need a different type of competency to sell to hospitals between 500 and 1,000 beds? Is that the type of thing that we can help train them on? Or are we going to ask them to recruit new people? Then again, we can say, "Our strategic goal is for all of our distributors to be selling a little bit more to larger hospitals. What we need from you then is to hire a salesperson who is competent enough to sell to these bigger customers."

Or we say, "We're going to really do an educational push to help train you so that you're able to sell better to this target group of customers. We'll take on that responsibility. We don't anticipate that you will hire new people for this, but we do anticipate that you will send people to our training and that they will learn from this training and get better at what they're doing."

Those are ways of handling that. Again, we could say, "We're going to push you to be hitting more meetings. Maybe what we're seeing is that you're not managing your time well enough. Can we help you out with time management training?" Or, "We will see if we can help you to better identify who the prospects are so that you won't be wasting your time on the wrong customers."

You will find distributors who resist change, who really put their foot down and fight. Once I even had a situation where I had seven or eight legacy partners, distributors I'd inherited, who pretty much said they weren't going to cooperate. I said, "You're done." They said, "You're not going to be able to fire all of us." I called it the strike. It put me in a really uncomfortable situation because I'd been there for less than a year and these legacy partners, some of whom had been working with my company for 30 years, were threatening just to ignore me.

They were all from Latin America, they were all about 20 years older than me, and most of them had played golf, in some cases for years, with my CEO, who didn't really like me very much at all. I tried to explain how much value they could get from tweaking their processes, but they were adamant.

As a group, they complained to my CEO that what I was asking was unreasonable. They really put up a fight. So I said to all of them, "I will terminate one of you randomly. You're right, I can't terminate all of you if you don't do this, but I can terminate one of you, and I'm not going to tell you which one it's going to be. It's not necessarily going to be the biggest or the smallest or the worst. I will choose a name out of a hat and terminate them. So you have a one in seven chance of being terminated if you guys don't get back to work and do what I say." They folded.

Because once again, we had a good product and nobody wanted to lose the line.

They also knew that what I was saying made sense. Now the one who gave me the most trouble, who put up the biggest fight, increased his sales by about 300% within three years. Actually, the value of his company was driven way up, and it was his plan to retire and sell the company and give the proceeds to his kids. I put a huge amount of money in his pocket by pushing him to sell harder. But he hated me in the beginning. He didn't understand why I was pushing him. He didn't understand why I was so "rude" to him. I was asking him for information that he didn't think was fair, all of that. By the end of it, he loved me.

After I left that company and after he retired, we stayed friends and we'd still have dinner a couple of times a year when I was in his country. So that's how making change will be perceived in the long run. But in the short run, everybody hates change, and most people are probably going to put up a lot of resistance to it.

We've talked about our funnel and how we use it to manage distributors, communicate to our team and our bosses, etc. Let's talk a little bit about how we use it for planning, even just sitting by ourselves working with it. After we've been working for a while, we will have a funnel and will be able to see how successful the different distributors have been in closing deals from reading the funnel, how accurate they've been in their predictions, and possibly even how truthful they are in what they're reporting to us.

I can look now to the funnel and I can say, "My distributor in India has a weighted funnel of $1 million worth of opportunity." By that I mean he has, say, $5 million of total opportunity in his funnel but he weights the probability of each project in a way that it looks like $1 million will close in the next fiscal year. In previous years, his forecast has been consistently 20% low. I may be able to assume from this that this year he is also lowballing me, but I'm not sure I'm willing to take the risk on assuming that is the case this year. But now I have a good forecast from his market.

When I take a look at the whole number of what's in my weighted funnel and I compare it to what I'm supposed to finish this year, that'll give me a good idea of where I stand. Depending on my sales cycle and how good my distributors are at this point in the process, I can tell how close I will be and what I numbers I need if I have to work harder and make changes. I'd like to have this information as early in the year as possible.

There's another fuzzy element to this, which complicates things quite a bit. I like to keep track of all the markets I'm working with—what the structure of their economies is and what macroeconomic issues may impact my sales year. The biggest elements could be related to war, extreme weather conditions, and commodity price. Several years ago, there was a major tsunami in Japan and a lot of Japanese companies were not in a position to do any buying for a period of time. It was actually even worse than that, because a lot of other customers that bought Japanese components were now frozen until those component manufacturers came back online. Effectively this meant that a huge part of the market was shut down. But by understanding how this could impact sales, I was able to react and push for sales in other parts of the world, shifting resources and focus to make up for the lost sales.

Then in 2014 oil prices dropped, and many of my customers were in countries that had a large position in oil and gas from a revenue perspective. Hospitals are often funded by public money and in many oil-rich extraction economies, all the public money is tied to oil price. Luckily, I've always been very careful about not putting all my eggs in one basket and I've always been very careful about trying to keep my eyes open to things that will potentially damage my market, so I had about 40% of my customers, or more accurately about 40% of my revenue coming from customers who were in non-extraction markets. By shifting resources and efforts early in the fiscal year, I was able to salvage that year from what would have been complete disaster.

My point is that you need to evaluate the market and keep an eye on anything that might impact you going forward in the short and medium term so that you can react in enough time to salvage your year.

I look at my sales numbers, but I also look at the activities in the various markets. If last year my distributor in Saudi Arabia did 100 customer calls and produced 10 purchase orders, each worth $100,000, and this year it is my expectation he produces $1.2 million, I want to make sure that he is making 20% more calls from the beginning of the year or he has an alternative plan to produce that additional revenue. If he is making fewer calls per month than he did last year or every project is progressing through the funnel either with less chance of success or at a slower rate, I would like to keep track of that earlier in the year rather than waiting until the end of the year. I'm using the Saudis as an example, but I want to be doing this with every country.

I can put a graph on the wall that shows me how many of each activity my distributors are doing, how many customer calls they are making, and how many opportunities they have in the funnel. Then I'll compare it with last year at this time, which will give me an idea of where I stand with everybody.

Let's say I have these numbers, what do I do about them?

Unfortunately, one of the issues with channel management is that our remedies usually are just a big stick. We can ignore when our distributor doesn't do what they're supposed to or goes against our distribution agreement or isn't selling—or we can terminate him. Typically, that's the way people look at it. It's binary: you can ignore, or you can terminate.

But there are alternatives. If you build your discount structure correctly, you can offer a higher discount off price list to better-performing distributors. Sometimes even just a few points of discount is enough to drive the behaviors that you're looking for. A while back when I was struggling to get distributors to put their deals into my funnel system, I said that starting in six months, anything that wasn't in the funnel would get 10% less discount off price list than projects that were in the funnel. Within six months everyone was putting all the projects in the funnel. So if you put together a reasonable plan to use compensation rates, commission structures, and discount levels to drive behavior, there is a good chance that you won't actually have to use the plan. Just having it in your pocket makes you safer.

I have given warnings to distributors a few times. I don't like doing it, because I'm of the belief that if you will fire somebody, then fire them. That said, giving somebody a warning tied specifically to an activity has been very effective every time I've done it. Often the way this looks is "I need you to replace the salesperson; he's not effective", "I need you to offer more sales training," "I see a specific weakness in your sales process," that kind of thing. You're giving them 90 days' or 180 days' warning, or you're just telling them that if they don't fix this, you won't renew their contract the following year.

On the flip side, you can also reward them if you see that somebody is exceeding their commitments from the agreement. You can give them extra discount, you can give them access to a better line of product, you can reward them with prizes or awards or medals.

One thing you have to be careful about is that most distributors do not want you giving any type of bonus or compensation to their salespeople, certainly not without asking permission. This is the type of thing that can really destroy the relationship between principal and distributor. So if this is something you'd like to do, discuss it with the distributor's sales manager or owner and make sure that they are in agreement with it.

Never tell a salesperson that you were planning on rewarding him but his boss wouldn't let you.

Over the years I have practiced something that a lot of people do in international distributors sales: culling the lowest-performing distributors. What's very common is to terminate and replace the 10% of distributors that are most poorly performing against their goals every year. That may be a Jack Welch kind of method. In my last company, my CEO very strongly disapproved of this. Although I thought he was wrong, I did what he said anyway.

Now I believe it was actually very helpful because it forced me to work with the weaker distributors to get better results. Aside from one distributor, every distributor I wanted to fire I was able to turn around and improve their average performance up by a little bit more than 300% in a few years. If I had gone out and every year found a replacement and onboarded four or five distributors, I think I wouldn't have achieved the same numbers and I would've used up a lot more of my time and effort in doing it that way. So you live and learn. That said, I'm not sure that that's a system or method that is effective for every circumstance, and terminating the weakest distributors every year is probably a lower-risk and less-expensive activity.

When somebody is performing weakly, that doesn't mean that I have to terminate them or push them aside. The other option is working with them on training and coaching. I can take a look at the evaluations for that market and decide that this market requires a strong training session or that the regional manager needs to spend more time there.

I may even, in some circumstances, push the regional manager to act in a semi-direct manner. Let's say we are working on one very large project or a very important project in a territory. I may decide that the distributor in this particular territory is weak and cannot handle this deal. I may decide that I want the regional manager to take personal ownership of this project (even in this case I'm not going to dispute the distributor's piece of the pie) and I will get to this decision through my evaluations of the distributor's capabilities. I will use this evaluation also for the team meetings with my regional managers and headquarters when I evaluate and compare the quality of the different distributors.

Let's say I have a distributor that simply can't be pushed to improve. What do I do? Once I have decided that I will warn the distributor that I will terminate him if he doesn't improve his performance, I will give him a formal written warning, which may be a one-year warning, 180-day warning, or a 90-day warning; it depends on the agreement that I have with him. Even if I have a 90-day warning in the agreement, I might give him longer than that because I'm really trying to do what I can to help him improve. He may very well at that point tell me that he is not interested in improving or changing and that he's going to resign. Sometimes they say, "I'm not going to resign. This is my country and I have good lawyers and I will make it very difficult for you to terminate me." Once you've given them the warning letter, you want to talk to them face to face, and often they come to understand that this isn't a good fit. Literally 9 times out of 10 over the past 30 years, when I've said to distributor, "This isn't working out I'm not going to renew you next year. Why don't you resign the line and I won't tell anybody that I wanted to fire you. You can tell people that you resigned the line," they've written me the resignation letter right then and there.

If they don't and I have to improve their performance, then I will follow the legal structure of our termination letter. This really is the only important part of the agreement: how you get out it.

In every case the distributor has more rights than you do because he's a citizen and a taxpayer and a businessman in the country that you operate in. He's probably registered with a government body that he is your distributor and it's going to be very difficult, if not impossible, for you to change that without his agreement. You can put various clauses that you believe protect you in your contract, but it's very difficult to get out of a representation agreement in many countries. You may want to get the US Commercial Attaché involved or see if they can recommend a lawyer. I've never really had anybody really dispute termination to the extent that I used a lawyer, because I planned the termination from the beginning in the agreement. Usually they ask you to buy back their demo unit or they ask you for some type of compensation for the efforts they've made. If you're replacing them with another distributor, you can ask the new distributor to buy the demo unit, which may save you a little.

In general, I'd say if you can make this easy rather than difficult, it's just going to make your life a lot better. You don't necessarily need to be fighting your distributor over anything. Again, depending on what your legal department says or how much of a footprint you have in the market, you may want to do some type of specific type of advertising that you've terminated the relationship. I've never done that. Typically, if my distributor has done a good enough job so that the general market knew about our relationship, I would never terminate him.

You want to pick up from the distributor any type of marketing material, devices, and demo units that they might have. You should have a system in place in the company that closes off any access they may have to things like your online playbook, your price lists, or an intranet that gives them access to information.

## Distributor meetings in market

Meetings are the key element of the ongoing management of my distributors. I would do this in a uniform way. My regional managers would be meeting with the distributors on a regular basis. They'd be doing ride-alongs constantly. Let's say each RM is managing 10 or 12 or 15 distributors, so essentially, every month or every two months they were spending a couple of days with each distributor, and that drove that relationship. The RMs push the distributors. They manage the sales processes, and so on.

But I would meet with my biggest distributors once or twice a year. What I tried to do was meet with them once at a centralized location, a trade show for instance, and then once I would get out to their market. With the really good ones, I might get out a little bit more than that.

I have a standard structure to these meetings. First of all, we would set them a little bit in advance, and I would set them so that I could hit multiple markets. I might hit 10 countries over the course of two weeks day after day, because I didn't want to spend too much time with anybody. Often this was the type of thing that would annoy my distributors, especially at the beginning of our relationship. They'd say, "Zach, you're coming in for one day. How come you can't come in for three or four days? Come out to the countryside for the weekend with my family," etc.

Over a period of time, I tried to spend as much time as possible with the distributors, especially the big ones and the ones that were more culturally driven towards this type of deep relationship. They wanted to take me out to their country house, they wanted to take me out on their boat, that kind of thing, and I would do that. But I also really had to hustle because I had a lot of distributors, and I had to get to as many of them as possible over the course of the year.

Typically, I would come out. I would send them an agenda ahead of time, or I would have that come from the regional manager. We would come out, and we would do about a two-hour funnel review. I would try to have the salespeople there. Let's say my distributor had four salespeople. I would spend a half an hour or so with the distributor, sales manager, say the owner and the sales manager, or sometimes just the sales manager, sometimes just the owner, depending on the company. Then we would bring in each sales manager to go over his funnel. He would basically talk about all the opportunities he was working on, where they stood, the opportunities that had dropped off since the last time we had spoken, the opportunities that had closed.

I will sit with the head of the distributor company. That could be the owner or the sales manager or both. And if possible, I also want to sit with the salespeople, and if you have three or four or six salespeople, you might have them rotating in, not necessarily watching their colleagues, although you could do it that way. It might be embarrassing or uncomfortable for them. So you could decide if you want to bring them in just for their section or you want to have everybody around.

But I then will say, "Let's walk through your funnel. Let's walk through all the different prospects in your funnel. Where are they? The last time we spoke, you had these. How many of these have fallen off? How many of these have closed? Who's moving? Why are they moving? Why aren't they moving? Are you finding that you're having difficulty?"

While doing a periodic review, I can take a look at the graphical representation on the funnel, and that is going to help me understand what's going on in the market. Let's say you take a look and you say, "Okay, great. We are getting a lot of initial meetings. And we're getting initial meetings that are asking us for a proposal. And then we're losing them at the proposal stage." Or, "We're getting a lot of initial meetings. We're doing a presentation. We're then meeting with the technical team to discuss it. And then we're seeing people drop off at that point." Or, "Every presentation is getting us a request for a proposal."

From those types of things I can really gain some insight. I can understand if customers like our presentation, if they like the product, if the price is a problem. Maybe we're not establishing enough value. Often you'll hear the distributor say, "Everybody has asked me for a discount in this market." And I can take a look and say, "Okay, in this market, I know we're expensive, but we're competing with the same people. We're competing in another market. That other market has very similar per capita GDP and a very similar spending pattern. So I don't see any reason we should be getting asked for so many discounts, unless we're just not establishing value. What can we do to be establishing value better?" Maybe some of the other markets are doing a better job of establishing value and this particular distributor salesperson or this particular distributor isn't establishing value. Maybe I can learn that from the graphical representation of a funnel. And then I can discuss it in the periodic review. And the periodic review can then help me build a training plan.

I can say to the distributor, "This particular salesperson isn't very good. I think you should replace him or maybe shift him to something else. He's just not able to close business as well as some of the other salespeople that I see in different territories or even in your market", or, "This sales guy is doing a fantastic job. I'd like to use him in my distributor training or distributor meeting. I'd like him to speak a little bit about what he's done." It's a great motivator and really helps build morale with people if you say, "Hey, you are doing such a great job. I want you to present at our next meeting, specifically about what you did here because I think this was a really a great job."

But the periodic review typically takes the structure of my coming into town or the head of international sales coming into town, meeting with everybody, looking at the sales funnel, and then going project by project through the sales funnel. What happened? What's the next step? What might hold it up? What are the chances of successfully closing this?

And we do a similar thing with the regional manager more often. Whereas the head of international sales might do this once or twice a year, depending on the size of the potential market, the regional sales manager will probably do this four times a year at a minimum. So the regional sales manager will talk to each of the salespeople at least once a week or every two weeks. If you're not reaching out and talking to the region, to the salespeople, every two weeks, it's probably a mistake or there's probably a problem. And if they don't respond to you, if they're not willing to talk to you, then there's definitely a problem.

But you should aim for approximately once every two weeks, no less than that. If you say, "This particular regional manager has 10 distributors. Each distributor has two salespeople. So that's 20 salespeople in this territory. Two hundred working days a year, can we spend five days a year in the field with each of the salespeople (as much as we may like to, we won't spend every day of the year in the field on ride-alongs; there are other activities). Will that work out?" So the RM's going to do a ride-along with the salespeople, and then on a quarterly basis he's going to do a review. This is how you will structure this type of review in your system.

If a large deal had been lost, typically I would draw a line. I would say that if the deal represented 25% of their annual sales target, I might come in specifically to do a postmortem. Talking about why a large deal was lost with the vice president of international sales is the type of thing that makes a huge impression on the salesman and on the company. They learn a lot from it, but they also don't want it to happen again. Nobody wants to be in that position where the head of international sales of your principal is coming out to talk to you about why you lost the deal.

But they can also be very informative. Sometimes we identified what the problem was, and then we were able to really teach a lesson to the distributor and to the salesperson about what had happened and why there was a problem. That was what I was aiming for. If I could do that, then we were in a good position.

You can determine that any one project we lose in the funnel that's valued at more than 25% of the overall annual goal for that distributor requires a postmortem. You could draw that line at 10%, you can draw that line at 50%, you could do it per salesperson or per company, but the idea is if you've lost a big deal, you want to understand why.

I can tell you about the best postmortem that I ever had. This salesperson had a lot of experience and thought that she was really fantastic. She really thought she knew everything, and I went down and met with her, and she had put a huge amount of effort into this deal for about two years. It was the biggest deal that she had ever personally been responsible for until that point. As soon as I heard that she lost the deal, I flew down, and I arranged my own interpreter, so that I could be sure that everyone understood every part of what we were talking about.

I told the saleswoman what I wanted to do. She said, "I don't want to talk about this. This is really painful for me. It really killed me that I lost this deal. I want to move on. I want to work on the next deal." And I said, "No, we have to talk about this." And we did.

This was a woman, about 60, who had great relationship skills, but she wasn't great at strategy or at sales process skills.

We talked and talked and talked, and after a few hours we identified exactly what the mistake was: she was dealing with the wrong decision maker at the customer. There were multiple decision makers in a complex sale. She was focusing on one but apparently one of the other ones was more important.

On top of that, her competitor kept talking about high-end features in a very offhand way when he was quoting a very basic system, and our saleswoman quoted a very high-end system that was fully loaded. The person in the customer organization that my saleswoman was talking to loved all the shiny features, but in the end she didn't have the budget. The person who ultimately made the decision wasn't really convinced that they needed a high-end system and was much more worried about the costs. My distributor salesperson had not established the value with the relevant decision maker, so they didn't want to pay for our high-end system. If we had done a better job of establishing value or had quoted a lower-end system, we might have done better. We could have come in with an offer that was very attractive if we had understood that in the end, the decision was going to be made based on a lower budget. We didn't. We came in with a much higher, much more extravagant, powerful system, which was above budget and we didn't know enough to fix that. So it was crystal clear what had happened and how we were outmaneuvered. As painful as it was, the lesson was unbelievably valuable.

This was the point where we were tricked and outmaneuvered, and from this fork in the road, instead of presenting and proposing a medium-level system at a low price, we presented a very high-end system with a very high price. This particular saleswoman did fantastically because she never made that mistake again and she was able to increase her sales dramatically. So I'd like to think that particular postmortem was extremely effective in helping her turn around.

In terms of the routine meetings, we would go over the funnel. You want to go over the funnel, and you want to use a format that you're using for your normal reporting. If you're using an Excel sheet that divides it up or you're using the CRM, you will use that as the basis. You will put that project on the wall and talk about it. I would always go and say hello to the staff, the supporting staff, the marketing people, the administrative people, the shipping people, the payment people, all those people within the company, and they would often have something to talk about. For example, they would say, "A lot of countries shifted to plastic pallets about 10 years ago, and the US didn't." We would have people saying, "We really need for you to ship on plastic pallets because it's difficult for us legally to import this way," those types of things. There would be questions like that, and it's good for the boss, essentially, somebody who everybody respects and sees as an important figure from headquarters to come out and talk to people.

I would do some ride-alongs. You have to be very, very careful about this because often what the distributor most wants is to get you out in front of customers. This can swallow up your time. You have to make sure that they're using you for the most important customers. You can also try and make this into meals or something like that. Let's say you go to Mexico City or São Paulo or Kuala Lumpur, getting around to three hospitals can be crazy with traffic, but having dinner with five customers at the same time isn't hard.

On the other hand, this can be valuable to help sell. There is value to the customers seeing that somebody important is coming out, for the market has to see that you as a manufacturer are aligned and standing behind your distributors. So having you go out can help in the sales process. If you think back to what I was talking about in terms of the elements, this is a great tool for building up trust between the manufacturer and the market.

One of the things that I try and do, and this is something that doesn't come quickly, is to learn a lot about the cultural elements of the different markets I work in. I spend a fair amount of time studying the local religion, food, literature, history, etc., and my customers and partners appreciate it.

Having that cultural understanding and showing it to the market while you're in territory can be very helpful. Part of your visits to the market should be just showing the customers, the end users, that you are committed to the market and committed to your distributor. Those things are very important.

# Follow up

I take good notes during my trips. I'm very careful to document anything that's a follow-up either from the distributor or from end users. Keep in mind, you may be doing 10 cities on a trip. The paperwork adds up, and the follow-up can be brutal. What I try and do is take notes, and then right away, in the evenings, try and start the follow-ups. I keep a to-do list and try and reach out to my headquarters and say, "We have these things to follow up on" and hand out tasks.

# Reports

What type of reports do we need for evaluation, the feedback, and the work that we are doing? Every meeting should generate a report. But I don't want to waste a lot of potential sales time. On the other hand, we need to keep track of this information. Why do we need to keep track of this information? Because we're not immortal. Somebody could leave the organization, somebody could get hit by a bus tomorrow and we need to know what's going on. So typically I put together a format of the reports I want, and it can be very basic. What I look for is whether we moved from one part of the sales process to another successfully.

Have we moved forward? Have we fallen out? Is it clear to us? We identified, for instance, that the customer doesn't have a need for our product, and we know that this customer or this prospect is not going to be a customer. But that's a very important piece of information for me to have identified. Now we have a basic format for a report, which we'll deal with.

Who am I talking to? What points were discussed, what was agreed upon, what are the follow-ups? And then we might say, "This meeting falls here in the sales process"." So there are specific things that we want to do for this meeting that we might not do for all meetings. And there may be questions or bits of information that I want. So we could add to that report specific questions and say, did we get the answers we were looking for?

And this is very important because we're always looking to the salesperson in the field to be feeding us back information that will help us understand, build our strategy, and plan out the next steps. Our expectation is that a distributor salesperson will tell us that when he got to a customer, they asked certain questions and got the information that we needed. And if we're not able to get our distributors to follow this type of reporting structure, then we might have the wrong distributor.

And this should be documented in the sales and the distribution agreement. The regional manager should be working with the salesman to coach and make sure that they're going to get this information and feed it back.

In the report we have what was discussed as we've moved through the sales process, next steps, answers to specific questions that we might have. And usually I will have a whole shopping list of information that I want, and that information is essentially tactical: how we are going to build our plan for this particular project based on this discovery, the questions that people are asking, and how to get those answers and feed them back to whoever owns the sales process with that particular customer. It could very well be the salesperson who is meeting with these customers is the one who wants the sales process and then I still want them to gather that information and document it for their own use because they can't do everything in their head and they can't just do everything playing by ear.

What we really want is for them to be able to get that information, document it, and think it through and then maybe work with a regional manager who is going to coach them to closing the deal.

# Distributor meetings (group)

Let's separate distributor meetings from sales trainings. What I've tried to do is have a global distributor meeting every two years, and then in alternate years, regional distributor meetings. It's difficult to get distributors to put people on a plane every year to the United States or someplace centralized, but you can do it probably every two years if they see enough value in your company and your product. By having this type of meeting, you are building fantastic mindshare with the distributors. Then in alternate years, you have them regionally.

Let's talk about how we go about doing these distributor meetings. First of all, I want to have them in a nice place that doesn't involve a lot of plane changes. For instance, in the United States, I want it to be near a fairly busy international airport like New York, San Francisco, Los Angeles, Miami, places like that. Let's say that you're from Jordan; you fly Jordan to Frankfurt, Frankfurt to New York, and then I'm asking you to fly to Chattanooga. You might have to change planes another two times, but if I do it someplace that is easier for you to get to, it makes it easier. It makes it a little bit cheaper. It takes away one more obstacle that distributors might have to sending their people to this. Again, I want the distributors to send as many people as possible. If possible, I want to get all the sales reps as well as the managers.

Here's the pattern that's going to happen. Maybe for the first meeting you have, it's going to be the owners and the sales managers. Maybe by the second or third meeting you have, everybody's going to show up, or at least their best people will show up. Then maybe after a couple of times, you will get everybody. Your goal is to get everybody who's selling your products to show up to these meetings, because the more people you have, the more mindshare you will get from all of this.

The other part of this is I want to hold the meeting in a nice place. Ideally, people will show up with their spouses and maybe even their kids. Think about the power of mindshare. If your distributor's salespeople all show up with their partners, the partners hang out together. The partners are making friends with other partners who are all involved in selling your product. It has a sticky element that these sales reps are never going to want to leave your "family." They're never going to want to stop selling your product, because their partners will have friends who are the partners of other distributor reps from other countries, and they're going to say, "I want to go back to this meeting in two years." There's a huge element of power involved in having these meetings. They're very expensive, but they're very powerful for driving mindshare. I've had distributor meetings where people brought their kids. I did it in Miami, and people brought their kids and then took them to Disney World. Then their kids know me, and their kids remember the name of the company, and their kids are excited about this. So doing a distributor meeting in a place that you get families, you get wives, is a fantastic, powerful tool.

I will have the distributors pay for their flights and the hotel rooms where I'm doing it, but I will provide the meals and the entertainment. Before I go into the work part of it, let's talk about the fun part of it. I will have an awards dinner. That's a given, and the awards dinner is going to address all the different successes that the different distributors have had. The awards dinner, for me, is almost the most important part of this meeting. I will have different types of awards, because let's say I have a distributor from Saudi Arabia who's selling $6 million and I have a distributor from Jordan who's selling $600,000. There's no way that the Jordanian is ever going to get the biggest number, but I can give a prize for best growth. I can give a prize for the first company to sell a new product. I can give different prizes to different people.

You don't want to give just participation awards. You want there to be some meaning behind it, but you also want that feeling that these people will be pushing and competing to get an award. I had one distributor saleswoman who was a little bit older and very set in her ways. It was very difficult for her to get some of the new techniques and to sell our more highly priced products, but I kept encouraging her. This woman really was invested in the product even if she wasn't the best salesperson in the world. She really liked wearing amethyst jewelry, and I promised her once, "When you do xxx, I am going to give you an amethyst necklace the size of a baby's fist," and I told that to other people. Every time we had a meeting, I would call her up on the stage and give her something with an amethyst until she finally hit that big number and I did get her a giant necklace and presented it in front of everyone.

One year I was introducing a new product line. The new product was much more expensive than the old product by a factor of 10, and everybody was scared of the new product. They were suddenly dealing with a totally different price point, a much more complex sale, different people in the customer organization, that type of thing. The first year, I chose a handful of salespeople who I knew were really sharp but who were also in some of the more affluent markets. I worked and coached them to sell one of the new systems before a distributor meeting.

At the meeting on the first night, I gave everybody who had sold the new product for the first time a trophy, and I gave everybody who had had their best year ever a trophy. Then I also awarded the biggest growth, the biggest sale of the year, and things like that. First thing the next day, in a meeting I said, "Everybody who got a trophy for selling the new product for the first time, please raise your left hand, and everybody who had their best year ever, please raise your right hand." Consistently around the room, everybody who raised their left hand also raised their right hand.

Then I said, "If you didn't sell the new product this year, take a look around at everybody else, and now you can understand the value of selling the new product. Over the next couple of days, I'd really like it if you tried to chat with the people who have sold the new product and see what they have to say about how easy it was for them, what they needed to know, etc." I also arranged lots of activities that brought the people into contact over the next few days, so that people would talk to each other. By the next year, every one of my distributors had sold the more expensive product, and my sales of the lower-priced product dropped dramatically. The overall number in terms of revenue of the company shot up a few hundred percent in that year just based on the fact that we were driving the distributors to sell this more expensive product that they had been very hesitant about.

I would almost say that the key to that year's sales was the dinner where people got awards and then that next morning where the correlation between having your best year ever and selling the new product sank in. These are the types of things you want to do with the distributor meeting that are really almost intangibles, because you say, "We're getting people together. We will train them on this, we will do this." What's really important is this element of social life.

I like to control every piece, pretty much every minute of this distributor meeting. I remember having a huge argument with my boss years ago over one of these. It was funny. She was really into things like working on the menu. She would spend a lot of her time dealing with the menus of all the different meals and stuff like that, and I said, "I just don't care about the menus." But I was dealing with the details of things like the social events we were doing, and that part drove her nuts.

She said, "Let's just get an event planner to do this," and I said, "I don't trust the event planner to get me what I really want." This sales meeting drove my boss crazy and really, by the end of it, she hated me, but it was fantastic for driving sales.

I had a game day that was based on *The Amazing Race,* where I took teams of four and five people and had them do essentially a scavenger hunt around the greater Miami area. They had to get a picture of an alligator. They had to catch a fish from a river. They had to learn how to salsa dance. They had to learn how to mix a rum drink. They had to win $25 worth of chips in a casino. They had to build a sandcastle. They were running around all day and they were having a lot of fun, and I set the teams. Every team had at least one person in it who had sold the new product. Effectively, what happened was you had a group of four or five people who didn't know each other, stuck in a car all day together doing this adventure, which was a lot of fun. It was strenuous.

It got the adrenaline running, but they had four or five hours of riding around in the back of a Jeep between missions where they could talk, and what they wanted to talk about was selling the new product. So by the end of that distributor meeting, everybody was sold on the idea that they could sell this new product, that it was going to be easy, that this was how they were going to make a lot of money next year, and that they would, by the next meeting, all win prizes. It was an incredibly valuable meeting from that perspective.

Aside from social events, what else do I do at these meetings? I hold trainings. Again, this was a little elaborate. It was the type of thing that drove my boss and a lot of people in my company crazy, but it was insanely effective. I did a really high-production game show on questions that were related to the sales deck for the new product. Basically, I wanted everybody to have memorized every element of the sales process and the sales deck that they were going to use to sell the new product, and the ones who learned it better got prizes. The grand prize was a brand-new iPad at the time when iPads were still very expensive. So there was an intense, tough competition for this.

In general, salespeople are extremely competitive, so when you get them together, you have to be watch out for injuries. I've gotten hurt myself during a game; I tore a muscle. I've seen a lot of people get hurt. We've had broken legs and broken arms and such, so you want to be as careful as possible. But getting that adrenaline running at the sales meeting really gets them to internalize the value of you as a company, the value of your product line, and how they're going to sell this product line.

These distributor meetings are an extremely powerful tool. They're going to be very expensive, but at the end of the day, they really pay off when you're trying driving huge growth.

Before you plan this meeting, it's important to ask yourself what your strategy is for next year, or for the next two years. I'm also going to use a little bit of the time to do one-on-one meetings with all the distributors because we have them together. We can do a funnel review, so this might not be the most fun part of it, but it's an opportunity also for the distributors. We can do the funnel review with my boss, maybe even with the CEO.

One of the other benefits of these distributor meetings is that it gives the distributors a chance to meet people from headquarters that they would otherwise never meet. The vice president of R&D is going to be there, as well as the head of finance, all sorts of product managers, etc. I want to get as much interaction between the distributors and the headquarters people as possible because this doesn't happen normally. Again, anything that is going to give the distributors a feeling that they are part of a family is going to be helpful for everybody.

After the distributors meeting, I sometimes take my best distributor of the year and his wife, plus my wife, for another two days at my expense to a hotel someplace for a little bit of extra face time and vacation. Again, that's another little added benefit of building up this bonding and this feeling of deep relationship between the distributors and the company.

## HQ meetings

We've spoken about how the regional manager meets periodically with the distributors and the head of international sales meets periodically with the distributors. These are parts of how we control and update what's going on in the territory with the distributors. The next level is to have team meetings where we evaluate everybody on an ongoing basis. This isn't only about competition; it's more about making sure that we're putting a few extra eyes on what we're doing. In most companies where I've done this, it's an annual thing or possibly twice a year. If somebody above the head of international sales feels the need or wants to get involved in this more often than once or twice a year, I think they should seriously examine their motivation because I believe it's a waste of time and counterproductive. If the CEO believes that he knows enough about international sales to want to get involved in a sales review on a monthly basis then he's probably mistaken, or he may need to replace his head of international sales. I've seen situations where the CEO, with no sales or international experience, wanted to have weekly phone meetings with the regional managers. This was a completely counterproductive activity driven by poor management skills.

For an annual or biannual sales review, I typically put everybody together: the CEO, the person (if there is one) between the CEO and the head of international sales, and other relevant people such as the VP of R&D or the VP of manufacturing. Depending on the company, you may have people from forecasting who need to be present. I see this annual meeting as inclusive in order to flow information.

The structure of the meeting should be to go through each territory; then summarize trends, political issues, major problems, major wins in the market over the previous year; and then go through the funnel. Most of the products I've dealt with over the years have been more than $200,000 per purchase order on average. So for me, doing a funnel review was a reasonable process going into every potential order. If you're dealing with products where the purchase order is $25 and you have a million of them a year, you won't review each one. What you want to be doing is reviewing how they're being sold to points of sale. For instance, you may be selling a thousand units to a chain of stores in Kenya; you would talk about that as one deal. I can see different industries or different markets where this system would simply not work, so it's not set in stone. Play around with it to find a way to make it work for your industry.

Having a global final review with people from outside the sales process once or twice a year can be valuable. Keep in mind that there are operational reasons that people need to be aware of. Your sales funnel and your sales forecast in a small to medium-sized manufacturing company poor forecasting can literally sink the company, so forecasting is very important. I had an aunt who was very well educated and very well traveled. She taught social work and had never worked in anything commercial or business related. Years ago, when I was very young, she asked me what I did when I wasn't in the field selling. At the time, I worked for a manufacturing company as a regional sales manager, and I told her a few things including forecasting. She asked me what I meant by forecasting. I said, "I have to forecast sales for the coming 12 months. We are dealing with a product with a 12- to 18-month sales cycle. We need to buy components for this about 12 months in advance from a dozen vendors all over the world, to make sure we have all of our components, and we may get paid as late as 12 months after we ship. Here we are, a company with a turnover of about $20 million. We have more than $2 million going out every month and we have to balance that against the money coming in every month, but we may pay for something today that we will effectively get paid for 36 months from now on the outside. So the more we can control our forecasting, the more likely we are to survive and thrive."

I think I astonished her with the complexity of the business process as much as she used to astonish me coming back from trips to Africa with pictures of animals. But that is the importance of forecasting. In my career, I have had many years when, using a funnel system, my forecasting was razor accurate, most of the time over 90%, when I had colleagues who didn't use a funnel system and whose forecasting was less than 80% accurate.

With these periodic meetings, it is very important for you as the head of international sales to control the tone and the flow of the meeting. I can guarantee that if you have six or seven regional managers, there will be one or two that don't like each other and will try to use the opportunity to embarrass the other in front of the senior brass of the company.

If this happens, it doesn't look good for anybody—not you or your team or your boss—so you want to try and control it. There will also be people from the company that will ask questions, typically related to them, that show a lack of understanding of what you do, and you want to answer them politely and try and steer them to information that is relevant and useful to them.

What do I mean by that? International sales management is one of those things that nobody understands and yet everybody thinks they understand. As Americans, many of us feel that we understand sales even if we've never sold anything, even Girl Scout cookies. And it seems like pretty much any American who has a passport and has taken his honeymoon to Paris believes that he has a great understanding of international markets. So what's often going to happen at these meetings is somebody is going to talk about something that they read in an article at one point or another, like "Are you sure that are distributor in India is of the right caste for people to be willing to work with them?" Or "I've heard that many people in South America don't like Argentinians; are you sure we should hire a regional manager from Argentina?" You just have to keep calm and answer the questions and not let the waste of time get to you. Most of these people are simply curious and interested in trying to help, but they also want to show off the little bits of knowledge they've acquired about the global market.

In these periodic meetings, I like to use those graphical tools that I talked about earlier. It gives people a solid feeling, for instance, when they can see the global funnel report graphically, and it's a good opportunity for me to matrix the various distributors and discuss it with people.

# Ongoing strategy or management sessions

Whether or not we do this with the group outside of our team or just within the team, periodically we will have to evaluate the direction we're taking in terms of our distributors, our messaging, and our markets. Continuing without evaluating how effective we are is never a good idea. On the other hand, changing direction without good reason is a disaster. I cannot possibly stress enough how important it is to not change direction without a good reason. Why am I mentioning this when it seems like it's probably common sense? Because we're dealing with something that a lot of people don't understand and conceivably see more or less as voodoo. People are always going to be coming up with ideas that to them make just as much sense as your strategy does. This is as good a time as any to discuss this.

We discussed in the beginning how we chose our markets. This is key to success in choosing and focusing on the correct markets. Every false market we throw investment into makes it that much harder for us to succeed. Every good market we don't put effort into makes it that much harder for us to succeed. As you start work, you will be constantly bombarded by people who want to distract you into alternative markets that you didn't plan on. Effectively, 99% of the time there will be no good reason to make this change. People within the company will discover that they have a friend who does business someplace, or they'll see a TV documentary about the growing economy of Rwanda, or they will decide they want to take a vacation with their wife to Japan and it might be a good idea for you to send them as a technical representative. It is very important for the success of your mission to push back politely but aggressively on all of this. The single biggest risk to global expansion doesn't come from outside the company; it comes from well-meaning but ill-informed people inside the company.

The same thing applies for distributors. As you start expanding internationally, people will discover that they have some family or friends with connections to people who distribute or who work in your target markets or other international markets. And you will be constantly bombarded with requests from everybody from board members to manufacturing line workers telling you why you should give distribution to a friend of theirs.

Again, it is critical to your success that you learn to avoid this as politely as possible, making it clear that this is completely off the table. This is one of those things that has aggravated me my whole life. I don't go down to manufacturing and tell the VP of engineering what type of oil he should use to lubricate this machinery, and I don't want somebody who doesn't understand my side of the business trying to tell me how to do international sales. I found that it is a slippery-slope disaster working with anyone that somebody in the company has a personal relationship with. To be fair, I will most of the time evaluate these recommendations, but it is almost 100% unheard of that somebody introduced me in this manner turns out to be somebody I want to work with as a distributor.

People who do not sell may be very confused by the whole concept of the sales process and sales forecasting. I found that I have this argument on a regular basis with new companies I work with. I worked recently for a company whose CEO was an engineer with an MBA. The first time we reviewed our sales funnel and talked about sales forecasts, he said something to the effect of "I don't believe it's possible to forecast sales. Sales isn't engineering." I said to him "Forecasting is literally in my contract. You are paying me to forecast. I believe forecasting is definitely something that's possible to do. I've been doing it for 20 years." Within a very short time, my forecasting with that company was at about 93% accuracy, whereas my colleague responsible for domestic sales, who didn't use the type of forecasting methodology I did, was coming in at about 76% accuracy.

At the end of these periodic meetings, there's a very good opportunity to talk about what the next year or years will bring and to generate some kind of statement that indicates buy-in from everybody. What I mean is something like "I'm glad we all had a chance to discuss this, and I believe we're all in alignment as to what our goals are for the coming three years." And see if they argue with you; at that point you have it in writing.

This is also an opportunity for the salespeople talk to headquarters people and vice versa about potential areas of friction and/or what might be needed to improve sales. As an aside, I like to tell my salespeople that it is their job to sell the current product and not to worry about what future products will be. I don't want my salespeople putting off sales or slowing down in a territory because they perceive that a new or better product that will be easier to sell and/or more profitable to sell will be coming out very shortly and they'd rather sandbag the market and wait for the new product.

That said, if we are designing a new product or new products, or if our company develops new products on a regular basis, I want my people involved in the product development discussions. This can be one of those areas of contention between sales, engineering, and marketing. Sometimes engineers may be not converse as well or internalize information received from a conversation as well as they might think they do. Salespeople typically are fixated on the last project they lost. So a not uncommon interaction between a salesman and a product managing engineer is the salesman saying, "I need the product to be blue or we'll never be able to sell any more of it" and the engineer believing that and thinking it is imperative to change the color of the product to blue, possibly with the effect of shifting the product roadmap around. As head of international sales, you need to moderate these conversations and make sure that you don't end up making major product changes based on a single sale that was lost because the regional sales manager was able to speak the loudest and most emotionally.

I've also discovered that I will need help from people within the company who might not necessarily be management or sales and might not really see money coming in from my sales into their pocket in the short term. So I'd like to really try and keep a good relationship, as much as possible, with the people from engineering, from shipping, from production, that kind of thing.

Remember in Chapter 1 I talked about having a pizza party? I have a pizza party once a year where I invite pretty much everybody from the company to have lunch in an auditorium or large meeting room. I bring in pizza from outside, and basically run up a projector with a short, looped presentation about our international successes and the needs of our international customers. It also covers why we might be asking for specific changes and why we're doing things the way we're doing them.

Very often, you're dealing with people on the administrative side or the manufacturing side or even the engineering side who aren't really aware of what you are doing. They're not thinking about the idea that people live in different time zones, so you say, "Our regional manager based out of Singapore and our regional manager based out of Egypt don't have overlap during the day. For the guy in Egypt, 8:00 a.m. Chicago time is actually toward the end of his day. If you get back to him by noon, he's actually off already and trying to spend a little time with his family. The guy in Singapore, if you get back to him at 10:00 a.m., he's already in bed for the night."

I like to give a very shallow lesson on cultural differences where basically I'm saying, "Here we're a very individualistic culture. We don't necessarily show overly strong amounts of respect to our leaders, that kind of thing, whereas in some countries, people won't argue with their boss—ever. People don't like to make decisions on their own. They like to have a group of people make a decision." We want to give people a basic idea of the differences in culture that we might be facing because they'll come and say, "How come when we asked this question, this guy won't answer? He says, 'I have to ask my boss.' This should be something he knows." And I get that a lot.

Many Americans don't truly understand that there are other cultures; they've spent their whole lives dealing with only Americans. So giving a very basic concept of this gives them a picture of the complexity of the things you do and what's involved with that.

What we're trying to show them is the value to the company and the value to them if we are successful internationally. If we can grow the top line of the company by 50%, if we can grow the value of the company by 100%, how will that impact them? And this is what we're working towards.

I used to keep track of how many manufacturing jobs were added at my company every year based specifically on international sales growth.

And I would say to people, "Last year we added 17 manufacturing jobs specifically because of the international sales growth. This year, we added 22 manufacturing jobs" and people got very excited about that. And in one place I worked for, the company would add a bonus to everyone's 401(k) account if international sales hit a certain target. One year, the only reason that we were able to get that bonus was because of international sales growth and the CEO was kind enough to mention that in an end-of-year letter to the whole staff. I made sure to talk about this to people and made sure that people were aware of it: "Change equals more money in your 401(k). There's reason to embrace it."

We're also not going to jump into a 100% change; we're dealing with incremental change. I've looked at sales improvements over the course of my whole life as lots and lots of little, incremental changes.

# Basic Concepts
# Processes drive sales and sales growth

The Funnel is the best graphical representation of sales opportunities. Used correctly it will give you most of the information that you need.

Running your workday and your team/ territory management around funnel management isn't a bad idea.

Setting a baseline is the hardest part, and you may find that you made mistakes, but better to be off than not set a baseline.

Your distributors will fight providing you information. Make it part of your agreement, and enforce it, terminate if needed.

Teach your team to use reports and CRMs. Enforce it.

Being in the field and interacting with the RMs and Partners is key.

Drive uniformity in structure of reports. It is key to scaling up.

# Meetings

If your product doesn't work well, try to keep your Partners separate. If your product works well, work to have your Partners socialize and cooperate.

Trainings and social events with Partners drive mind share.

Good salespeople are competitive. Leverage that to drive mind share.

The biggest danger to international sales is headquarters. Use strategy and planning meetings to protect your project.

# Chapter 7
# TRADE SHOWS

Trade shows are one of the most powerful and important parts of what we do. First of all, let me talk a little bit about the philosophy of trade shows, because what I find is that most people seem to be going to trade shows either for the wrong reasons or without a real strategy.

Why do I go to a trade show? For me, it's not so that random people can walk into my booth. I've never sold a product that really could be sold at trade shows. That said, a lot of products are the type of products that anybody could buy, and there are trade shows and conferences that are a really good fit for those types of products. But I'm typically selling B2B, complex products that go to a very specific group of people.

For the past three decades, at 95% of the trade shows I go to where I'm paying for the booth, my primary goal is to have meetings with people I already know or meetings with people that I've identified. Those people could be distributors or customers. But they are named individuals who I know I want to meet, and I've already planned those meetings and scheduled them. I find that at a trade show, unless you are selling a product that anybody can buy, having people walk into your booth randomly is an extremely poor way to spend money.

Obviously, there are exceptions to this. Imagine a conference of cardiologists and you sell a product that most cardiologists would be interested in, or a trade show specifically for the pipefitting field and you sell a pipefitting tool. This means anybody walking down the aisles of the trade show could conceivably be a customer for you, and then your show strategy would be very different from the strategy that you would have when you are selling the types of products I'm selling, or when you're looking to expand internationally.

In terms of utilizing trade shows for international expansion, particularly in an area where you are using distributors as your sales assets, most of the shows you attend where you pay for the booth are designed for manufacturers to meet with distributors. I would be surprised if there are any industries that don't have a few shows like this. In the industries that I am most familiar with—healthcare, telecommunications, and IT—there are large shows like this. The worldwide show is usually in Europe, and then there are big shows for Africa, the Middle East, Asia Pacific region, Latin America, and sometimes North America. North America is an outlier in this type of business because it's less common in my experience to have manufacturer-to-distributor shows in North America than it is to have manufacturer to end user shows.

I probably pay for four shows in a typical year. These are all global or territorial shows with the express purpose of meeting my existing or new distributors and a secondary goal of meeting with end users. Aside from those, I'll probably attend six to twenty small shows that are designed for local distributors to present in their local market to end users and I will be a guest at the booth.

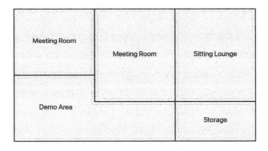

So let's start at the very beginning. When I know I will be entering into a market or territory and I will be looking for distributors, I will consider a show to be an important part of this activity. At this point in my career, there are very few shows that I attend that I haven't been to before. But let's say that's not the case. Let's say that I'm faced with three or four shows that are supposed to be the biggest shows for what I'm looking to achieve and they each advertise themselves as the global show or the European show for my particular industry and I don't know which one is better. So the very first thing I will do is get some people's opinions. I would ask the people from the US commercial office.

I'll start with this because I'll be talking over the course of the book about government people who can advise you. There will typically be somebody in Washington who is the lead for your industry. So, for instance, if you sell plumbing supplies, there is certainly a construction industry lead in the commercial office in DC, but there may even be a plumbing industry commercial lead in your city. These people are usually relatively accessible. You can find them on LinkedIn, or you can call the commercial office and explain what you're trying to do and who you're trying to find, and they will identify that person. As an aside, you really should know that person anyway; it is very helpful to know the key players in your industry in the US commercial office. You can ask this person what the value of each of the different shows is and that's one opinion, but a pretty good opinion.

If you know additional sales managers in your industry, call them and ask them. This is the type of thing people discuss and share a lot. You can check your competitors' websites and see what shows they will. You can actually check online to see who attended the various shows last year and get a feel for the number of attendees, the number of countries they came from, etc., but you can also see who the exhibitors were and if your relevant competitors were there. You can probably also see how big their booths were. If your biggest and most important competitor had a 50 meter booth at one show and a 12 meter booth at another show, that gives you an indication of how important they believe the different shows are.

Depending on your timeline, how much money you have, and what your short-term goals are, you should try to attend every show at least once as an attendee before you take your booth there. You never know from the marketing material exactly how good that show is going to be, and there's nothing that makes you feel stupid more than spending $25,000 to go to an awful show. I once almost went to a show that was advertised as a really great show. It was a European offshoot of a Middle Eastern show, and the Middle Eastern show was a great show that I had been attending for years. I decided just to visit and walk around, and I literally was the only non-exhibitor in the entire building for about 15 minutes. All the exhibitor salespeople came out of their booths to try and pull me in as I walked around. That's how empty the show was. I'm very happy that I decided to visit before I actually spent money.

Once I've decided where I want to show this year and I know what my goals are for each show, I will figure out what kind of budget I have for each one. At the end of this chapter I will talk a little bit about techniques if you are working on a shoestring budget, but I will hold off on that and start with the way I would normally handle a show in a good situation.

I will decide on what type of the booth I want based on my product and my goals. With some shows, it doesn't really matter; I will have to start with what the show will give me. The best shows are typically sold out year after year, so they aren't going to give you a good spot if you're exhibiting for the first time. The best way around that is to go with the US commercial pavilion if there is one or even a state pavilion, although most states won't be able to give you much space. I would say you go with the state when you are on a shoestring budget and you cannot afford a booth—or just to get a better location. The other advantage with going with the US commercial pavilion is often you do not want to be next to your biggest competitor. If they have a giant booth and you have a small booth, when you are next to each other it's easy to compare. If you are a midmarket US manufacturing company, you may show in six or ten shows in the US and three shows internationally, but your biggest competitor in Europe or Asia may only show once, so they're putting all of their budget into a giant, elaborate booth and if you have a booth that will make you look small. Of course, going with a pavilion will also be easier in terms of the logistics.

If you have a standalone booth, you will want to understand the traffic pattern of the trade show building. This is another reason that walking trade shows can be helpful for you before you buy your first booth. If you don't walk the trade show, you at least want to look carefully at the map and get a feel for how traffic flows. I go to a trade show every year with hundreds of thousands of visitors and thousands of booths spread out over 18 very large buildings. If you are 20 meters off the main pathway, you will get about half as much traffic as somebody who is in that pathway, and you might not be paying significantly less for your booth. How can you tell from a map? Typically, you can see where the doorways of the different buildings are, and when the doors, for instance, of three buildings all line up, you know that along that line there will be heavy traffic. This may also not be relevant for you if your goal is not to get passersby into your booth, but it will make it easier for your invited guests to find you if you are on a good path.

Either with the standalone booth or a booth as part of some other sponsoring organization, you want to make sure you're in the right building or pavilion. Some big trade shows will have, as an example, six buildings, and each one is dedicated to a group of similar products. Then they will have two or three buildings that are for national pavilions, and then they may have an additional two or three buildings for people who signed up too late or it's their first year or the organizers just think they don't need to treat them fairly. Those last buildings are the ones that will get the least traffic and the traffic from the least important potential customers.

Assuming that we've figured out what hall we want to be in and we've gotten a pretty good position in that hall, let's think about what we want our booth to look like. Let's take two extremes as examples. I've had booths where it was pretty difficult to tell what we did, and they weren't inviting at all for passersby, but they did have very good meeting rooms and my goal for the show was to have quiet, comfortable meetings. So it was a perfect booth for me. As an aside, I found that it was actually important to write on the walls what it was that we did because otherwise people would get too curious and come to the booth and interrupt our meetings to ask what we did.

In a booth like this, I would have two enclosed and relatively quiet meeting rooms that would hold about eight people, because I found that it wasn't uncommon for distributors to come with four people and sometimes I would want to pull in one or two other people from my side for a meeting. I would also have a demo area that wasn't visible from outside or from the aisles, where we could do demos and discussions about the actual product for the people who came into our booth. It is very difficult to avoid having product in your booth unless what you sell is just so big and unwieldy that everybody understands why you don't have it there. One of the products I sold was very difficult technically to set up and get running in the booth, so we always had to bring a technical person just for that. That became very expensive. On top of that, over 10 years she screwed it up for various reasons three times, so what we found was we might spend $10,000 to add a demo to our booth, spend 48 hours frantically trying to get it set up before opening the booth, and then not even have a working demo.

My solution to that was to put in place large flat-screen TVs with some very good video options, and then very good animation and actual pictures of the product could be maneuvered 360°, so by using technology we were able to avoid having any real demo for several years in our booths. That just made life a lot easier, but this really is dependent on what you're showing what stage you are in the market. Keep in mind that if you are new to the market and/or you have technology that people haven't seen before, not having a physical demo will probably hamper building trust. It will make you seem a little suspect.

Most of the meetings I have had in recent decades at trade shows have really been about my distributors. And as I will mention this rule in another chapter, but if you're not sure about the quality of your product, you don't want your distributors talking to each other, but if you're confident in the quality of your product, you want to encourage your distributors to share information.

For me, it is very important that my distributors consider me sort of a home away from home or their most important, closest principal to their heart. This is key to my overall strategy. Your distributors will represent multiple products—in some cases, maybe as many as a thousand product lines. The more valuable you are to them in a wide range of ways, the closer you are to their heart; the more they feel part of your family, the more they're going to sell for you. You can't always be the easiest and most profitable product for your distributors to sell, but with a small amount of investment you can be the principal they like the most.

For years I have put a small lounge/waiting room in my booths for distributors. It adds to the expense and it can sometimes add to the work, but the return on investment is enormous. Picture a booth that is divided into four: two meeting rooms, one video room with a deck and videos to do presentations, and one room with two couches and a coffee table, a water fountain, and a chair that my distributors can come and hang out in. Additionally, I make sure there is enough comfortable storage for my distributors to leave their bags and coats in my booth. If you come in within an hour of opening time at a big trade show or you leave within an hour of closing time, you will wait 15 minutes to half an hour in line for the cloakroom. Your option then is to carry your bag and your coat around all day, and it can be pretty uncomfortable. So if you let all of your distributors' salespeople know that they can leave their coats and bags in your booth, they will always come to you first thing in the morning and last thing in the afternoon. Again, if your goal is to make them feel part of your family—and I'll give you a hint: yes, that is your goal—this is an excellent investment of money if you can afford it.

Let's think about a different type of booth for a different type of industry. So let's say that your product could be sold to anybody who comes in and anybody could be a business partner for you. That booth might look totally different. You might want a booth that's very inviting and encourages people to come in to see your product. Again, depending on your product, you might have a lot of actual physical product around the booth or you might have other props that can be used to demonstrate your product. Years ago I sold some laboratory equipment that was about as exciting as oatmeal and it really didn't look different from anybody else's equipment. At the trade show I filled everything up with colored water (using food color) and about half of the products had movement, so there was swirling and sloshing colorful water around the booth, which created a very attractive and inviting environment.

If you're showing and demoing or explaining to passersby what you do, then you might want to set up as many positions as possible that are designed for people to come in to see the product. I find that the tables that are about four feet tall are a perfect platform to discuss and display small physical objects, and you can also use a tablet or a screen to present PowerPoint and videos on a table like that. Again, depending on the size of the booth, the amount of traffic you expect, etc., you may have one position like that or you may have eight.

When the goal of your booth is to attract people to come in, the design will typically be very different from the type of booth that is designed specifically for meetings. This is probably the first thing to think about: making sure that you know what your booth looks like from every angle and especially from the angles with the most foot traffic. When we design a booth before the show, we are often focusing on the wrong angles as it relates to direction of traffic. I am not a designer, but from an aesthetic perspective, I like light-colored booths because of their ability to be attractive to traffic. Most of the time that I've been with good companies, we have had a color scheme and we have used that color scheme on a light blue, white, or light gray, which I believe is very attractive to passersby.

Of course, not all booths are one or the other, and often we will want a booth that will be somewhat attractive to passersby, will allow us to do demos and presentations, but will also have meeting space. Instead of having three meeting rooms, we could have one meeting room and one large demo area.

One more thing about design is the text on your graphics. Keep in mind that people might see thousands of booths over the course of a day, depending on the size of the show. Depending on how much frontage you have and where you are and how fast people will go by, you really can only expect that they will be looking at your booth for a couple of seconds. So your graphics should be clear, especially the ones visible from the outside of your booth. You want people one way or another, whether they're coming in or not, to understand what the name of your company is and what it is, more or less, that you do. If they are potential business, that will drive them in. If they aren't potential business, that'll keep them out (so they don't waste your time), but if they don't know what you do, there's a chance that they'll come and ask what you do and interrupt your real meetings.

With graphics inside the booth, you pretty much can go wild from an aesthetic perspective. Simple might be better, but I've seen some really great and effective uses of very heavy verbiage on the walls inside the trade show booth. For instance, a really smart salesman wanted us to print the names of all the great reference sites in his territory on the inner walls of the meeting room in the booth. The idea was that people would sit there and see an almost endless list of sites and customers and would realize how serious we were and what a great installed base we had. It was a very effective tool.

I am a big fan of pounding home specific messages to my sales team, customers, and distributors. There's a great story about Cato the Elder in ancient Rome, who used to end every speech with "Carthage must be destroyed." Even when he was having lunch with friends and they started talking about different-quality figs and what their prices were and where he could buy them, when they were done with the conversation Cato said, "Carthage must be destroyed."

I think repetition is a very powerful tool for sales and training. For instance, if I have an overriding strategic goal that involves getting my distributors to shift from a lower-end product to a higher-end product (let's call it the R5), I will put a powerful, simple slogan about that new product on every surface in the booth. Then when people are sitting in the booth, they look at the wall and will be reminded for instance that "last year every distributor salesman who exceeded quota also sold his first R5" or "all the top-performing distributors last year sold their first R5." The idea is that if my distributors are in the room chatting and relaxing, they're going to see the slogan and maybe it'll burn a little bit into their subconscious.

So we have a booth design, we've chosen the booth, we've chosen the location, we've chosen the show. What's next? Let's think about who from our team should be at that show, and again this comes down to identifying our goals. For most shows I go to, the overriding goal is to meet my existing distributors, review their funnels, and talk to them about the coming year's strategy. My secondary goal is to meet new potential distributors and discuss with them the possibilities of working together in their territory. My third goal is to meet with unscheduled distributors from specific countries who may come by the booth. I will address the issue of unscheduled drop-ins later. For now, let's talk about my first two goals.

If what I want is to meet with scheduled people, the key person for those meetings is me. If we are so busy that we will be running parallel meetings, the people who can run parallel meetings are important to have. If I am meeting partners who work with regional managers from specific territories, the correct thing to do is to have those RMs in those meetings. This means we need all the sales assets who typically will be running or participating in the final review meetings with scheduled partners.

We also need somebody just to take care of the booth while the meetings are going on. On the other hand, that could be a position to outsource. If all that person is going to do is get coffee and water and make sure people don't bother you while meetings are going on, you can probably get a local person for less money than if you bring somebody with you. But if you need somebody who's going to do demos at least some of the time, you probably want to bring somebody with who you trust to do these demos.

Another viable option is to ask your distributors' salespeople to each put in a shift at the show. Keep in mind that if you're doing a trade show in

Frankfurt, for example, the cost of every person you bring is going to be probably about a month's salary for a salesperson when you take into account flights, hotels, and the opportunity cost of keeping them off a normal work week, so you want to keep the number of people at the booth as exact as possible. You don't want to have too few people, but you also don't want to have too many people and waste money. Most big trade shows can cost a company $100,000 or more, which really can be a little crazy.

Depending on how complicated what you're showing is, you may very well have a technical person at the booth to keep the demos going and to manage the IT. When something goes wrong at a trade show, it's almost always related to technology. When you're trying to show how reliable a product you have, if it doesn't perform correctly in the demo you could be completely defeating the purpose of the demo, and you may be doing a lot more damage than you would by having a good narrative with a video and a PowerPoint and talking about your solution. But you have to weigh how important it is. There are certainly a lot of products and a lot of industries where you simply can't avoid having a working demo in the booth.

If one of your goals is having passersby come into the booth, you need to have enough salespeople staffing the booth to cover this. I have a family member who had a great rule for taking kids to the pool: they needed a number of adults that was equal to the number of children plus one. That is sort of what you want for the trade show. If you will have three demo positions, you're probably going to want four salespeople on duty at all times. If you have eight demo positions, you will want to have nine salespeople, etc. If you're dealing with a four-day show, that is eight hours a day and the expectation is that you will be entertaining at night (which is as strenuous, if not more so, than booth duty), you probably want 1.3 to 1.5 people for every person you need on the booth at any given time. So if you have eight demo positions, you will need nine salespeople, a booth administrator, a technical person, and anybody who's going to be involved with business meetings at that time. So let's say you have 12 people on the booth; you will want a team of 18. Now that's giant for just starting out, but it really depends on your industry. If what I'm looking for is mostly meetings, then I will probably have a three-person or a four-person team, and I might get a local person to serve water and coffee and keep strangers out of my booth.

If three regional managers are coming in and between them they have 20 distributors coming to the show, each one of those regional managers is going to need time spent away from the booth with their distributors. Going back to what I said before, if what we want is that the distributors consider us their most important or favorite principal, then we will have to entertain them and spend time with them at the show. This could be an expensive proposition, and it might not be a strategy that you're in a position to pursue right now, but this is where you want to be eventually.

The return on investment for every beer you buy at the show is astronomical. If you have three regional managers and you believe that they're going to have to have lunch with their people every day (or they're going to be out drinking very late every night), plan for this in the schedule. It might be that the regional managers don't have any booth time aside from when they have final review meetings with their distributors. Again, it all comes down to what your budget is and how much you are able to invest in the market. I happen to have very good stamina and I love trade shows, so I'm typically okay with this, but there is no shame in building the schedule around people's abilities and strengths.

I had a great sales manager once, who had fantastic relationships with his channel partners and end users. At trade shows, he would go out drinking all night, and he would be exhausted the next day. The first year I worked with him, I had tried to use this important trade show as an opportunity to have a strategy meeting with several other VPs from

HQ. This sales manager came to the meeting completely exhausted and got into a huge argument with somebody over something irrelevant and broke down in a very emotional display driven by complete physical exhaustion. Picture a middle aged top performing sales shark, with tears streaming down his face yelling at a marketing person over a poorly designed brochure, with me trying to separate them and keep the meeting going.

After that year I realized that it is important to take into consideration the energy and work required to entertain, as well as the different stamina and energy levels each one of us has. And, if we go back to the strategic value of the trades show – what we are trying to do is build mind share, and so the late night entertaining is more important than the strategy meeting.

Some of your distributors and customers will probably want to go out drinking. You have to decide how much of that you will do and how much you will shift onto other people on the team. I'm enjoy drinking and I love my distributors, but it's critical for me to have a clear head for final review meetings so I will be careful about how much drinking I do at night.

Who else am I going to have along? Trade shows are an excellent opportunity for people in your company to get to know foreign markets, partners, and end users as well as competition. I love to have a competitive intelligence person on my team, but not all companies can afford that. A reasonable alternative is to have a part-time business intelligence consultant working for me. One way or another, it's good if I can have somebody from competitive intelligence at a trade show. It's a great way to gather information about competitors. Most cities with large trade shows have companies that will offer the services of competitive intelligence people. Often your competitors may know your competitive intelligence person if he's been with your company for a while, so using a local person who is unknown can be helpful.

I love to bring along people from product development so they can get a feel of the market and our competitors. These people can take a role on the trade show booth as well. They may not be able to sell, but they can answer questions and probably do a demo, and they can be used for a lot of the booth activities if I'm already paying to bring them out. They can probably cover all of my competitors in one day and then in the evenings or at meals still have a chance to talk to my distributors to get more market insights. The rest of the time they're pretty much free, which means I can utilize them for something at the booth. Alternatively, I might just bring them in for just one day if the show is in a place where hotel rooms are very expensive. For instance, I go to a trade show in Düsseldorf (Germany) that overtakes the city, and hotel rooms are extremely expensive. For that show it makes sense to bring in four different engineers from headquarters, each for one day, so that they only use a single hotel room even though their flights will be expensive.

If I'm the head of international sales, I may also bring in the overall head of sales to meet the distributors. It really doesn't pay for the head of sales to travel around the world too much; the return on investment usually isn't that great. But bringing them to a trade show once a year to meet all the distributors is a great return on investment. I might even bring out the CEO or other members of senior management. An excellent person to bring out is the head of R&D. It's great for the distributors to meet these people and it's great for these people to get a feel for our markets and to put faces with names of people we do business with.

There is a danger here that these people won't know how to talk to distributors or customers or international people, and it may be difficult to keep them from unintentionally doing harmful things. If a distributor asks the VP of R&D for a product change and the VP smiles and says something like "That makes sense, let's see," your distributor may very well think it's a done deal, while your VP may think he was just being polite. It is critical to avoid those types of mistakes. The best way to do this is provide a good briefing for the people who aren't usually in sales. (I speak about this in depth in Chapter 1).

Let's talk about the timeframe of a show. The first thing we're doing is figuring out what our strategy is because that's going to drive everything. Are we going to be at the show? Is it worthwhile to spend our money on this show? What type of booth are we going to have? Who are we going to bring? Once we have decided those things, we will engage a booth designer. Again, I've been talking like I am made of money. Our booth may also just be a fold-up stand 9 feet across, and I've certainly been to dozens of shows with a booth like that.

We will decide on marketing material that we will take to the show, and that will be based on strategy and what we are trying to achieve. Maybe we have 20 products in the company but we are only focusing on two. We may be focusing on all 20, we may really not be addressing the general public and passersby, or maybe that's the focal point of our attendance. These things will drive our marketing material.

A quick word about marketing material at trade shows. People are always burdened with too much, and when you give them paper there's a solid chance they're going to throw it away. Instead you can give them a way to download material from the internet, such as a barcode that they can scan that will lead them to a Dropbox, or flash drives with your company logo and telephone number on it that are loaded with the material you want to give them. All of this comes down to making a cost-benefit analysis of how many people you believe will come to your booth or that you're interested in giving material to. But most of the paper that you hand out won't make it out of the trade show city.

In terms of giveaways, I would say that there are two types that I like. One is directly relevant to your product. For instance, if you want to give somebody a lot of white papers, you give him a flash drive full of material. I also love to hand out things that people can give to their kids. A lot of people fly in for trade shows, fly out, don't have a chance to do any shopping, and feel guilty about it. The big trade show facilities often have toys stores or souvenir stores specifically to address this issue. So if you make available or give something that your prospect can take home, that's actually very nice. I'll tie those two things together. I've been in medical product sales for a very long time, and one of my favorite giveaways is a flash drive with a little Lego-type figure of a nurse or doctor. I can give that customer a flash drive full of material, he can take it home, download the material, and then give the little toy to his child. People seem to love those. I'm always trying to avoid buying anything to give out that I think is going to get thrown away, obviously. I'm trying to get the best investment in the trade show.

As we approach the time for the trade show, I need to be sure to ship what I need for the booth. In a lot of cases, I can get the booth built by a designer based in the city where it's needed. For instance, if I will the same trade show in Dubai every year, my booth is going to be built and designed by somebody in Dubai and then stored. You do want to check the shipping and storage costs because it's actually sometimes cheaper just to throw out the booth every year and rebuild it than to ship it or store it.

I learned a long time ago that I should have a disaster recovery plan. With modern technology, this is actually pretty simple. In most cities with major trade shows, if your booth gets lost or stolen or damaged, with a credit card you can replace it in 24 hours or at least get something reasonable put up. On a flash drive in my pocket and in the cloud, I like to have all my graphic files as well as files that that could be helpful if I had to throw together an emergency booth.

Years ago I used to carry a fold-up back-up booth to every show I went to. This really isn't a bad idea even today, but it may be a little bit of overkill. Likewise, if you believe that having a demo is critical to your success at the trade show and you're shipping it by air, you should carry a spare with you in your suitcase or preferably your carry-on. I've found that things like the right cables or the right adapter may be critical for your demo and I'll carry a spare set of those, as well. In some cases, with medical products, communication products, or IT products, you might need things that aren't going to be available in every hardware store. This means that if one of those things gets lost, you need to be able to have a backup for anything that you don't believe you will be able to replace in 12 hours that is mission-critical.

There are shipping agents who typically work trade shows. Like rock concerts, trade shows are very specific for shipping. Going back to a theme that I hit multiple times in this book, your shipping guy probably doesn't know how to ship product to an international trade show and get it there successfully. So you really want to be working with somebody who can do this confidently and can get the product in and out safely. You don't want to show up at the trade show and have your stuff either get lost or held up and cost you a show because you are saving money shipping with somebody who doesn't know what to do. This is incredibly common, and your people will probably find it insulting that I'm suggesting they don't know how to do this, but they have to suck it up. It is critical that you get what you need in place on time for the trade show, and you can't have a messed-up show if you want to keep people happy.

In the time leading up to the trade show we need to make sure that nobody is going to surprise us from the team that is going. I like to give people about 90 days' notice that they're expected to come to the show. Again, if they're not mission critical, I will make it clear that they can opt out but that they should let me know so I can replace them if I need that spot. That gives them time to make sure they have passports and visas if needed and that they don't have a conflict.

I send out a briefing document a week or two before the show. The document starts out by clarifying our primary mission (and if there are secondary and tertiary missions) for this trade show and how they tie to our overall company and department strategy. This is critical because you want to make sure that people know what we are trying to achieve and why they're coming to the show. If you have salespeople who aren't very strategic (and that isn't meant to be an insult—there are a lot of salespeople like that) or you are bringing technical people or non-salespeople to the show, your strategy may be confusing to them or fit their expectations. You don't want to have this discussion on the booth at the site. If they have questions or they disagree with on anything, you want to have this discussion before you leave home.

Next, the document will address things like target markets. I might say that my tertiary goal is to meet distributors from five countries that I have identified in advance of this meeting, and if they come to the booth they should be treated a certain way. Let's say I already have a distributor in Saudi Arabia that I have no intention of switching at this time, and so a dozen people will come to my booth who are distributors from Saudi Arabia. They should be treated politely and we will collect their cards, but we don't really want to waste time and effort on them. But I am very interested in getting a distributor for Oman. So if a distributor from Oman comes into the booth, I might specify in the briefing document that someone needs to grab his card and try to schedule a meeting. I may even say this target is important enough to interrupt me in a meeting that I'm in.

In the briefing document, I will also talk about how we treat our competitors. At trade shows I like to be very courteous with my competitors, but I don't want them interrupting or disrupting my routine business. I've actually had this happen to me at trade shows where salespeople from my distributors have disrupted meetings that I've been having with end users. I want to give my people guidelines for what to do when competitors come to the booth. Typically, I like to invite them to come back the following morning before the show starts, and I promise to give them a demo. That way I can give them a controlled demo without any end users around. I can control what we show them and what we don't show them. I'm being courteous but I'm also getting them off my booth.

I will be very clear in the briefing document about dress code. I'm sending the document out a week or two weeks before the show, so this allows enough time for people to get anything that they might not have. For me, how people dress on my booth, how people look, is something that I want to control. Sometimes I've been with companies where everybody wears khakis and a matching golf shirt. That's perfectly fine, but that's typically not my dress code. Whatever the dress code is, I want everybody to know about it early enough so if there's something missing, they can replace it or they can tell me and I can make a decision whether I will allow that exception or not.

I'm also going to outline how I want people to act on the booth. I don't want them using their phones or eating or drinking on the booth. It's been a long time since anybody thought it was acceptable to smoke in the booth, but I used to tell people not to smoke on the booth as well. At some shows we drink water and coffee and at some I have beer, depending on the market. But all of that is going in the briefing document so people are aware of this ahead of time.

I will typically make a schedule telling people when they're expected on the booth. That may go out with the briefing document or more likely it will go out a few days before the show. I like to distribute the stress so that not everybody is getting up early every day and working late every day, and I also believe that everybody appreciates knowing in advance that they're going to have a few hours for sightseeing and shopping. Everybody who comes to a trade show and doesn't come to that city on a regular basis is thinking about how they're going to get sightseeing in, and if you don't give them a schedule with a block of time for sightseeing, there's a pretty good chance that they will be thinking about it on the booth and/or trying to sneak out, and really you want to avoid that. If you know your people well, you could also set it up so that they have the same breaks as the people they are friendly with.

Once we get to the week of the show, I like to stagger the way people travel. Having exhibited at hundreds of shows over 30 years, I have seen every kind of problem. So if you put everybody on a plane, I'm not so worried about that plane crashing, but let's say they connect to an airport where there's a strike. Then you have half the team not make it. (That's better than the whole team not making it!) I like to get to the destination city (or have somebody else in charge get there) about 36 hours before we start building the booth. That's just me, but I like to be on site just in case problems come up, and I take that opportunity to check on all the entertainment and make sure all is set.

Let's talk about extracurricular entertainment. If I have a booth at a trade show and I have distributors or even if I'm just starting out and I'm interviewing distributors, I am going to have at least one meal that I invite people to. In the early years this might not be a very impressive dinner party, but I've had many years where I've had 50 to 100 people at my dinner table at a trade show. Entertaining people for dinner and for drinks or other activities is key to the rapport and relationship building at trade shows. Going back to my strategy of having distributors meet each other, talk to each other, and share ideas, this is an excellent opportunity. As a matter fact, at some trade shows I'm hosting a dinner every night for different groups of distributors just because there are always different meals and parties going on and if somebody can't make my party one night, I want to give them another option. In cities where there are large trade shows, getting restaurant reservations for 12 people can be very difficult; when you're looking at 70 people, it can be really difficult.

The cornerstone of my philosophy is that business entertaining isn't about me—it's about business. So most of the time, I'm choosing food that I might not choose for myself. I'm choosing it because I believe it will create a good experience for my distributors and any end users that will be there.

My biggest trade show is in Düsseldorf, Germany. I will have distributors there sometimes from as many as 40 countries and some of them will be from the Middle East. What I found was that the people from the Middle East who are Muslims don't want to be in a restaurant that serves pork. Most of them will be fine if there is wine on the table, but they're very concerned that if the kitchen serves pork, the server might accidentally serve them pork or something that touched the pork. So every year I have one evening where we go to a Lebanese restaurant that is halal and doesn't serve any pork. That is comfortable for everybody. The atmosphere is very familiar, and this particular restaurant always has a belly dancer, which people enjoy. I've been getting a reservation for 25 to 70 people at this restaurant year after year for very close to 30 years. Every year I make my reservation for the following year the night I'm having dinner. So at this particular trade show, every year on the second night we go to an Italian restaurant, on the third night we have Lebanese, and the fourth night we have German. Every year I make the reservations for the following year. And there will be some overlap. Some people will eat dinner with me three nights that week and some will only join for one night, but they all know that those are the options and those are all good restaurants and they're all very good experiences. I started this practice in my 20s when my boss didn't have restaurant reservations one night and we couldn't sit down with the distributor and his wife for dinner—very embarrassing. I never wanted that to happen again and I've never had to experience that again.

Obviously, if you're new to this trade show, you can't do that, but you can reach out to the concierge of your hotel before you arrive or to the local tourist bureau to look for recommendations for restaurants and make reservations. You can also take the opportunity the day before the show to visit the restaurants and check them out. If you don't like them, see if you can find an alternative. The first years, you probably won't have such a big party so you might not have a problem finding restaurants that will accommodate you. Over the course of the trade show you can scout out places that will be good for following years.

Another thing that I will do the day before the show is the various administrative tasks, like making sure we have badges for everybody and have the communications devices we need. That issue is getting to be less common because everybody has a cell phone, but in some places, you might need Wi-Fi scratch cards or something like that. I will oversee and possibly participate in the building of the booth. Again, that really depends on where you are and what type of company you have and what your budget is. For a long time now, I haven't actually had to get down on my knees with a screwdriver to build a booth, but I have certainly done it dozens of times, and sometimes that's what you have to do the first few years before you hire somebody to build your booth. Some companies do that forever because that's just the way they are. But you want to make sure that everything goes correctly and that there are no problems. At more than a few trade shows, I've ended up having to make an emergency hardware store run because something broke or something was stolen or something didn't make it. I always make sure that we have a set of tools on the booth just in case; you never know what types of crazy things can happen.

I like to have what I call message boards at a trade show. This isn't my invention. I was introduced to this by somebody I worked with more than 20 years ago at a trade show, and it's a great idea. Let's say we have the key message that we're presenting, a key benefit that is what we're strategically interested in talking about this year, that goes on the message board. We might have eight of those messages, although that would be a little much.

As a sales organization we might tell the company's origin story or possibly the product origin story where we are telling the world how much we sell, etc. It is critical at an international trade show that everybody on your team is telling the same narratives in terms of these types of fact. Why? Because you are building trust and rapport with the new market and nobody trusts you to begin with—it's as simple as that. For American manufacturers that have solid market share and a reputable reputation at home, this is always surprising, but nobody knows you internationally. People are looking to figure out if they can trust you, and even if they have been doing business with you for a while, trust is always a key issue. I worked for a company whose founder had essentially founded a half-dozen companies over a 15-year period. And at one point they sort of merged and were cleaned up and became one company. Crazy as this sounds, there wasn't really agreement on what year the company was founded. So you could go on a trade show booth and one person would say the company was founded in 1919, somebody else would say 1947, and somebody else would say 1925. When people hear that, they find the whole company a little suspicious. So the founding year goes on your message board. Likewise, what do we tell people if they ask us what our annual sales are, what our market share is, or what some of our best reference sites are. Documenting these on the message board and then using them in the morning briefing is a very powerful tool for consistency of messaging on the booth.

I also like to tell people how they should greet people who come to the booth. I hate to say it this way, but don't assume that your people who aren't in sales will act in a way that seems reasonable to you on a trade show booth. So don't give them too much leeway. Give them guidance, and usually they will be fine with that guidance.

For instance, I tell people a good greeting is "May I give you some information about our product line today?" Or "Are you a customer of our product?" And I give people a very basic script. I don't want to make them feel uncomfortable or stilted, but for instance I tell them I want to make sure that they ask people where they're from within about 15 seconds, because if they are a distributor from a country where we're very happy with our distributor, I don't necessarily need to waste time on them. If they are a competitor, I want to treat them one way, and if they are a distributor from a country where I may be looking for a distributor, I'll treat them a different way. If somebody who is already using my product comes in, I'd like to greet them and talk to them and make them feel special.

In this briefing I will also go over the rules that I put in the briefing document. Again, never underestimate the stupidity of people. You want to make sure they know that they're not supposed to do things like eat at the booth if that's your rule. I also like to reinforce what Ray Kroc, the founder of McDonald's, is said to have repeated: "If you have time to lean, you have time to clean." I am fanatical about a clean and orderly booth. I hate seeing a booth where things look disorganized.

Now considering that I already said that I invite my distributors to hang out at my booth, these are two very conflicting positions because given the chance, the distributors will make my booth look like a pigsty, so I and everybody on my team are constantly cleaning and organizing the booth.

When I'm running the booth, I like to be there every morning at opening and most days when it closes because I like to do both the briefing in the morning and a quick discussion at the end to summarize how the day went.

Around the booth during operating days, there are a few things that I'd like to have out, but typically I try to put them in places where they're handy but not completely visible to passersby, just to keep the booth looking neat. For obvious reasons, I like to keep hand sanitizer very easily available around the booth. A few times a day I'll just yell out, "Everybody use hand sanitizer." I will put out high-quality, mass-produced ballpoint pens, something like a Pilot, so that everybody who needs a pen has one whenever they need it. Don't confuse this with giveaways; I just want to make sure that if somebody needs to write something down, they have a pen.

I write certain key points on notepads before the show and put the pads on clipboards around the booth so that if somebody does come in or if somebody's in a meeting, I'm not dependent on whether or not that individual has a pen and pad and I don't have to worry about information getting lost. If, for instance, I have a high priority of finding a new distributor from India at this trade show, I will put a note in a contrasting color on the pad saying, "Remember: we're looking for a distributor from India." Just in case somebody walks in the booth and I don't talk to them but somebody else does, I want to make sure that the people talking to the passersby who do come in are following my procedures and my priorities.

I'll also spread boxes of mints around the booth. I'm a big believer that salespeople should consume eight or ten mints every day during the trade show. You never know when your breath is a little off and you're not noticing it.

I use a position that I call booth captain. Nine times out of ten, when I'm at a trade show I'm the booth captain, the person with the ultimate responsibility for the success or failure of the show. That person is responsible for the team and for everything running smoothly. As VP of international sales or the managing director of an international sales unit, I also would attend shows where one of my regional managers was the booth captain. If the show was Middle East–specific and I trusted the Middle East RM, I would make sure that he was booth captain.

What does the booth captain do? Well, pretty much everything I've talked about until now comes down to decisions that rest on the booth captain: what shows to attend, what are the strategic goals of that show, what type of team do we need for that show, what type of booth, how do we design the booth, etc. The booth captain sets the schedule and typically is going to be on the booth all the time. The booth captain sets the message boards. Of course, depending on the size of the company, it's very possible that the booth captain won't actually be taking a marker and actually making the message boards, but he will be coming up with the strategic guidelines for those messages. Many times I've had people over me in rank at a booth, but my expectation is that if my

CEO is on my booth and I'm the booth captain, he's my asset while he's on the booth. Likewise, I expect my RM to treat me as an asset if I'm on his booth while he's the booth captain. That means if I have to make a coffee run or clean up a spill or do a demo, that is the correct way of using me.

I said before that, for the most part, I don't go to shows to meet passersby. I will start maybe as much as six weeks before the show reaching out to the people I want to meet. There are essentially three groups of people that I may want to meet:

1.   *My existing distributors.* For most of the shows I've paid for over the last 20 years, the meat and potatoes of why I was there was to meet and manage my existing distributors. So I will send them an email that reminds them that we will the show and talks about the social events that we will do. So if I'm inviting them to dinner one night or possibly more, I will mention that. If I have a distributor lounge on my booth and I have room for them to leave their coats and bags there, I will mention this in the email. I will also invite them to a specific time slot for our review, and I will ask them to reply by a certain date and mention that if that particular timeslot is not good, I can find another one. So if we're looking at a four-day trade show, I have approximately 32 hours of booth time. I will be aiming for probably 20 hours of set meetings, depending on how many of my distributors are showing up. Typically, I want an hour with each distributor, and I want a few minutes in between meetings. I will talk about a typical distributor review meeting in chapter 6, but these meetings essentially follow that pattern.

2.   *Potential distributors.* In chapter 4 where I talked about finding potential distributors, I discussed how I identify the people I may want to work with. Depending on the priorities of market, my available time, and my available budget, I may or

may not have been able to meet with all the distributors that I would like to in the market. I may have been working with a distributor and it didn't work out and now I'd like to talk to my number two choice again, or I spoke to somebody but that market was less of a priority and we were not able to close an agreement and now it's more relevant. So there are a few reasons I might be meeting with somebody who isn't my distributor but now I'm interested in having them as a distributor. These meetings will again follow very closely the pattern of a meeting that I would have in market with a potential distributor. I prefer to interview distributors in market because I really like to be able to see their offices and I like the possibility of going to an end user with them during the evaluation stage before we start working together. I recognize that this isn't always possible because of budget, time constraints, or even issues of personal safety. (I don't travel to some countries like Iran, Syria, and Sudan. If a war is going on in the area or the US government doesn't want me traveling to a country, for legal reasons I won't go there and then my preference is to interview the those distributors at a trade show in a neutral third country).

For potential distributors, I will also have a one-hour meeting where I will have prepared specific questions. I will have a presentation and I may use the opportunity to get other people involved who may be at the booth, for instance, my boss, head of regulatory affairs, etc.

3. *End users.* Again, it really depends on the type of show and your strategic goals. You may find that the majority of your visitors are end users. For me, this is not typically the case and hasn't been for most of my career. That said, trade shows are an excellent opportunity to meet with end users. Often the highest-ranking people from an end user organization will be at

the trade show, and if I can I try to set a meeting with them, even if that meeting is more of a courtesy call in the case of people who are very high up on the food chain. This may be an excellent opportunity to show them product or presentations when they are in the mindset to be open to this. During their regular working day, they may be very difficult to get hold of and they may be distracted.

Additionally, taking high-ranking end users out to dinner or other entertainment at the trade show can be very valuable. First, it's an opportunity to bond with them and strengthen rapport. It also shows our distributors our solid relationships with end users, and it gives our end users an opportunity to see and talk to other end users. As I've mentioned before, my rule of thumb is if you're not sure about how reliable your product is, you don't want your customers or your distributors talking to each other, but if you are happy with the reliability of your product, you do want your customers and your distributors talking to each other. If they have good things to say to each other, they will in general feel good about you and your product.

# Administration and logistics for a trade show

As I mentioned, you as the booth captain should be very familiar with and on top of issues that include shipping to the show and booth design. In the big trade shows I go to on a regular basis, I also like to get to know the people who provide services because you never know when those services will be critical for you.

Let's say you have a four-day show in Germany and you have six or eight people there. Your overall cost without the people (the labor) is going to be about $25 a minute for the show. I'd suggest that with the labor (not even looking at lost opportunity cost), you're probably doubling that to about $50 a minute. So every minute that you waste at that show is $50 wasted. We could also look at it a different way. Let's say you anticipate generating $2 million worth of business from that show. Every minute that you're not working on actually generating revenue, you're wasting $1,000. So one way or another, the time on your booth is worth something between $50 a minute and $1,000 a minute for a regular company, not even a massive booth with dozens of workers.

Why do I raise it this way and quantify it? Because anything that goes wrong isn't just an issue of aggravation; it may be an issue of losing $1,000 a minute until it's fixed. So you want to make sure that you have everything prepared and under control and you've considered every possible complication that could happen and thought through how you will prevent it and/or fix it. You don't want to be trying to figure this out at the cost of $1,000 a minute. So, as I said, getting to know the correct people beforehand is a good investment. There may be carpenters or electricians or various other people who work your hall or the people who set up your booth, depending on if you select yourself or outsource it, but you should know how to reach those people in case something happens. You should know who is responsible for cleaning your booth and how to reach them. You should know how to find people who can provide office services, communications support, etc. Again this might sound a little obsessive or over the top, but you don't want your booth to have to shut down for two hours while you're trying to solve some emergency that came up.

There are just a few more things to cover about the trade show. One of them is what we're doing in the day-to-day work if we don't actually have meetings set up. I will assume that not everybody on the team is taking part in these meetings and that most people aren't running their booths the way I typically run my booth—certainly not at the beginning of international expansion.

You want to give off the impression that everybody is neat, orderly, friendly, and professional, and that isn't easy. Every time I do a trade show, I wonder how people get through a career working in retail because it's very hard work standing and smiling all day. I say that very deliberately. I don't like to have people on my team sitting at the trade show if they're not in a meeting and that might require me to rotate people because it's hard for many people to stand for eight hours in a row. But that really is required to keep the booth looking neat. Once your people start sitting down and, even worse, once they start opening their computers and working on their computers or looking at their phones, your booth's appearance dissolves into chaos.

A few years ago at a trade show in Brazil, I saw a booth that belonged to a company that was run by a friend of mine. The people on the booth were dressed in a very slovenly way and they were all sitting and staring down at their phones, so I took a picture and texted it to my friend. Within seconds, phones were ringing on the booth. People do get lazy and part of the responsibility of the booth captain is to keep up that discipline. One serious end user seeing your booth in disarray can cost you a sale, because would you want to do business with a company that has half-eaten sandwiches all over their booth at a trade show?

As people do approach the booth, you will greet them. As I said, I like to have a uniform greeting for the booth that is inviting and mentions what we do but isn't too pushy. So something like "Good morning. May I give you a little information about our product line?" is a good greeting.

As an aside, I've noticed that when I'm walking through a market in a developing country the people who do best at getting my attention are opening with a question. Now once the people answer or don't, we can give them a short, clear pitch about what we do and then ask them what they do. That conversation could go something like this:

"May I give you a little information about nurse call this morning?"

"Sure."

"We help hospitals provide better patient care and improve their patient satisfaction goals through better communication, and we are in some of the largest hospitals in the world. May I ask you what you do?"

At this point, the customer may say, "This has absolutely nothing to do with what I do. Thank you very much," and leave. Or the customer may say, "As a matter of fact, I sell to hospitals in Peru and I don't carry a line of products like this. This could be interesting" or he could say, "I work in a hospital and we may be looking for a solution like this in the coming years," and that will lead you to where this conversation will go next.

The reason I want everybody on the booth to have access to a pad and pen is because if this person doesn't turn around and leave at this point, I want to document who they are and what they're interested in, and I want to make it as easy as possible for that to happen. I'll make basic questionnaires that help guide the team on what questions that they should ask. At the end of the day, we should have a stack of pages of my questionnaires that are filled in and stapled to people's business cards. At the end of the show, the booth captain will take copies of all of those pages, then divide them up and distribute them to the relevant regional managers or the people who should follow up.

We should have a stack of every relevant employee's business cards, including yours, so that if the booth captain is not present, somebody can give a visitor their card. Relevant employees can include various regional managers and managers of other areas such as regulatory affairs, operations, logistics, purchasing, R&D, etc., just in case certain questions come up. Another thing we need to have at the booth is a small stapler—two or three of them if possible.

I am fully cognizant that I've been talking about a pretty luxurious lifestyle with trade shows. I know that not everybody is in this position and I've spent part of my career not living so high off the hog. So let's talk briefly about what else we can do at trade shows.

I've started several times new with a company, and often I haven't wanted to show at the trade show right away or I haven't had the budget to show. Over the years, I've worked for some startups as well. Probably the lowest cost possibility is this: I've set up meetings at a trade show at a coffee shop inside the show. I met people at a national pavilion meeting area and beforehand I gave a tip to one of the catering employees to let me take over a table for a few hours at a time. That way I knew that there was a location where I would have workspace and it didn't really look that bad. In this way, I was able to meet the potential distributors who were at the show, talk to them, and present to them. In a few cases I was able to make deals and close distribution agreements.

The next step up the food chain is to take a hotel suite in the city where the show is going on and set up your demo and a presentation in the living room of the suite. It does require some understanding of the geography of the city, because people will not go out of their way to meet you, but if you know that the hotel is very close to the trade show or is very close to the central entertainment district of the city, it's not that difficult to get people to agree to meet with you. Obviously, people will find this a little unusual, and you can explain it away by saying that you were late registering for a booth because you are new with the company, or you can even say that you are a startup and you are working on a budget. People will understand that, and it's not a bad way to work. I have actually done plenty of business this way. I'll even say that it's not uncommon, even when I have a booth, for me to take a suite with additional space because it's cheaper or more effective than getting a larger booth. One year we were even trying to keep our competitors from seeing what we were doing, so we had the demo of that new product line in a hotel suite, away from prying eyes.

There are various options for being in other people's booths. I mentioned the national pavilions. You can rent a booth in the American pavilion, and the same thing is possible in the Israeli or German or Chinese pavilions in various shows now. What you get in that situation is typically better services and less worry about dealing with things like set-up, cleaning, etc. But the cost per meter is much higher, probably three times as high. But they also often offer the ability to get just a desk spot that is very reasonably priced, and they usually give it a fancy name like the CEO Service or the Platinum Service, so you can say to people, "I will be at the US commercial service pavilion in their CEO Room. Can you meet me there?" It doesn't necessarily look like you're trying to be cheap, but you'll be saving 95% of the cost of having a booth. Of course, you won't have a lot of space to demo or anything like that, but if you are starting out and what you're looking for is a place to meet potential distributors, that is an excellent, cost-effective option.

I would also look, if you are with an American company, for state and regional booth possibilities. For instance, New England often has a booth, as do the states of California, Pennsylvania, Florida, etc. Again, your cost is dramatically lower, but you don't really have any space to demo your product.

Speaking of costs, when a large trade show is going on in a city pretty much anywhere, hotel and transportation costs will skyrocket. One thing that works especially well in Europe, where cities are often quite densely located and public transportation is fantastic, is to fly in and out of another city and. You can typically shave 30% to 50% off flight costs. I have in the past used Airbnb, but even before Airbnb, I stayed in private apartments during some trade shows to save money.

At my big trade show in Düsseldorf Germany, the price of hotel rooms is about three times what it normally is. Going from the trade show center to the train station in Cologne is just about 15 minutes longer than it is to get to many neighborhoods within Düsseldorf, so if I get it close to the train station in Cologne, I can get a hotel room for about half the price of my room in Düsseldorf and I won't miss much sleep over it.

All these things can be balanced out to try to save money. If you're going by yourself, it doesn't really matter that much, but if you have an eight-person team going for six days, an extra $150 a night on the hotel room becomes a great deal of money.

## Basic Concepts
## Bonus videos:

https://www.youtube.com/watch?v=L1-tG1HDWxk

## Tradeshows

Always know what you want to get out of a trade show. Have primary, secondary and tertiary goals and everyone on the booth should know them.

Have a booth captain.

Your goal should be that 50 % of your time should be set with meetings before the show starts.

You don't have to pay for a booth, there are ways to game the system.

If you can, visit a show before you pay for a booth.

The location, design and color of a booth can impact your return on investment.

Use message boards to drive uniformity of message.

Know how much every minute of the show costs you before you start. It will keep you focused on your return on investment. Think of every person as an expense that must be justified.

Chose giveaways rationally.

# Chapter 8
# TRAINING

Sales training is one of the most important elements here of getting your people up and running and working correctly, and there are a couple of different parts of this. I'm also going to start off by saying if you run a good sales training program for your distributor reps, it's going to generate revenue, and it's going to contribute towards positioning you as their very best or their favorite principal. Good sales training is the type of thing that attaches your reps to you, connects them to you, makes them feel really a part of your family, and if you train them well... we go back to what we said before. What are the distributor reps looking for? Ease of selling, profitability, and trust that you will stay in the market.

If you run a good sales training program, you're showing commitment. You show that they can trust you and they connect to you. It makes selling easier and more profitable. The sales training element is one of those things that solves most of your problems as a new principal in the international market. A good sales training program is key to creating explosive international growth for you. It's the type of thing that most principals don't do. I can tell you that 9 out of 10, maybe 99 out of 100 principals that are trying to sell internationally don't do sufficient sales training to achieve the goals that I'm talking about, and you can do it. It costs a little bit of money. There are ways of doing it more expensively or less expensively, but really, the investment returns itself dramatically. I've done this with every company I've worked with for years, and a good, solid sales training program is key to establishing you as a global leader.

What am I looking for in a sales training program? First of all, let's divide this into two different parts. We're dealing with how we sell our product. What everybody expects is, "What's the product? How do you do a demo of the product? What do you present of the product? What are the key features and benefits of the product?"

We will start off with that. That's sort of the kindergarten or the first-grade part of it. Depending on your product, this might be something you can handle in two hours. Or it might be something that takes two days, but you have to start off with that, and that's what everybody's going to expect from you.

You go from there to "What's the sales process? How is this product going to be sold?" I like to talk through the whole sales process, and I like to workshop it so people can talk about it and people can say, "This is how it works in my market. We can talk about where there are variations in the different markets and what people are doing today."

What am I going to do in a sales training? First of all, I want to get a group of people together. Now, I've said this over and over again: a manufacturer that believes in their product and believes that their product works wants to get their distributors together and talking to each other and sharing information.

It can happen that you're dealing with a product that you might not trust right now. That's not the end of the world, and you have to work with it. If you're not sure that your product is sufficiently stable, sufficiently robust, and you're scared of that, then you don't want to have a group sales training yet. You don't want to have salespeople together, talking about the deficiencies and the problems of the product. You might want to do trainings in smaller groups, online, or one distributor at a time to begin with.

But let's assume that you do have a robust product and you trust it and you think it's good. What you want to do is get your people together. I usually put them together in pods. I like to do a sales training for South America. I like to do a sales training for Europe, one for the Middle East, one for Africa, one for South Asia, one for Southeast Asia, and one for Australia. You don't want to ask people to travel halfway around the world multiple times, although I will talk later about distributor meetings, which are a very powerful tool. But right now, what we're talking about is sales training. Let's imagine a sales training in the Middle East for my Middle Eastern distributors.

Ideally, I will bring them together in a nice place that they're going to enjoy. That could be Dubai. It could be Sharm El-Sheikh or Casablanca. It could be someplace with a beach. I will try to get the head of the distributor company if possible, the sales manager, but what's really important is for me to get the salespeople.

This might be an argument. Think about what I said about distributor agreements. I want it stated in the distributor agreement that the distributor is obligated to send their salespeople to this, because often they just want to send their sales manager. But if it's just the sales manager and not the salespeople, you're not getting all the benefits.

If you find that your distributors are being cheap about this, then you say, "Let's not do the whole Middle East, let's not do it in Dubai. Let's divide this up into two groups, and we'll do them in cheaper locations so people don't have to fly so far or they don't have to stay in hotels or whatever," but I really stress the value of bringing people together at a nice physical location. You also want to get the benefit of the camaraderie and the unit cohesion of getting your salespeople feeling that they're part of your family, part of your company's larger sales organization.

For the most part, distributor salespeople, not the distributors themselves, are earning less than the manufacturer salespeople are, and they feel somewhat less important than the manufacturer reps. Often, distributor reps dream of going to work for a big international manufacturer, so bringing them together and making them feel that they are part of a family is a very powerful tool towards getting mindshare from them and making you their most important and their favorite manufacturer.

Let's talk about the administration and the logistics first. There will be shared dinners. There may be an evening or a morning where we do a game or something like that. I've done what we call Beach Olympics, which is where everybody plays silly games together on the beach. It's fantastic for bringing people together, for giving the distributors this feeling that they are part of your family and part of your team.

In a lot of cases, these distributor reps might not actually spend a lot of time with other people from their company. They might be in the field all day, and they don't feel that they have a team or a family at work. If you can make the unit that they associate themselves with your team, your unit, your company, that goes a very long way towards building mindshare with distributors. That's the first step.

Now we've gotten them all together. We have them in a hotel. I will get a conference room in the hotel. I might have 10 people. I might have 40 people, or 500.

I use the funnel and the periodic reviews essentially to help set up my training structure. What do I mean by that? I take a look at how people are being successful, what we might call their conversion ratios from stage to stage of the funnel. From this I can get a clear answer to questions like: Are they successful with one product line and not with another? Are they having trouble doing presentations? Are they having trouble finding enough customers? Are they having trouble identifying people at the right stage? Are they having trouble perhaps identifying when they should cut bait and give up on a customer who isn't going to buy from them? Typically, the funnel is going to give me a huge amount of information about what that distributor salesperson is experiencing and where they might be having difficulties. That's where I will try and supplement with training.

If you see, for instance, that they're just establishing value well enough for your high-end product line and you're getting hit over and over again by requests for discounts, the best remedy may be to teach them to deliver a presentation better or to work with them on preemptively attacking objections. Maybe you can teach them to tell better stories around the presentation or to teach them to establish what the cost of the inactivity among the customer may be. I've seen dramatic successful results on things like this. You basically say, "The focus this year is that all the distributor salespeople will learn five good stories to talk about in terms of what the cost of inaction would be." If the distributor doesn't buy this product this year, they try and wait a year. What is the potential downside of that? And just by teaching something like that, you can see a flurry of sales growth. Or you work on how they can better identify the right potential prospects who are in a better position to buy.

We can take the corporate goals and use those to build a training plan, as well. So let's say we're launching a new product line, and it's more expensive but we realize that this is what we really want. We want to be driving the customers to be buying a more expensive product as opposed to a cheaper product.

We can then say, "This year we will focus on teaching people to be more comfortable selling the higher-end product. Everybody is very comfortable selling the lower-end product. Can we teach everybody to sell the high-end product?"

And we set up a multiyear training based on the shift to the new product. And we will set up that this year, the coming year, and the year after that, our training will be around identifying the proper customers for the higher-end product, qualifying who could be a good customer for the high-end product and for the low-end product, and what level of trust, perhaps, is needed to sell the higher-end product. Then we might go through "How do you present the high-end product? What are the objections people might raise? What are the questions that you can use to help people understand the value of the higher-end product? What are the stories you might tell? How can you utilize the slide deck to present and help the customers really understand the value of the higher-end, more expensive, product line?"

These are the types of things that could be based around strategic goals of the corporation. If the strategic goal of the corporation is to increase selling the high-end product by 20% every year, then your training program should be built around getting people to be more competent and comfortable selling the high-end product, at least 20% more a year.

As head of international sales and even as a regional manager, a large part of what you're doing is coaching, recruiting, and training the salespeople who are out selling. They say that's basically what sales managers do: recruit, coach, and train, as well as set strategy. And the fact that you're dealing with channels doesn't really change that. They're all part of your sales assets. So the training is going to be a big part of this. Now let's say we've established which competencies we want to see in the salespeople who are selling our product. For example, we can say, "We really would like them to be spending 25% of their time on our products." That's not something that you can really coach them in. You can try and push them to make sure that they are giving you the right amount of time.

And the second part of that is they have to have the relationships. They have relationships in the market. And again you can push them to form relationships. Hopefully, they started out with the right relationships. We can't necessarily teach them to have those relationships. On the other hand, there are a lot of competencies that you want them to have that you can train them on.

You can train them on things like developing relationships. You can train them on making better use of their time. These are the types of training goals you should have—training them on your product, on the benefits of your product and on how to sell it. Training them on your deck and the stories you will use. And training them on how to best manage their time and how to establish and maintain relationships.

In a lot of cases, what you will find (and it's perfectly understandable) is either the salespeople or the sales managers and the distributors saying, "This is none of your business. Don't try and coach my people on their time management." On the other hand, if you can bring them something of value and they can use that to generate revenue for other products, you've suddenly made yourself a key principal. And this is something I've tried to do my whole career—to make sure that I am bringing to the distributor salespeople the tools that will make them make more money, even with other people's products. And it's not that hard to bring in somebody to do a training for all your distributor salespeople in a distributor meeting that's going to teach them to manage their time better or to take notes better or to ask better questions.

We can simplify that. What if you, as head of international sales, curate this information and you attend six workshops a year, you learn new skills, and you put together enough information so that you can then help teach this to the salespeople? These are probably seminars or workshops or trainings that the distributor owners aren't going to pay to send them to. So you're in a position to bring them something very

330 | ZACH SELCH

valuable from the perspective of the distributor company, because if you are teaching new general sales skills to the salespeople that they can use for other products, then everybody can be happy here. The distributor manager is going to be happy, the distributor salespeople will be happy, and they're going to bring in better results for you.

On top of that, we are also going to train them on our product, and we can tie these things up together. Let's say you take a course on asking questions as part of establishing rapport in the sales process. Then you work on questions that are specific to your product and then you hold a training session during your annual distributor meeting. That is the type of thing that everybody's going to find valuable, but it's directly tied up with your product; you're already giving them the questions that they can ask to sell your product and you can use those questions later, in the coaching sessions and that kind of thing.

The next big thing that we will do is talk about the sales process. Map it out. We will workshop it, talk to everybody about it, and then we will execute the different elements of the sales process. I will present, again, from the very beginning. How do we find customers? How do we do prospecting for the particular type of customer that we want?

I once worked for a company whose product was essentially installed in the walls of hospitals. We found that if a hospital was doing renovations, they were probably at least four times as likely to buy from us than a hospital that wasn't planning renovations, because if they wanted to buy our product but they weren't doing renovations, they had to break walls and install our product, fix the wall, paint the wall, etc. But if they were already doing renovations, the added cost of putting in our system wasn't quite so high. If they had a plan to do renovations, it was actually a relatively easy sell.

Brainstorming with my RMs and some people from my team and my intel person, I said, "Let's work on ways to figure out how to identify hospitals that are planning renovations." We put together a plan and a system that was pretty effective all over the world for identifying hospitals that were planning renovations. Then we put together training for all the salespeople on this system. We said, "This type of prospecting is a key element of your sales process—identifying hospitals that have already made a decision to do major renovations."

And again, that little incremental change in their sales process helped dramatically increase sales for a lot of distributors.

Now if I had to let my distributors discover this by themselves, maybe they would, but it would have wasted time. It would have slowed down the velocity of sales. By teaching my distributors this element of the sales process, I was helping them out and I was making it more profitable and easier, and I was building trust. They would say, "Wow, Zach really understands how to do this act. Zach is really somebody who can mentor us," and I became, in effect, a trusted advisor to my distributors. I was somebody that they looked up to and respected, and they wanted to work with me. They trusted me. They wanted to bring me into this.

I can't stress enough how rare it is for a manufacturer's channel manager or international sales manager to be in this position with their distributors. This is really what drives that huge growth that we're looking for, to get to the point where the distributors really respect you, value you, and see you as somebody who can help them make more money. So we will go through every element of the sales process like this and try and give them tools to help them from the prospecting part, from the introduction part, from the discovery part, going through the different types of presentations you will do and going through different types of stories. So those types of things you can really teach and identify the need for that knowledge or that teaching.

I can tell you about a sales training that I did once where I was talking about how to develop a sales story that was very emotional and powerful to connect with the customers. And in this case, for instance, we had a product that made nurses' work easier and more pleasant; it essentially took away a lot of the administrative work that nurses had to do. We talked about how you tell a story that nurses will hear and think, "Wow, this is a tool I really like. This could change my life. This could really improve my life."

One of the guys in the training wasn't an experienced salesperson. He had actually spent about 15 years as an engineer. He had studied engineering and then moved into sales, and he'd only been in sales for a couple of years. We went through this whole workshop of building up a story. He was normally very introverted, a nice guy, but not anyone I would have thought of as a stellar salesperson.

He told one of the most beautiful stories I've ever heard in a sales training framework. He began, "My wife always wanted to be a nurse, and she spent her whole life dreaming about being a nurse. Then she went to nursing school and became a nurse, and she hated her job because more than half of her time was spent on paperwork. She would come home every night and say how miserable she was. This wasn't what she dreamed about when she was a little girl. She didn't dream about doing paperwork. She dreamt about treating her patients, and she isn't treating her patients because she's so busy with paperwork and her life is miserable.

One day, she finally came to me and said, 'Do you mind if I stop working and just stay home with the kids because I really hate my job?' And so we decided that she didn't have to work and that she'd stay home. We gave up the income, and 10 years later, she would talk about how she regretted not being a nurse because she had always wanted to be a nurse as a little girl. If my wife had had access to this tool, it could have changed our whole life. It would have made her happy. She would have had less paperwork. She would have continued working as a nurse. She would have fulfilled her childhood dream..."

I was almost crying when I heard this story, and I was amazed that this guy, who on the surface was a very quiet, very introverted engineering type, had come up with this beautiful sales story as part of our story workshop. Everybody else came up with good stories too, but this was a great story.

Over the years, I've done workshops on the value of asking questions in the sales process—for instance, open-ended questions. A lot of salespeople, especially in certain cultures, are not familiar with the concept of open-ended and closed-ended questions. I've done trainings on that. I like to go in and get people to work on their questions. We will come to them with suggestions for questions for the different parts of the sales process, and then we will present these in the sales training and then we will workshop it. We will have everybody practice. We will have people asking each other questions. We will work through these questions and we will role-play, and this is going to be very helpful. We will go over all of the different sales tools from the sales enablement toolkit so that everybody's very familiar with how to use them. By the time they finish the sales training, everybody should be very familiar with everything that they have and how they're going to use it.

This is what you might call the product-oriented sales training, and this is the cornerstone, or the meat of our training. In today's world, we can gamify this too, and that's very helpful. What do I mean by gamifying? Including game shows in sales trainings. For instance, you have people come up and you ask them questions about the products and you give them points, and you'll have a winner. Or you'll have different people do different parts of the presentation. You have them improvise and you award prizes. You have everybody do it in front of each other. You get excitement going, you get a feeling of urgency going. All these things working together will help make the training more memorable and really bring everybody together and get that mindshare, that excitement, and also help the salespeople internalize all the different elements.

A while back, I was working for a company that had one product, and let's just say that that product sold for about $100 per hospital bed. Then we shifted to a product that sold for about $2,000. We added the product line that was much more expensive. It had a lot more features and benefits, but now the whole system for selling it was going to be different. There was much more to learn, and there were people who were extremely comfortable with the early product line, the simpler product line. They were very comfortable at that price point. They were very comfortable talking about it, and they were terrified of the idea of selling a product at such a high price point. They really did not like the idea of selling this new product, even though it would be much more profitable.

There was a lot of information to learn, there were a lot of benefits of the new system, so we spent a few days going over all this information, how to talk about it, how to talk about the benefits, how to relate those benefits to the customer's needs and the customer's workflow. Then we gamified the whole thing. In the game show we asked, "If you're talking to somebody like this, what are you going to say? What are the different benefits? Who can name five benefits of this feature? Who can name five benefits of this other feature? Who can name three benefits that this particular individual within the purchasing process might be looking for? What's something that this individual within the purchasing process isn't going to be interested in? What do you not say to this guy? What do you say to this guy?"

The game really helps the distributors internalize all this information. If you just give it to them in writing or you just present to them and you don't give them a chance to talk about it and discuss it and present it themselves, it's going to be very hard for them to learn it.

I also like to have everybody present in front of the group and then have the group give feedback. You have to be really careful with this part. Different cultures express criticism differently. You might find a group of, say, Germans, who are direct about their criticism, talking to Egyptians, who are very indirect about their criticism, and you might find a real clash of culture. So you have to be a little bit careful of how you bring together different cultures for this element and feed them ground rules so you don't have fist fights breaking out in the class.

Once we've gone through the product-specific things that are the meat of the training, I always like to add some less traditional, unexpected things—especially tools that the salespeople can use to sell my products as well as other people's products. If I can give sales reps some tools that they're not going to get from anybody else, this is going to build mindshare. It's going to cement me as their favorite and most important principal.

Another thing that I will talk about is a specific way to report information. For instance, often I'm using a funnel system and I will ask for people to report to me, for the distributors to give me information a certain way. I will put that in my playbook and I will handle that as part of the basic sales training. In some companies, we might even give the distributor sales reps access to our CRM or a seat on our CRM so that they can input information about their prospects directly into our system. If we're not doing that, I will ask them to report in a specific way through an Excel sheet or something. Again, we will set all these expectations. We've put these expectations in our distributor agreement, and then we will make sure that we train people on how to meet those expectations.

I add different things to the sales training that aren't necessarily specific to my product, my product line, or my systems. As I mentioned, this is going to help the salespeople sell better and help me reach my goal of building mindshare, of making myself the preferred vendor of my distributor's sales reps.

I've done trainings on note taking. I've done trainings on time management. I've done trainings on the structure of an elevator pitch. I've done trainings on a lot of things that can be used not just for my products, but also for other products. At trade shows or in my travels around the world, I will run into salespeople who worked for my distributors 20 years ago, and they'll remember that I was the one who trained them on these things. That is extremely powerful in terms of achieving your goals of being the preferred vendor, of being somebody who has solid mindshare with your customers, with your distributors, which then gets you into the market and gets you more sales. This is how you drive explosive growth.

We will start off with the basics. In a sales training, you might set aside the first day for brand new people, and then the second and third day are for everybody, including the people who've already attended one sales training. There are basics that you might not necessarily want to run over and over again.

One of the cool tools that I've used before is to say to more experienced people, "I'd like you to help out the first day. You know how to demo really well. Can you help teach people the basics of the product because I need a few extra hands around." That can be helpful. Very often, I will bring people from headquarters with me—technical people or clinical people or the type of people who don't necessarily see customers that often. They get to meet the distributors and the distributor reps, and they feel connected to the international expansion project. I'm trying to build this mindshare backwards and forwards, backwards within my company and forwards within the reps all the way out to everybody who is involved in selling.

We get everybody together. The first day or the first part of the training, depending on how complex your product is, we talk about the product features, how to demo it, what it looks like, how to make sure it works, that type of thing. You should expect that you're always going to have distributors that are quiet and distributors that are argumentative, and this really goes market specific. Years ago, the first time I did a session like this multiple times, I did a training program in Asia and then one in the Middle East. I found that the people in Southeast Asia and Confucian Asia really did not ask any questions. They sat there very quietly and took a lot of notes.

In the Middle East, all the Arabs had lots to say, lots of questions, lots of discussions. It was a cultural difference. It was much livelier, but you also should expect people to say, "I don't really like this feature. Maybe you can change the product." It's almost like being in stand-up comedy, where you have to expect hecklers sometimes. You have to be ready for that. I've sold products that had fundamental product flaws where suddenly, a distributor sales rep is saying in front of everyone else, "I don't know if you know this, but there's a problem with the product." You have to be ready for that. That's definitely something that happens.

My standard answer to that is "I don't want to talk in these sales meetings about what's going to make the product better. We will have a session for that. Maybe we can talk about it with the product managers. We can talk about what we might want to change for future products. I don't want to talk about that in the general sessions because this is the product we have, and we all have to focus on selling the product."

What you don't want is a situation where a sales rep says, "It would be much better if you made it blue," and somebody from headquarters says, "Hey, that's a great idea. Maybe we'll do that." At that point, everybody is going to wait for that product change, and they're going to think, Why should I try selling now? If the product is going to be improved, it's going to be easier to sell. I'll wait for this improvement.

If somebody from headquarters gives any indication that they might change this product, everybody's going to expect that the product change is going to happen imminently, and you're in trouble. You want to make sure that your people from headquarters know not to agree or indicate or even be overly polite about the idea that changes have been requested and that those changes might happen quickly. You can say, "This is a great idea. We will file this. We will think about it for the next product line, but we're not looking at doing this right away," because, again, once you say that it's something that could happen right away, you're in big trouble in terms of your short-term sales. People will just decide that they're going to wait for you to make these changes, and that's a big problem.

## Training tools

One thing that I found to be extremely helpful is sales training videos.

There are a variety of different elements that you will use in your sales process. Twenty years ago we would have been talking about a deck; nowadays we are talking about a combination of slides, videos, questions, scripts, and a variety of other elements. Now let's assume that if you're successful, you will have 200 people around the world in 50 or 60 countries selling your product. You'd like them to sell using a uniform system, and you have to assume that there will be some attrition of the team. (One thing I've noticed is that salespeople in distributors' positions change jobs more rapidly than they typically do with manufacturers.) You're looking at a situation where you need to train hundreds of people, and maybe 30 to 50 of those might be new people every year, spread out all over the world.

Ideally, we will do at least part of the training in person, but if we're limited to doing it face to face, we're really limiting our ability to scale rapidly and to keep all of our distributors selling, even when they have changes of personnel. So we will set up video clips to help us—a clip for each separate component of these tools that I use for sales training for selling.

Let's say in my deck I can divide this up into seven or eight different pieces. This might include an introductory piece; it might include a problem that is specific to a specific type of customer (let's say I'm talking about a 250-bed private hospital that caters to medical tourism) that may warrant three specific slides in my deck.

Likewise, there may be specific components that deal with objections. I will do a short video clip speaking exactly as though I'm talking to an end user, and I will do another clip that explains why I said what I said, because from my perspective every single word, my body language, my pauses, are all going to be designed to help out the sales process and I would like to try to teach these things to my salespeople. Remember, I'm talking about a perfect world. Say I have 200 salespeople around the world. Maybe 40 or 50 of them will learn this like it's the Bible, maybe 40 or 50 will completely ignore it, and the rest will learn some of it but not all. Anything they learn will help me generate more sales.

I will create training videos for the different questions that we use in the sales process.

I will probably know more as the head of international sales of the manufacturer about how my customers typically use my product and how or more accurately what their problems and needs are in their day-to-day then my distributors will early on. My distributors may know better, for instance, what an Egyptian hospital looks like. I will know more about what the workflow of the specific clinician who uses my product looks like even in different markets.

Maybe you don't feel that you are there yet... that is ok, but that is what you should be aiming for. The most powerful groups of questions that you can ask are those questions that really establish you as understanding the day-to-day needs of your customer. If I come into a factory manufacturing floor talk to a shift manager and I asked her a question about her workflow that no other vendor has asked her before it's immediately going to establish credibility in her eyes and it's going to take me be in position of a trusted advisor. If I know these questions can I pass them on my distributors' sales reps?

One of the most powerful tools I have to establish my credibility is to ask questions specific to the workflow of the clinicians that buy my product. Let's say I'm selling to operating room nurses and I go in to talk to them about their specific workflow at a very high level. And I ask them questions, maybe questions that no other vendor has ever asked them before, maybe questions that a surgeon might not even ask them but that I've picked up over the years. And when I ask the clinician—the customer—these questions, it's going to establish me as very credible, and it'll bring me a big step towards being a trusted advisor. And this is what I'm looking for.

Now, if I know how to do this, can I pass this on to my distributor reps, who don't know how to do this? And if I can teach them how to do this through a video, then we're all going to be happier and we're all going to be going towards better sales. So can I do videos that talk about these types of questions?

Can I do videos that talk about the discovery questions, for instance? There might be five or six different groups of questions that I want them to ask. And I'd like to talk about the questions, why they should ask them a certain way, etc.

Now we've covered what I would call questions or videos that are specific to the sales process of my product. And these are the most important ones, and these are the ones that really you have to have.

Another group are videos that teach general sales skills. I've found that often distributors don't invest a lot in general sales training. If I can teach general sales skills to the distributor reps, they're going to love me, they're going to make more money, they're going to love my product, they're going to put more effort and time into my product.

Often I will "curate" sales information. I will read sales books. I will go to sales courses. And I've been doing this for 30 years now, so I can actually put together a training that's going to help them with the skills they need to sell my product. And they can use this to sell other products too. The fact is they're going to pick it up and they're going to appreciate it and it's going to help me sell.

I've done this already now for three or four different companies. When I come in and put together a group of videos like this, this is rounding out my sales enablement toolkit.

Let's think about the various other things that a salesperson might need to hand to a customer. There will be proposals. Let's say you have 50 distributors. Do they all give different-quality proposals? Some distributors I've seen do phenomenal proposals. Some of them do really lousy ones. I'm not a great person for that type of stuff. I'm not really artistic, I'm not really good with those little details. I never had very neat handwriting or anything like that.

But what I've been really good at is looking at the different proposals for my different distributors and borrowing them to create a "best of breed" proposal book. Again, you have to ask permission to borrow from the different distributors. Sometimes the distributors will feel some competition with each other, so you don't want to take anything without asking. But if you can then put together the "best of breed" proposal template, you can then make that available to everybody as part of your sales enablement toolkit.

This is fantastic because if you know that every distributor is going to be handing over a really nice, neat proposal to customers, that also puts you in a good position, because people buy emotionally and when they see something neat, that could very well be the type of thing that's going to help out.

And then today's world, again, is different than the world was 20 years ago. You might even be giving suggestions for different types of emails that your distributors will use with end users. So you could say, "Maybe there are 10 different emails that are typically used during the sales process. Can I give templates of those to my distributors?"

I want to take away any guesswork. I want to take away any administrative work that I can, and I want to take away any inconsistencies I can. Ideally, my distributors in Nigeria, Brazil, and Singapore will effectively be approaching their customers in a uniform way. Now again, this might not happen, but this is what I'm aiming for. And I speak from experience because I have achieved this multiple times. This is the type of thing that drives huge growth, when you can provide this level of effectiveness in the tools that you're giving to your distributors.

# Basic Concepts
## Training

Training is a key part of your job, it will drive competency in your team and Partners; it will also drive mindshare. The more you build sales competency in your partners, the more you will build mindshare.

Questions are an often forgotten part of training. Good questions are one of the best ways to establish trust. Training people to ask the right questions is the best way to scale up trust.

## Training Tools

Videos, a system to deliver videos and an instant video chat application drive competency and mind share.

# Chapter 9
# SALES ENABLEMENT TOOLS

## Deck

The deck is of course the star of this folder of tools. Over the years, people have been using decks less and less. Let me tell you my philosophy on the deck.

The primary structure of the deck should be based around problems. Exaggerating and isolating that problem, and explaining how we can answer that problem, should be the meat of the deck.

Another thing we have to realize is that we have a very limited window of opportunity to get focus from the audience. People always forget that and squander that attention. Imagine the attention span like a hammock. We start off having the attention of the of the customer. We introduce ourselves, we talk for two or three minutes, and then the attention level drops like a saggy hammock. Half an hour later we say something like "and in conclusion," and the attention level shoots back up to the level it was at the beginning. But what's in the saggy middle? All the important stuff that we want the customer to hear. So, first of all, I'm not going to waste any time on anything that isn't critical to working with the customer or helping them internalize that I can solve their problem.

If we want to address solving the customer's problem, we have to make sure that the customer identifies that he has a problem, that he is worried about that problem, and that the problem is something he's thinking about how to solve. We all have 100 different problems that are going through our head. Let's say 80 of them have to do with work, maybe 10 of them have to do with things we're worried about like health, and 10 of them have to do with our home life and our families. Our spouses are pushing one way, our bosses are pushing another way, and maybe our feet are sore from the weekend and we're thinking a little bit about that. Now imagine I'm a customer. A vendor comes in and he's talking about one of my 80 problems, but it's something that my boss hasn't mentioned in months, it's not really hurting me, and I have a lot of other things that I'm worried about. Why should I buy anything for a problem that is so far down on my list of priorities right now?

So what do I do about this as a salesman? I want to accent, isolate, and exaggerate the problem that I will solve.

Coincidentally, what's the best way that I can pull the attention level of my customer back up to the starting point, to its high point? By using fear, or at least emotion, so if I can pull together the problem myself with emotion or with fear, I'm reaching several goals at once. I'm making sure that the attention of the customer is where it needs to be, and I'm helping the customer realize the cost of inaction.

My deck should be based around "This is a problem. As a matter fact, this is a really huge problem. Oh, my! This problem is bigger than I thought it was. Wow, it looks like this problem is really going to hurt me! Aren't I lucky that Zach has a solution to my problem and somebody else with the same problem used Zach's solution and it worked out really well! Now that we've established that, let's learn a little bit about Zach's company."

We're hitting the customer with their problem and showing what could happen if that problem is not resolved and is not addressed—how that problem could get worse and worse and really hurt the customer—and then how we can solve that problem. At the very end we will tell the customer a little bit about the company and possibly tie up with the issue of trust—why they can trust us to deliver.

If we do this correctly, the attention level of the customer should look sort of like a wave dropping a little bit down and then going back up, and then dropping and going back up, over and over again during the course of the discussion without dropping too far down.

Let me make a couple of other points about decks for international sales. There are very few cultural issues that I will let impose on the structure of my marketing material, but there are a few things that you really do have to accept and adapt to. Some cultures need to see an argument being built up before they see a conclusion, and some cultures prefer it the opposite way. In my experience, typically it's the French-educated or continental countries that need to see the argument being built up before conclusion is reached, and it is the British-descended cultures that prefer to see it the opposite way. In each case, having it in the wrong order antagonizes the customer, can create stress, and can cause people not to pay attention. If you are selling in multiple countries, I would suggest that you make a separate deck for each structure of this argument, but really you can use all the same slides. The difference is going to be in the order.

The other big cultural difference in building and moving an argument forward is that in Asia, people are used to seeing more context, which typically means that they want pictures of people to show more context about their environments. They also want the arguments to relate to a more holistic picture.

This may sound a little confusing, and I'm trying to be short with the very long subject of cross-cultural selling, but imagine this paragraph:

American: "There's water shortage. Over recent years, rainfall has been decreasing, and with less rainfall there is less water."

French: "The more rainfall, the more water. Over recent years there has been less rainfall. Therefore, there is a water shortage."

Confucian Asian: "Society needs water for agriculture, hygiene, and human consumption. There has been less rainfall in recent years. There is a shortage of water. Many people are suffering and do not have sufficient water for personal hygiene, and the cost of food has gone up, creating suffering among poor people."

If you can structure three different sets of the same deck with just a slightly different slide order, with more photos and verbiage for the Asian one, you will make the deck a more powerful tool for selling to customers all over the world.

I like to take most of the verbiage out of slides. For me, each slide should contain a picture and then maybe 5 to 25 words, no more than that. In reality, most of my slides don't even have that. They have less than 10 words. Part of this has to do with my philosophy of selling, but a large part has to do with the fact that most of my customers speak English as a second or third language. I don't want them to be working on trying to translate or understand something when they could just be absorbing it. So this is something to think about in the structure of the deck. You can tell a lot of stories with just the right pictures.

That said, I will make available to my distributors slide decks that can be translated into their local language easily.

A lot of us have a tendency to put very heavy graphical files with a lot of verbiage on slides—lots of charts and lots of words, and I think that's a big mistake. It loses people and it becomes confusing. You can always have slides available at the end to answer specific questions, so you could have an 18-slide deck with no verbiage, and follow it with a series of slides specifically to answer questions. People shouldn't be reading data off of your slides. We like to think that they do, but they simply don't get their data that way.

Here's the danger if you don't have a lot of verbiage on your slides and you're dealing with channel salespeople. Are they going to remember what to say? That's a very valid question. That's why training is so important, and typically I will make a sales training video series for the deck. Picture a series of videos—anywhere from one to five slides based around a specific subject, with somebody presenting the slides to the camera, then another video where the presenter explains why he said what he said. So, for instance, I might talk about a specific benefit in a specific way, but I have a very good reason that I'm using that specific language, because I want them to take it away and I want them to have learned that point. If I wasn't using the accurate language, maybe they wouldn't get the point.

In my training video of it, I will point out to people the importance of that accurate language and that if my language had not been accurate, maybe the point wouldn't have been internalized by the customer.

While this sales training video for the deck might seem like an awful lot of work, the return on investment is huge and the same training videos can be used for coaching again with a huge return on investment.

## Bonus videos:

https://www.youtube.com/watch?v=8JoOl9rHwfI

https://www.youtube.com/watch?v=BMO2Fu_Wy9g&t=2s

## Playbook

Using a playbook in a static format usually turns out to be a mistake, because things change, especially things like who does what, or how you expect things to be done, or price lists, or even things like presentations. People are very unlikely to update their playbook on a regular basis. They'll get one and they'll use it for years, and you really have no way of getting them to replace it, unless at every annual meeting you give them a new hard-copy playbook. But having one that can update automatically, whether it's online or whether it's on an iPad or whether it's on some other electronic tool, really is a very powerful tool. But obviously, not everyone has the budget for this.

Your playbook should cover, at an absolute minimum, the salesperson's primary sales tools. How do they manage the sales process? What are the elements of the sales process? Who should they be looking to talk to? It should cover the presentations, either through videos or decks or stories or whatever you're using to sell. It should cover the questions that they might want to ask. The last couple of playbooks I've written have had libraries of hundreds of questions that would help lead the salesperson through the different elements of the sales process at different times. What questions should they be asking at different times in the sales process? This could be very helpful.

The playbook is going to deal with all of your interactions between the distributor and your headquarters. Who do they talk to? Who should they be reaching out to when they need something? Is there a process for setting up a site visit? Often, some companies have very complex procedures for site visits, and that can tie up a salesperson, a regional sales manager, or the head of international sales. It can tie them up for an hour, four or five times a month, to handle the paperwork for setting up a site visit. And if you can divert half or more of that paperwork to the distributor salesperson, you will save yourself a lot of time and aggravation.

Be sure your playbook includes product price lists.

Next we're going to put in everything we want the distributor to know about the sales process. We will map it out step by step, name all the different components, and talk about what we're trying to do with each part of the sales process. And we will talk about what we expect the distributor to do, where they can ask for help, where the RM should step in, those types of things, with the idea that we want to give them a clear map of everything that's expected of them during the sales process. And the more detail we can go into, the better.

We will attach to this all the different pieces of sales enablement tools that we've put together. All of this is going to go into the sales playbook. And what I like to do with this sales playbook is put it online.

The biggest problem you have with a sales playbook is keeping it updated and keeping it fresh. A lot of these documents have to be up to date, and revisions have to be managed and controlled. What we say about our products, or our solutions, or the market situations, has to be up to date. And with certain products, especially medical equipment, healthcare devices, communications, transportation, defense and security, those types of things, sometimes there are legal requirements.

In today's world, often a playbook is going to be made electronically. The absolute best I've seen are put onto an iPad or another tablet. You could set them up so they'll essentially renew every time there's a change, or they'll renew periodically so that you can feed new information to them.

Giving your distributor salespeople a tablet is a really cool little perk. You can tie that up to a training or something. You'd say, "Everybody who finishes our week-long product training boot camp or presentation boot camp will get a tablet. We will load that tablet with the playbook as well as our library of videos and presentations," as an example.

That might be a little expensive, but on the other hand, if you had 20 different requests for information coming from a distributor salesperson to your regional manager, then moving up to your head of sales, just that savings in time is easily going to pay for something like a tablet or an iPad.

The other way of doing it, obviously, you can do a little cheaper. You can just do it online. It can be an app, which they can then use on their computer or smartphone, or it could be on a website.

What else goes in your playbook? You will have things like how to interact with your corporation. That could include an address book. Who are the different people they should be contacting within your organization? What do they do? How are those people going to be able to help them? What are their functions? How do you get certain materials? Do you need a demo unit? Who do you order a demo unit for? Do you need more brochures? How do you order brochures? What are you allowed to print up? Do you have all the different graphical pieces so that you can print your own brochure in your own language?

If you don't have a playbook, or you don't put the contact info in the playbook, people will be contacting the regional manager constantly to ask for what they need. The regional manager will either be able to deal with it or will be contacting the head of international sales and saying, "Can you get me a logo for this guy? Can you get me some new brochures? Can you arrange this? Can you arrange that?"

## Value dossier

This is actually something that I went through almost 30 years of my career without having, and I was introduced to it by somebody from the pharmaceutical industry. So it's sort of a new thing for me, but it's a very powerful tool. Imagine a book that contains everything the end user needs in a way that's going to fit how the end user in that culture and that organization processes and internalizes information to go through their purchasing journey. What you might find is that you need two or three structures of value dossier. The differences are more going to be in the order of the material included, more than anything else. To clarify, each structure may include 90% identical material, but the order it is laid out may be different. You will layer the white papers, the scientific documents if you have them, the explanations, etc., and put them in a nice, orderly document that looks attractive and neat and is bound nicely. You could make it an electronic file with printing instructions so that people can print it locally or you can print them up for people.

The value dossier is a really nice tool to give to customers. Sometimes, especially with complex sales, you might have somebody within the customer organization that you expect is going to show this document to their colleagues, what we may refer to as a champion or mobilizer. Sometimes, as much as you would like to be there for the internal presentation, you won't get invited. And by you, I mean also your rep. Nobody from your sales organization is going to be there; it's going to be just people from the end user organization.

So if you can put together a really nice value dossier, a nice folder of material that is going to be used internally by customers to internally sell this to other customers, that's going to be really helpful.

# Remote coaching tools

Coaching your reps is hugely important, and this should be one of the primary jobs of your regional managers and of the head of international sales. Ideally, we will do this face to face. But if you have 200 sales reps selling your product around the world, the cost of doing this face to face can be prohibitive. On top of that, the time factor might make it very difficult to get out to all those people, depending on how many regional managers you have. But if you do this remotely, one of the best ways to do this is through video.

My favorite way of doing this is matrixing out every element of the sales process and every type of end user individual that you might encounter during the sales process. Imagine that you have a sales process with 12 pieces. It includes prospecting, identifying the customer, and trying to qualify the customer. It includes your initial meeting for discovery. Every element of that sales process is put down on the horizontal x-axis. And on the vertical y-axis are the different individuals you might be meeting.

Let's say you have a simple sales process and you are selling to individual proprietors. There's one decision maker. That's pretty simple. So all you really have are the elements of the sales process and the one person. But most of the products I've sold are more complex. You're typically going to have a minimum of three and probably as many as eight to ten people that you're involved with in the sales process. So imagine your x-axis has the 12 different pieces of your sales process. The y-axis is the 10 different people you might be dealing with. So you have 120 squares on this matrix.

For each one, you can put in all the materials that you think are necessary for that element. If you're going for a discovery meeting, where you are talking to the financial person within the customer organization, then that square of the matrix would include everything that a sales rep might need for this meeting plus three or four short videos explaining what the best practice would be during this meeting. And then the head of international sales, the RM, or whoever is responsible for this element of coaching, knows that on Tuesday, the sales rep is going to carry out this meeting. You can send him this packet or more likely, a link to the packet on a cloud-based server like Dropbox. And then he can go through all the different files, watch the videos, read the material, take the material that he needs.

You can call him and say, "Did you read it? Are you ready? Let me ask you some questions. What are you going to say? How are you going to do it?" And you can coach him and prepare him for this meeting. Then, after the meeting, you can call them up and say, "Let's debrief." About 99% of channel managers and international sales managers will say this is not the way they do things. Or even they'll say that the distributors simply won't stand for it.

What I've found is they *will* stand for it. They like it once they get used to it, especially if it's been consistent and successful. If they understand from the very beginning that this is the way you do things, they will follow up. They'll be happy to work this way, they're going to see much better results, and they're going to treat you more seriously. They're going to consider you a much more important part of their whole portfolio. They're going to consider you possibly the most important and the most organized principal that they're dealing with, and they're actually going to like this and it's going to pay off in the long run for you.

## Other sales tools

What other great tools are there? You can do things like a simple laminated sheet, which is sort of like a message board of your product. On one side is the primary benefits people should remember. The other side has the sales process: who you're talking to, at what point, where you're going, the different steps of the sales process, etc.

I have shifted, over recent years, to using a lot of videos as sales training and coaching tools. You separate the coaching from the stuff you will do for an individual need or working on a certain position in a particular sale. The training would be more broad-based and used for more people, but again, you can do these videos either professionally or by yourself. If you learn how to manage basic videos and basic video editing, you can pump out videos relatively simply, or you can get a professional to make a set.

Typically, I've created a number of three to ten-minute videos that deal with different elements of the sales process and different elements of the deck. First, I'll show what I'm doing. Let's say I'm talking about a certain three slides of the deck and the stories I tell with them. Then I'll do another video that asks, "Why did I say this. What was the importance of this particular sentence? What's the importance of pointing this out?

Why do I always point this out during the presentation? Why do I ask this question? What am I trying to achieve?"

That can be really helpful. Then as a basic starter, I will ask the salespeople to watch the videos at least once or twice. It really gives them a good starting point to do the presentations, to talk with the customers, to represent their products.

When we're considering that our distributors are essentially our sales force, we need to provide them with the same type of tools that we would provide our sales force, and these tools might even have to be more elaborate, more carefully thought out, and better designed than we would do for our salesforce. Because we're dealing with people who aren't our employees, if the tools don't make it easy for them to sell, they might not sell our products. On top of that, they have to keep track of multiple product lines, so from their perspective if somebody else has better tools that make it easier for them, they may put their effort into that product line. If they don't have good tools, they also might not remember what they need to sell our products. So we need to give our distributors excellent sales enablement tools, and this is the type of thing that people often either overlook or ignore with distribution partners because they're thinking, The distribution partner salespeople aren't our employees, so why should we put effort into providing the tools?

We want to provide them with a folder of tools. One of the best ways to do this is with an online folder that we control and they can download from. This way we can update the materials whenever we want to and make sure that the materials are always up to date and accurate. What I would also do is put as one of the first documents in the folder a catalog that lists everything and explains what the best uses of everything would be and when and where in the sales process one would use it. For instance, you may have a master deck with 40 slides, but the typical pattern would be to use it with between 15 and 22 slides, depending on who you're talking to and at what point in the sales process you're talking to them. And then you would list them all separately in the folder so somebody could pull them out and use them according to that suggestion.

Likewise, let's say that I have 10 or 20 or 100 white papers or pieces of collateral that would be used to answer specific questions or at a specific point in the sales process. You will find that, on a regular basis, distributors' salespeople will be calling up the regional manager or the head of international sales and asking for a specific document. The better this is organized in our library, the less time we will be wasting on it. This becomes pretty important. Imagine if you have 200 international salespeople selling your product and they're each calling you once a week asking for help finding a document. You might not be able to get rid of that completely, but the more you can curate this collection, the more time for selling will be available for everybody.

In this folder you'll also have images and terminology that can be used by the distributors to make their own collateral, brochures, signs, posters, etc. The reason you do this is to control everything being used by your distributors, and if you give them photos and phrases, etc., they won't make up their own stuff. This can also be enshrined in the distributor agreement. More than once, I've seen a distributor just make something up and put it on a sign at the trade show. It's not accurate, but that's what the customers are learning. Then, later on it can become a problem even if it's not an outright lie. It's better if we control our messaging because we also know what benefits we want to present and how we want to phrase those benefits.

Of course, this part of the package is where you can find things like the approved logos and so on. You will clarify with the distributor what they're allowed to do with that logo. Often the distributor is going to have your logo on his business card, not as his company logo, but perhaps he might have the five lines that he represents displayed on his business card or on the sign in his office and at his trade show booths.

There should be a range of what you might consider raw materials or components in this file. I've seen distributors take presentation videos, dub them into their language, and use them, so if we're giving the distributor approved materials to work with, that's best for everybody. By the way, there's nothing as bizarre as seeing a video of yourself speaking in Portuguese when you're pretty sure you don't speak Portuguese!

I use a lot of stories, and I don't necessarily want people to copy or adapt my stories because they are mine, and if somebody tries to repeat my story as his own, it might not sound very believable. But having a video library of stories and some explanations allows people to develop their own stories, and this can be a very powerful tool. This should also be in this file.

Questions are a very important part of the sales process. I also know that thinking up questions and asking them are two of the biggest weaknesses salespeople have. You might have a salesperson who is fantastic at presenting his deck and at doing a demo, but he can't think of good questions for the life of him.

I like to have a file of questions in this folder, divided up again by who you're talking to, what stage of the sales process you're in, and what you're trying to achieve. You might have 40 sections of questions. This may seem like a lot of work, but it is very powerful for the distributor to be able to get this kind of information and ask these questions.

Depending on the type of product you have, there may be tenders as part of the purchasing process. If you have a good representative and good relationships, there is a good chance that people within the customer organization will ask you to help them write the tender specifications, so you should have a series of spec examples in the file as well.

Depending on the product, short video clips can be very helpful in the sales process. Again, it's really good if you can make these for your partners and make them available but also put them in a format that will allow dubbing or subtitling in the local language.

Ideally, you want to give your partners all the marketing tools they need so they don't have to worry about it themselves. In some cases, you might find yourself a distributor that has a better marketing department than you do. I've had that a few times myself, but that is pretty rare in today's world. Anything that your partners will use for sales and marketing and you think is going to be helpful, you should make available to them in a controlled manner.

# Basic Concepts
## Deck

"This is a problem. As a matter fact, this is a really huge problem. Oh, my! This problem is bigger than I thought it was. Wow, it looks like this problem is really going to hurt me! Aren't I lucky that Zach has a solution to my problem and somebody else with the same problem used Zach's solution and it worked out really well! Now that we've established that, let's learn a little bit about Zach's company."

It's useful to understand how to shift the order of slides and the graphics on slides when you present to different cultures.

## Playbook

A static playbook always causes problems, electronic delivery is the way to go.

## Value Dossier

This is a great tool to help channels or champions (or mobilizers or what ever you want to call them) within the customer organization.

## Sales Coaching Matrix

Build a folder for every stage in the sales process (for example first technical demo) and for every possible customer profile (for example 250 bed critical care hospital). Aggregate the material that can be used for that piece of the matrix, deposit in a file sharing app and then you can send it to the relevant sales assets at the right time.

# Afterword

The idea for this book was to bring together what you would need to know to explosively grow international sales for a small to mid-sized manufacturing company. I have always felt that there is no better way to grow the value of a company, to expand your manufacturing team, to create jobs and value, than by growing the international sales footprint. But for decades I have seen that the knowledge on how to do this is not easy for people to find; schools don't teach it and it is hard to impossible to find a mentor. Companies get tossed around like ships trying to find a port in a storm.

When I was finishing up this book, I reached out to some people I had worked with over the years and asked them for quotes I could use in the book. I got a few dozen. I was very pleased with what people said, and it was what I was hoping for – some variation of "Zach helped me make a lot of money" through teaching or guiding them in driving their international sales.

There was a second element to the notes that I wasn't expecting, although I guess I should have. About half the people said some variation of "Zach's ideas seemed crazy and unorthodox but they really paid off". Over the past 30 years, I have spent a great deal of my time arguing and fighting with people I worked with about how to do my job. When I do a 360 survey, the results are always the same – 35% will say "I love Zach, he delivers sales" 30% will say "Zach seems nice enough, and I hear that he delivers sales but I don't really work with him that way" and 35% will say "I hate Zach, he has these crazy ideas, and he never wants to look at photos of my cat dressed in costumes". In the end of the day, these ideas drive results. Repeatedly, in different industries, in over 130 markets around the world. It seems to me that these should be the orthodox, textbook concepts. The concepts that don't work or drive weak anemic sales should be the ideas that are shunned, not the ideas that help everyone achieve their goals.

I hope that people will read this book, adopt these concepts, and create millions of manufacturing jobs based on exports. I hope that young sales managers will read this book and find the career that they were hoping for. I hope that people will use this book to build their 401K or the value of their company to leave to their grandkids.

I'd like to hear from you. If you have successes to share, or you find that you still need a little help, please reach out to me at Zach@globalsalesmentor.com I also invite everyone who has read this to join my closed WhatsApp group, which will give you a peer group to discuss international sales issues. Email me and I will send you an invitation.

Made in USA - Kendallville, IN
1211311_9781735913100
01.12.2021 1228